The Economics of Waste Management in East Asia

T0295707

The existing literature provides very little information on the real and current process of waste disposal and recycling in China. China generates a large amount of waste, and it covers about 20 percent of the world waste trade. This book focuses on China's waste management and recycling policy.

The book also examines the relationship between China's waste management and recycling industry and its legal structure. It fills in the gap by providing insight into topics such as how to resolve China's waste management and recycling problems, theories and empirical studies on waste and management as well as waste management policies in East Asia. It also includes comparative analysis through case studies on other Asian countries, such as Thailand and Japan.

Masashi Yamamoto is Associate Professor at the University of Toyama, Japan.

Eiji Hosoda is Professor at Keio University, Japan.

Routledge Studies in the Modern World Economy

The Economics of Waste Management in East Asia

Edited by Masashi Yamamoto
and Eiji Hosoda

Routledge
Taylor & Francis Group

LONDON AND NEW YORK

First published 2016 by Routledge

2 Park Square, Milton Park, Abingdon, Oxfordshire OX14 4RN

711 Third Avenue, New York, NY 10017

Routledge is an imprint of the Taylor & Francis Group, an informa business

First issued in paperback 2018

British Library Cataloguing in Publication Data
A catalogue record for this book is available from the British Library

Library of Congress Cataloging-in-Publication Data
Names: Yamamoto, Masashi, editor. | Hosoda, Eiji, 1953– editor.
Title: The economics of waste management in East Asia / edited by
    Masashi Yamamoto and Eiji Hosoda.
Description: Abingdon, Oxon ; New York, NY : Routledge, 2016. |
    Series: Routledge studies in the modern world economy ; 155 |
    Includes bibliographical references and index.
Identifiers: LCCN 2015039766 | ISBN 9781138805989 (hardback) |
    ISBN 9781315751917 (ebook)
Subjects: LCSH: Refuse and refuse disposal—Economic aspects—
    East Asia. | Recycling (Waste, etc.)—East Asia. | Environmental
    policy—East Asia.
Classification: LCC HD4485.E18 E36 2016 | DDC 338.4/
    736370095—dc23
LC record available at http://lccn.loc.gov/2015039766

ISBN: 978-1-138-80598-9 (hbk)
ISBN: 978-1-138-31793-2 (pbk)

Typeset in Galliard
by Apex CoVantage, LLC

Contents

Figures

Tables

Contributors

Simon Gilby is Policy Researcher at Kitakyushu Urban Center, Institute for Global Environmental Strategies, Japan.

Matthew Hengesbaugh is Task Manager, IGES Centre Collaborating with UNEP on Environmental Technologies (CCET), Institute for Global Environmental Strategies, Japan.

Eiji B. Hosoda is Professor in the Faculty of Economics of Keio University.

Daisuke Ichinose is Associate Professor at the College of Economics of Rikkyo University.

Shou-Chien Lee is Section Chief of the Recycling Fund Management Board, Taiwan Environmental Protection Administration.

Chang Miao is Associate Professor at Tsinghua University, School of Environment.

Jun Nakatani is Assistant Professor in the Department of Urban Engineering of the University of Tokyo.

Takashi Saito is Associate Professor in the Faculty of Social Sciences of Kyorin University.

Janya Sang-Arun is Deputy Area Leader of Sustainable Consumption and Production at the Institute for Global Environmental Strategies (IGES).

Kazuaki Sato is a Research Associate in the Faculty of Economics of Keio University.

Eiji Sawada is a Lecturer in the Faculty of Economics of Kyushu Sangyo University.

Takashi Sekiyama is a Lecturer at the Department of International Studies of the University of Tokyo.

Kenji Someno is a Research Fellow at The Tokyo Foundation.

Piya Wanpen is Director of Asian Coastal Resources Institute Foundation, Thailand.

Yirui Xu is Associate Professor in the Faculty of Economics of Senshu University.

Masashi Yamamoto is Associate Professor at the Center for Far Eastern Studies of the University of Toyama.

Preface[1]

Waste has been with us since the beginning of human history. Its appearance, however, has changed, especially in the last 30 years; these changes also vary among countries. What has not changed is its increasing importance. According to Kellenberg (2013), total waste traded in the world is approximately 200 million tons per year. We understand the impact of this figure when we compare it with the total debris generated by the terrorist attacks on the United States on September 11 in 2001(1.6 million tons) and by the Great East Japan Earthquake in 2011 (26.7 million tons). More importantly, the volume of trade has increased by 67 percent over the last 5 years.

These facts have attracted the attention of researchers in various fields, and the appearance of seminal books in the field reflect this increased attention. Buclet (2002) is a pioneering study in the field of waste management, which presents international perspectives. It focuses primarily on policy issues of municipal solid waste in EU countries. Fullerton and Kinnaman (2002), on the other hand, shed light more on economic analysis in the field of waste management as well as on policy issues in the United States. Furthermore, Shinkuma and Managi (2011) updated the theoretical contributions made during the 2000s and provided a summary of the related empirical analyses. Their interests were very general, with each chapter appealing to readers who are interested in a given topic.

Recently, more focused types of books have been published. The study by Kinnaman and Takeuchi (2014) is largely a collection of papers in applied economics featuring particular problems in various countries (or regions) around the world, while D'Amato et al. (2013) concentrate on Italy's waste management issues from the perspective of spatial econometrics. Kojima and Machida (2013) have produced an ambitious study that covers most of Asia, from more developed East Asian countries such as Japan, China, and Korea to developing countries such as Vietnam, India, and Thailand.

Although the title includes the term "East Asia", the main focus of this book is China's waste management and recycling policy. One of the main reasons for focusing on China is that China is the largest importer of waste in the world and it is responsible for approximately 20 percent of the global waste trade (Kellenberg, 2013). It is well known that China receives recyclables and waste not only from other Asian countries but also from the European Union and the United

States. Nonetheless, we have very limited information on the real and current process of waste disposal and recycling in China. BAN (2002) is probably the first work to note the negative side of China's cheap waste disposal process, which is run by informal entities. Because BAN (2002) had considerable impact, China's recycling industry has earned the attention not only of researchers but also of mass media.

More than 10 years have passed since the publication of BAN (2002). Since then, many policy reforms have been carried out in China's waste management and recycling programs, including the launch of the home appliance recycling law. Along with constant change in the global business environment, especially in natural resource industries, China's waste management and recycling industry continues to change rapidly. The flow of all these changes is explained in Chapter 4. A discussion of the revealing relationship between this rapidly changing process in the informal sectors and the introduction of proper laws is one of the final goals of this book.

For readers who are not familiar with the economics of waste, Chapter 1 should be read first. Most of the concepts specific to the field of waste management are covered through a comparison with western waste management policy, such as that of the EU. Chapters 2 and 3 provide a good summary of the literature on waste and recycling.

The remaining topics in this book were chosen because they concern solutions to problems in China's waste management and recycling programs. For example, some of the chapters are devoted to Japanese waste management policy because Japan is one of the biggest exporters of waste to China. It is important to grasp the status quo of both the supply side and the demand side to fully understand a market transaction. Other chapters concern case studies in other Asian countries, such as Thailand, because they may replace China's current leading position once labor costs in China become too high. We hope that all of the conclusions reached in this book prove valuable for other developing countries.

Note

1 This book is designated as the final report of a project funded by the Japanese Ministry of Environment (Research Fund for Environmental Economics and Policies: FY2012–2014) in which one of the editors (Hosoda) was the project leader. The editors and other project members are grateful for the financial support.

References

Basel Action Network (BAN) (2002) Exporting Harm: High-Tech Trashing of Asia. Retrieved from http://ban.org/films/ExportingHarm.html
Buclet, N. (2002) *Municipal Waste Management in Europe: European Policy between Harmonisation and Subsidiarity (Environment & Management)*, Springer, Netherlands.
D'Amato, A., M. Mazzanti, and A. Montini, eds. (2013) *Waste Management in Spatial Environments (Routledge Studies in Ecological Economics)*, Routledge, New York.

Fullerton, D. and T. Kinnaman (2002) *The Economics of Household Garbage and Recycling Behavior (New Horizons in Environmental Economics)*, Edward Elgar Publishing, New York.

Kellenberg, D. (2013) "Trading wastes," *Journal of Environmental Economics and Management*, Vol. 64, pp. 68–87.

Kinnaman, T. and K. Takeuchi (2014) *Handbook of Waste Management*, Edward Elgar Publishing, New York.

Kojima, M. and E. Machida (2013) *International Trade in Recyclables and Hazardous Wastes in Asia*, Edward Elgar Publishing, New York.

Shinkuma, T. and S. Managi (2011) *Waste and Recycling: Theory and Empirics (Routledge Studies in Ecological Economics)*, Routledge, New York.

Part I

Critical reviews in waste management: theory and empirics

1 Waste policies and related legislation in Japan

Eiji Hosoda

1 Introduction

Legislation relating to waste disposal has a long history. As an economy develops, its socioeconomic structures are transformed. Accordingly, the quality and quantity of the generated waste change. This process leads inevitably to changes in laws and policies around the appropriate disposal and recycling of waste. These changes have a significant impact on the modalities of waste disposal and recycling in the domestic context. In fact, waste-related laws and policies have followed a continuous, if at times meandering, reform path, while the circumstances relating to waste disposal and recycling have continued to change.

In this chapter, I discuss changes in the laws and policies around the appropriate disposal and recycling of waste, showing how waste management policies have interacted with the daily activities of waste disposal and recycling. Although this chapter's main topic is the basic issues of waste disposal and recycling since the 1990s in Japan, it also discusses issues in early waste disposal and recycling after the Meiji era (1868–1912). It includes these historical references because it is difficult to understand the *raison d'être* of the present legislation and policies in waste disposal and recycling without knowing the history.

I demonstrate that the present legislation and policies represented by the Basic Act for Establishing a Sound Material-Cycle Society, the Waste Management and Public Cleansing Act (hereinafter, the Waste Management Act), the various individual recycling-related laws, and other provisions have contributed to the reduction of waste emission and the conservation of landfill capacity. At the same time, however, I explain the limitations of the legislation and policies: a large amount of precious potential resources, such as end-of-life products (ELPs), parts and materials (called venous resources), are flowing out of Japan to developing countries. I also note that this export of ELPs in an invisible flow may be regarded as waste export that may cause pollution in developing countries and is strictly regulated by the international agreement known as the "Basel Convention".[1]

With these points in mind, I emphasize that without an appropriate degree of coordinated coupling between the "arterial" economy, which produces, distributes, and sells goods, and the "venous" economy, which collects and transports waste and engages in intermediate disposal, recycling, and landfilling, there will be no further progress in the sound and smooth circulation of resources.[2] To achieve a sound and smooth interface between the two economies, I underscore the role of product chain control (PCC), of which I give a detailed explanation in Subsection 4.2.

The chapter is structured as follows: Section 2 provides a brief overview of the changes in the Japanese waste management system. Section 3 details the current legal and policy framework relating to waste disposal and recycling, beginning with the Waste Management and Public Cleansing Act of 1971, and outlines the ultimate objectives pursued by these various laws and policies for waste disposal and recycling. Section 4 examines the impact on waste disposal and recycling of Extended Producer Responsibility (EPR), which was formulated by the Organisation for Economic Co-operation and Development (OECD) and introduced in Japan following various changes. Section 5 presents the limitations of existing legislation and policies relating to waste disposal and recycling and considers the systemic prerequisites for realizing the sound and smooth cyclical use of resources and constructing a circular economy, referencing policies being implemented by the European Union (EU). The final section provides concluding remarks.

2 A short history of waste-related systems

With any type of socioeconomic system, the present situation cannot be discussed without first reviewing the past: for better or worse, future development depends on the development that preceded it. Waste disposal and recycling systems are no exception, and they have developed in accordance with the policies and laws established to date. Any search for a new path toward a circular economy must be conducted with knowledge of the past. This section provides a brief overview of the transformation of the waste disposal and recycling systems in modern Japan.

2.1 Before the waste management act

During the early Meiji Period, foreigners who came to Japan in the employ of the Meiji government were struck by the beauty of the Japanese urban landscape. Although the houses and streets of the towns were beautiful in themselves, the foreigners' attention was attracted by the quality of sanitation and hygiene in the towns and cities. Rubbish, including house dust and kitchen refuse, was nowhere to be seen, and sewage was returned to the fields as fertilizer, meaning that it did not pollute the towns (Morse, 1917). In the towns and cities of Europe and other regions, where a wave of urbanization had continued since the 18th century, rubbish and sewage disposal were not adequately addressed, leading to unsanitary conditions for residents, who were assailed by a malodorous environment (Schwartz, 1983; Corbin, 1988). In contrast, old Edo, which became the new national capital, Tokyo, after the Meiji Restoration, provided a sanitary environment, and thus, it was natural that foreigners at that time were impressed.

Before the modern era, rubbish and sewage disposal in Japan was relatively systematic, accomplishing an extremely advanced cyclical use of resources. The effective utilization of sewage as fertilizer was noted above, and other resources, such as used paper, iron scrap, used steel implements, rice straw and wood, were thoroughly recycled and reused (Ishikawa, 2013). It is also worth noting that rubbish disposal and sewage treatment were conducted under the administration of local authorities (Oishi, 1988). There was often illegal dumping of rubbish in large cities, such as Edo and Kyoto (Ando, 1993). Local authorities also encountered difficulties securing landfill disposal sites. Yet, even with these various difficulties, issues related to waste disposal were by no means as serious as those witnessed in the modern era.

The above models of waste disposal and recycling largely continued into the Meiji Period. It could be said that the model for modern Japan's rubbish and sewage disposal methods had its origin in early modern times. However, once Japan experienced industrialization, as one might expect, the systems that had functioned so well were unable to address the realities of an era of expanded production and consumption. In response to this situation, rubbish and sewage disposal came to be controlled through the passage of various laws and regulations. In cities, police writs and other orders were also drafted, transferring waste and sewage treatment to the supervision and administration of central and/or local authorities (Mizoiri, 2007).

Even after these changes, the situation was not sufficient to ensure public sanitation in modern cities, leading to the 1900 passage of the Waste Cleaning Act. The two major characteristics of this act were as follows: first, it sought to promote waste management under the supervision of municipalities, and second, it recommended disposal by incineration (Ministry of Environment, 2014). It is worth noting that these two characteristics have remained in place and are included in contemporary waste administration policies. Incidentally, waste disposal by incineration was prohibited during the Edo period (1603–1867), partly due to concerns about fires. Thus, the encouragement of waste disposal by incineration can be regarded as an epochal change in waste disposal administration from the early modern to the modern period.

The rubbish and sewage disposal activities controlled by the Waste Cleaning Act remained in place after the end of the Second World War. However, it became increasingly difficult to appropriately administer waste disposal under the provisions of this law, which placed responsibility on individual municipal authorities. Cooperation and partnerships were required among national, prefectural, and municipal governments and citizens. In 1954, the Public Cleansing Act was enacted, creating a new structure for rubbish and sewage treatment and disposal in the postwar period. Under this new structure, national and prefectural governments were obliged to provide financial and technological support to municipalities for waste and sewage disposal (Ministry of Environment, 2014). Needless to say, partnerships and cooperation among stakeholders remain key elements of contemporary waste and recycling administration.

However, this law did not distinguish between municipal solid waste and industrial waste, nor did it clarify responsibility for the disposal of waste generated by industrial activities. Whether the waste was generated by households or industry, in principle, the responsibility for waste disposal lay with municipalities. I note that Japan would go on to experience unprecedented economic growth around the time when the law was enacted. While volumes of industrial waste naturally surged during this period of rapid economic growth, municipalities were unable to respond to the surge or take responsibility for the appropriate disposal of this waste. It soon became apparent that there were serious problems with waste disposal based on the Public Cleansing Act.

2.2 After the Waste Management Act

In approximately 1955, Japan began to experience unprecedented levels of economic growth, as already noted. Although there were fluctuations, from 1955 for a period of approximately 18 years, Japan recorded annual growth of approximately 10 percent; this is now referred to as the rapid economic growth period (1955–1973). During this period, a massive increase in investment led to expansion in the industrial scale and changes in the industrial structure. At the outset, growth was supported by the mining and textile industries; however, as time passed, major growth shifted to the processing and assembly industries for mechanical products, such as automobiles, and the chemicals industry.

The volume of waste produced increased in line with this economic growth. The 6.21 million tons of waste produced in 1955 increased 4.5 times to 28.7 million tons by 1970 (Ministry of Environment, 2014). Although household waste increased, the amount of industrial waste similarly increased. In an economy in which industry had become highly developed, it was difficult for industrial waste to be appropriately managed and disposed of under the supervision of municipalities. The need for household and industrial waste to be separately classified and disposed of was gradually recognized, leading to debate about the need to amend the relevant laws.

The period of rapid economic growth was also one in which industrial pollution intensified. Inappropriate disposal and illegal dumping of industrial waste generated environmental destruction. Additionally, another type of environmental pollution occurred: smoke, particulate matter, and waste water discharged by industrial activities led to air pollution and water contamination, and threats to public health thus emerged as a social issue. To respond to these serious threats, the 61st extraordinary session of the Diet, convened in 1970, passed 14 acts relating to the prevention of environmental pollution. One of these acts was the Waste Management Act.

The Waste Management Act has since been revised on numerous occasions; however, its underlying concept has remained largely unchanged, and its basic structure remains in place today. There are various differences between the Waste Management Act and the Public Cleansing Act; however, for the purposes of this chapter, I refer to the most characteristic difference: for the first time, a clear distinction was made between municipal solid waste and industrial waste. Industrial waste, which had previously been included in all-encompassing stipulations in previous legislation, was separated and categorized by type (there are currently

20 categories of industrial waste). The Waste Management Act further stipulates that the responsibility for this waste lies with the waste-generating business operators themselves.

In accordance with the separate classification of municipal solid waste and industrial waste, as already referenced, permission (a business license) to act as a waste collection and processing business or facility is also separately granted, another important characteristic peculiar to the Waste Management Act. Because the responsibility for disposal of municipal solid waste lies with municipalities, as during the time of the Public Cleansing Act, permission to engage in waste collection and transportation of municipal solid waste is granted by municipal authorities. However, the Waste Management Act stipulates that permission to engage in the collection, transportation, and processing of industrial waste is granted by prefectural governments. These two systems for permission are separate. Hence, even when a business operator with permission to collect or process industrial waste also has the capacity to address municipal solid waste, the operator may not process that waste without also having the additional appropriate license.

The above-referenced classification of waste under the Waste Management Act and its inflexible implementation made waste disposal and recycling in Japan extremely complex and inefficient. This will be explored in further detail in the next section.

3 Development of the legislation and policies of waste disposal and recycling

This section explains the development of the institutional infrastructure for waste disposal and recycling mainly after passage of the Waste Management Act. Here, an institutional infrastructure is defined as an institutional framework that regulates human behavior and actions, consisting of hard and soft laws. A hard law is a body of legal codes that enable the government to impose certain constraints with compelling power on the actions of people, firms, and other institutions, while a soft law is a body of non-legal codes and standards that constrain the actions of people, firms, and other institutions by means other than the compelling hand of the government. Shared moral codes, social norms, and business customs are good examples of soft law. Corporate social responsibility (CSR) and, recently, "creating shared value" (CSV) have become buzzwords, and these concepts can be thought of as variations of soft law. Through the harmonization of and complementarity between hard and soft laws, a socio-economy with a greater degree of socioeconomic welfare can be built.

The core of the hard laws for waste disposal and recycling is the Waste Management Act, and, as already noted, this law holds an extremely important position in the history of waste disposal and recycling. Hence, it is worth examining in detail how it has promoted proper waste disposal and recycling. This act may have a significant impact on the future development of resource circulation systems.

In this chapter, the word "waste" is used in a very specific way that may differ from ordinary usage. People are so familiar with the word that they may not feel a need to examine what it truly means or how it is defined. However, difficulties arise whenever one tries to define the word rigorously; consequently, I use the word in a narrow sense, as it is defined by the Waste Management Act. Care should be taken on this point because there may be cases in which this definition of waste differs from that used in daily life.

3.1 The precise definition of waste under the Waste Management Act

In this subsection, I explain how waste is defined under the Waste Management Act. As already noted, waste under the act must be understood in a specific way. The prime factor that characterizes waste is *bads*, which are precisely defined in terms of economics. Hence, I explain how bads are defined and how residuals discharged by economic activities are classified as waste by means of the concept of bads. Doing so helps us clearly understand the relationship between the law and economics in a *venous economy* (an economy relating to businesses such as those that engage in the collection, transportation, processing, and recycling of residuals) so that the concept of waste defined by the Waste Management Act becomes straightforward.

Suppose that some residuals are transacted in a market. If there is a sufficient amount of demand compared with the amount of supply, then these residuals are positively priced and are referred to as "goods" (or commodities). These transactions are often called "onerous" transactions (or "compensated" transactions). Used paper, iron scrap, and nonferrous scrap are examples of goods.

In contrast, if there is not a sufficient amount of demand compared with the amount of supply and there is an excess demand for those residuals at zero price, then they are negatively priced and are referred to as "bads" (or discommodities). These transactions are called "reversely onerous" transactions (or "discompensated" transactions) (Hosoda, 2008, 2012). Rubbish, including house dust, kitchen refuse, waste acid liquid, and waste toxic substances, are examples of bads.

Based upon the above conceptual background, I examine the waste covered by the Waste Management Act. The following definition of waste appears in Article 2:

> In this Law, "waste" refers to refuse, bulky refuse, ashes, sludge, excreta, waste oil, waste acid and alkali, carcasses and other filthy and unnecessary matter, which are in solid or liquid state (excluding radioactive waste and waste polluted by radioactivity).

Although the above sentence is simple and easy to understand, it is too loose to provide criteria for deciding what constitutes waste in the daily operations of waste disposal administration. It is almost impossible to determine whether used PET bottles, waste clothes, used batteries, and other items are waste only by this definition. Facing some difficulty caused by this loose definition of waste, the former Ministry of Health and Welfare (currently the Ministry of Health, Labour and Welfare) clarified the definition of waste as follows:

> Waste refers to items that have become unnecessary to the possessor of the items, being unable to use them by himself/herself or sell them for compensation to another person. When determining whether said items correspond to this definition, comprehensive consideration should be given, for example, to the intentions of the possessor and the character of the items, so that they cannot be objectively conceptualized as waste at the point when those items are discharged.
>
> (Notification from the Director of the Environment Promotion Division, Environmental Hygiene Bureau, Ministry of Health and Welfare, to the heads of waste-related departments in prefectural and designated city governments, 1971)

Examining the above definition, I emphasize that the first sentence refers to the economic character of the transaction of residuals. It states that the transaction in question is an inversely onerous transaction or a dis-compensated transaction, implying that waste is a bad (discommodity). Therefore, waste products must be bads. However, I note that bads are not only the characterization of waste: waste is not equivalent to bads even if waste is nearly equal to bads. The subtle argument around the definition of waste can be understood by reading the second sentence.

The second sentence states that "comprehensive consideration should be given", which implies that bads are not necessarily regarded as waste under the Waste Management Act. When we judge whether used items or residuals are waste, we take many factors other than an inversely onerous transaction into account.

The "comprehensive consideration" noted above raises a troublesome question: how many factors should we consider in deciding whether used items or residuals are waste? The answer may differ between regions or persons. In the course of daily waste administration, it is almost impossible to judge whether used items or residuals are waste, considering many factors comprehensively. Hence, bads are generally considered to be waste in daily waste administration. Consequently, I have noted that waste is nearly equal to bads. I call this characterization of waste the practical interpretation of waste. Indeed, following this interpretation, local authorities and municipalities decide what is and is not waste without the serious difficulties that they faced under the definition of the act.

The ambiguity of the definition of waste under the Waste Management Act seems to disappear by the above practical interpretation, which is logically consistent and clear from the viewpoint of economics. Even so, several questions persist regarding the definition. In fact, there is still discussion and even litigation on the definition of waste. Below, I comment on the characterization of waste.

First, I discuss the shortcomings of the practical interpretation of waste, according to which whether an item is classed as a good or a bad is significantly dependent upon market prices. The price of a residual that has resource potential fluctuates as prices of natural resources change. Hence, a used item cannot be identified as waste purely by its physical characteristics. Depending upon the place and time of discharge, the same item could be a good or a bad.

Transactions involving used lead batteries are a good example: these were bads and regarded as waste under the Waste Management Act around 2000. Because the price of lead was extremely low in the world market at that time, recycled lead was also devalued, and as a result, used lead batteries became bads. Approximately fifteen years later, however, the price of lead in the world market rose drastically, and used batteries became goods. Hence, they are no longer regarded as waste.[3] A similar pattern is also observed with old paper and used plastic bottles, causing confusion among citizens, government, and municipality administrations because in an extreme case, an item that was waste yesterday may not be considered waste today, and vice versa.

There is another problem with the practical interpretation. We find quite a few cases in which a used item is *not* purely a good or bad but consists of both goods and bads. In those cases, goods and bads are combined, creating one used item. Even so, the item may be subject to an onerous transaction or a compensated transaction, and thus, it is seemingly a good. Note that this type of process could occur intentionally or unintentionally. Should this item not be regarded as waste? This is a delicate question, and one cannot definitively state that the item is *not* waste. For example, it is often found that exporters intentionally mix goods with bads to make counterfeit goods and export them to foreign countries. This is nothing but waste export to foreign countries. Because revenue can be gained from the sale of the counterfeit goods, there is always motivation for exporting residuals, which consist of goods and bads. This situation arises especially in the case of exports to developing countries that have lenient regulations on the transaction of waste and waste disposal, although transboundary transaction of hazardous waste is strictly regulated by the Basel Convention.

Furthermore, there is a complication: some residuals or by-products[4] are classified as goods at the point of production but not ordinary goods when they are transported long distances. Although a cost-price balance is maintained at the point of production, the overall cost may exceed the sales price if these items are transported long distances and the cost of transportation is included. Because they have a positive value even if they are transported, they are nothing but goods. However, there is a deficit on the seller's side of the transaction. Whether these goods should be deemed waste requires deliberate consideration, and the comprehensive consideration must be referenced.

Iron and steel slag, which is a by-product of iron and steel production, provide a good example of this case. Whether residuals and other similar items are regarded as waste depends upon prefectures' judgment. Yet, in the current administrative interpretation, these residuals are goods *before* transportation so that they are *not* waste because they are priced positively regardless; however, the cost loss margins *after* transportation mean that they are actually the same as "bads" and deemed waste. Apparently, according to this interpretation, whether these residuals are regarded as waste significantly depends on transportation distances. The same residuals are not waste when they are transported short distances but are waste when transported long distances.

3.2 *Legal permission for handling waste connected with the definition of waste*

I have noted that problems remain around the definition of waste: the definition given in Article 2 of the Waste Management Act is not applicable to judgments regarding waste in daily administration. Although the Ministry of Health and Welfare has given a more practical interpretation with comprehensive consideration of the definition of waste, some subtle problems remain. However, we note that the mere definition of waste does not cause the problems; rather, the problems arise because one is required to obtain legal permission (a business license) from municipalities for municipal solid waste and from prefectures for industrial waste when one tries to collect, transport, or process used items, residuals, or other items that are deemed waste under the Waste Management Act.

Thus, if one seeks to transport iron and steel slag long distances, the transporters may be required to obtain permission from the prefecture because the slag may be regarded as industrial waste. If one seeks to transport it short distances, they are not required to do so. I have noted a similar phenomenon with used lead batteries, although the key factor in the judgment of waste is not distance but rather the price of lead.

Obviously, it is troublesome to obtain a license to handle waste from a local government, depending upon transportation distances, market circumstances, and other factors. Moreover, once used items, residuals, and other items are deemed waste, many constraints are imposed upon their collection, transportation, and processing. For example, municipal solid waste is supposed to be transported and treated within the relevant municipality,[5] in principle. Quite a few prefectures severely restrict the inflow of industrial waste from other prefectures.

One of the most awkward problems is that it is almost impossible to obtain a business license for collecting, transporting, or processing municipal solid waste from municipalities. This is because the transaction tends to be subject to the world of vested interests; business licenses are rarely granted to newcomers to the field of municipal solid waste transaction, partly due to the pressure from individuals already in the business. Therefore, there are no new entrants to the business of municipal solid waste and, consequently, no competition. An incentive to reduce treatment costs is not anticipated to develop, and inefficiency prevails without competition.

Additionally, the market for waste transaction tends to be segmented due to the restriction noted above, leaving little room for firms to grow and mature. This is particularly true in the business of municipal solid waste. Consequently, it is not surprising that Japan lacks big business in waste disposal and recycling similar to Waste Management (USA), Republic (USA), Suez Environment (France), or Veolia Environment (France).

The definition of waste and the related granting of business licenses for waste transaction and disposal, then, present perennial difficulties, and inefficiency prevails in the business of waste treatment and disposal. Sound and smooth recycling may be hindered by strict requirements for business licensing, and waste-disposal and recycling businesses do not mature easily. I also note that too-strict restriction on waste business creates an underground market for waste, in which informal businesses can become active and prosperous, causing environmental problems through improper treatment, disposal, or illegal dumping.

Obviously, it would be absurd if recyclable materials were not efficiently recycled on the grounds that they are waste and that their treatment and transportation is strictly regulated by the Waste Management Act. Here, I note that legal consideration is given to allow specific types of residuals to be recycled soundly and smoothly. For residuals that are transacted solely for the purpose of recycling, whether they are goods or bads, a business license is not required.

> Even in the case of businesses engaged in the disposal of industrial waste, existing collection businesses addressing waste solely and exclusively for recycling purposes, or in other words, addressing used paper, scrap metals (including old copper, etc.), empty bottles and old textiles, shall not be subject to licensing requirements.
>
> (Notification from the Director General of the Environmental Hygiene Bureau, Ministry of Health and Welfare, to prefectural governors and mayors of designated cities, 1971)

Although the above consideration is for industrial waste, a similar measure is in place for used paper, scrap metals (including old copper), empty bottles, and old textiles that are classified as municipal solid waste. Hence, a certain type of used paper that turned to bad from good in approximately the spring in 1997 was recycled without a license for handling municipal solid waste. I note, however, that this consideration is made for a limited number of items and does not apply to others – suggesting that inefficiency still remains in the recycling activities of some residuals.

3.3 Peculiarities in the classification of industrial waste

In this subsection, I demonstrate specific characteristics of the classification of waste. These characteristics are peculiar to the waste management system in Japan.

It must be remembered that waste is classified as municipal solid waste and industrial waste under the Waste Management Act. At first glance, municipal solid waste might be considered household waste; however, this is not true. Strangely enough, municipal solid waste includes certain types of waste that are discharged from business activities. I explain this in the following.

Under the current provisions of the Waste Management Act, industrial waste is classified into the categories shown in Table 1.1.

There are two different types of waste identified in Table 1.1: those numbered (1) to (12) and those numbered (13) to (19). The former type of waste, which is classified as "waste discharged from all business activities", is classified as a "non

Table 1.1 Categories of industrial waste

	Category	Concrete examples
	(1) Cinders and ashes	Coal cinders, incineration ashes, furnace cleaning residues, and other incineration residues.
	(2) Sludge	Sludgelike substances discharged from drainage-treatment processes and all types of industrial and manufacturing processes, sludge residues generated by activated sludge process, building-pit sludge, carbide residues, bentonite sludge, automobile-washing waste, construction sludge, etc.
	(3) Waste oil	Mineral oil, animal and vegetable oil, lubricant oil, insulating oils, washing oil, cutting fluids, solvents, tar pitch, etc.
	(4) Waste acid	Photograph fixing solution, waste sulfuric acid, waste hydrochloric acid, all sorts of organic acids, and other acid waste.
	(5) Waste alkaline	Photograph development fluid, waste sodium liquid, all alkaline waste liquid, including metal soap.
Waste discharged from all business activities	(6) Waste plastics	Synthetic-resins (plastic) residues, synthetic fiber residues, all solid and liquid synthetic polymer compounds such as synthetic rubber residues (including used tires).
(1)~(12)	(7) Waste rubber	Raw rubber, natural rubber.
(Non-business designation)	(8) Scrap metal	Fragments from iron and steel or nonferrous metals, grind residues, sawdust, etc.
	(9) Glass, concrete, and porcelain residues	Glass (plate glass, etc.), concrete from manufacturing processes, interlocking block residues, brick residues, waste gypsum boards, cement residues, mortar residues, slate residues, porcelain residues, etc.

(Continued)

Table 1.1 (Continued)

Category	Concrete examples
(10) Slag	Foundry waste sand, electric furnace and melting furnace refuse, spoil tip, inferior coal, powder coal, etc.
(11) Rubble	Concrete debris from construction, reconstruction or removal of buildings, fragments of asphalt debris, and other similar residues.
(12) Dust and soot	Dust and soot that are generated by the facilities designated by the Air Pollution Control Act or the Anti-Dioxine Measure Act or generated by incinerators of industrial waste, and which are collected by dust collection facilities.
Waste discharged from specified business activities (13)~(19) (Business designation)	(13) Waste paper	Waste paper from construction (i.e., generated by construction, reconstruction or removal of buildings), paper residues generated by pulp manufacture, paper industry, paper processed goods industry, newspaper industry, publishing business, bookbinding industry, and printing processes.
	(14) Waste wood	Waste wood from construction (the same as in waste paper), wood debris discharged from wood and wooden production industries (including furniture manufacturers), pulp manufacture, and wholesale imported wood, as well as lease companies, sawdust, bark, pallets used for freight, etc.
	(15) Waste textile	Waste textile from construction (the same as in waste paper), natural fiber waste such as cotton or wool waste generated by industries other than textile processing and clothing industries.
	(16) Animals and plants residues	Foodstuff (groceries), medical and pharmaceutical products, sweet residues from flavouring industry, size lees, brewing residues, fermentation residues, solid waste such as fish and meat residues, etc.
	(17) Solid waste from animals	Waste from abbatoirs, solid waste from poultry processing plants.
	(18) Excrement and urine from animals	Excrement and urine from livestock industry (beef, horse, pork, lamb, poultry, etc.).

Category	Concrete examples
(19) Corpses of animals	Dead bodies from livestock industry (beef, horse, pork, lamb, poultry, etc.).

(20) Waste that is generated from industrial activities and cannot be classified in the above categories (e.g., concrete solidified waste)

business designation". Thus, for example, waste plastics, used oils, and sludge generated from business activities are regarded as industrial waste, whatever business produces that waste.

In comparison, not all forms of waste discharged as a result of industrial activities are regarded as industrial waste if the waste is classified as "waste discharged from specified business activities" ((13) to (19) in Table 1.1). It is classified as a "business designation". For this reason, any waste discharged by a business other than a designated business is *not* classified as industrial waste, even if it was discharged as a result of business activities. It is classified as municipal solid waste and must be treated by people who have a license to handle municipal solid waste.

For example, used paper and wood products generated by offices, food residue generated by restaurants, and pruned shrub and tree cuttings from highways and airfields are *not* classified as industrial waste because offices, restaurants, highways and airfields are not in the category of designated businesses. These items must be treated as municipal solid waste in the same way as household refuse, so that they are collected, transported, and disposed of by businesses that have permission to transport and dispose of municipal solid waste.

This classification is artificial and not easy to understand. In fact, this peculiar classification of waste creates serious problems if taken literally. The transaction of used wooden pallets demonstrates the absurdity of this classification. Waste wooden pallets are categorized as waste wood, which is business-designated industrial waste. Because haulage, freight, or distribution businesses are not in the category of designated waste wood business, waste wooden pallets discharged by these businesses were not classified as industrial waste but rather as municipal solid waste. In the same way, waste wooden products generated by leasing businesses were also classified as municipal solid waste.

This classification caused a serious problem because most municipal solid waste disposal facilities and private municipal solid waste disposal facilities could not process vast quantities of waste wooden pallets and waste wooden products. In fact, those wastes were treated by industrial waste disposal facilities. Although this practice was illegal, there was no other way to treat them. Strangely enough, used plastic pallets discharged by any industry were classified as industrial waste because plastic waste were *non business designation waste*. Eventually, in April 2008, an amendment to the enforcement order of the Waste Management Act reclassified waste wooden pallets as industrial waste regardless of where they are discharged. In fact, we can find the item "pallet used for freight" in category

(14), entitled "waste wood" in Table 1.1, implying that it is classified as industrial waste at present.

Although the problem was resolved for wooden pallets, similar issues have been observed to a greater or lesser extent in industrial waste that is discharged from other specified business activities, as would be expected from the artificial categorization of industrial waste. It is incomprehensible that waste that corresponds to categories (13) to (19) in Table 1.1 and is discharged by non-designated business is classified as municipal solid waste and must be treated by the municipal solid waste facilities. This predicament demonstrates that the essential problem has not been resolved.

3.4 Development of and problems with the legal system for waste management and recycling

I have explained that some problems are caused by the tricky definition of waste, the artificial distinction between municipal solid waste and industrial waste, the peculiar categorization of industrial waste, and the immaturity of the waste markets due to the strict regulation of waste-disposal and recycling businesses. Except for those problems, however, the legal system and policy of waste management and recycling have worked well and contributed to solving waste problems.

Needless to say, the Waste Management Act is the core of the legal system for waste management and recycling. Thanks to its enactment and proper implementation, the transaction flows of waste are properly controlled and the sound and smooth disposal of waste is basically ensured, compared with the circumstances in the period of rapid economic growth. Indeed, proper disposal of waste was promoted and the amount of landfilled waste decreased drastically under the Act. Considering that a shortage of landfill space has been a serious problem in Japan, the role of the Waste Management Act must not be overlooked.

Additionally, the waste disposal industry, which had been a loosely controlled informal sector, was gradually formalized thanks to the waste management policy based upon the Waste Management Act. Here, an "informal sector" is a sector that operates without the protection of the legal system and that at times engages in activities that ignore legal provisions. Incidentally, the formalization of a waste management sector is a crucial issue everywhere, particularly in developing countries.[6]

Whereas the Waste Management Act may certainly have succeeded in advancing appropriate waste disposal and formalizing venous business operators, waste disposal in Japan now faces new issues. Waste that is discharged by consumers or firms is promptly and properly collected, transported, processed and disposed of by formal venous businesses. However, this venous business style has faced difficulties in treating products that rapidly change in terms of both quality and quantity.

New appliances and IT products, such as mobile phones, personal computers, and audio machines, provide an example. As products with new functions appear in a market, consumers quickly replace old products with the new products. Other advanced machinery products are also rapidly finding their way into family homes. Because the parts and materials of new products are made with new technology and thus the contents and composition of new products often differ from those of older products, it becomes difficult for municipalities or waste disposal and recycling firms to treat those new products properly when they reach the end of life.

Another troublesome issue is that materials in containers and packaging are becoming increasingly diversified. In the past, almost all beverages were packaged in glass bottles and sold. Currently, they are packaged in diversified containers, such as PET bottles, steel cans, aluminum cans, paper containers, or glass bottles. More efforts are now needed to sort them properly for recycling at the post-consumption stage. If different materials are mixed, sorting operations become more difficult, and thus, proper recycling may be hindered.

As for a material that has a blocking effect in proper recycling, I must mention plastics. Various types of plastics are used not only for containers and packaging but also for other products. Plastic products seem to be indispensable for modern daily life because plastics are easy to handle and hygienic. However, there are downsides to plastics: it is almost impossible to sort different types of plastic for recycling. Even if there is a label attached to a plastic product listing the materials used in the product, perfect sorting is not expected. Proper recycling of plastics, then, is a painstaking task, and a large number of used plastics are still considered bads and cannot be recycled.

Naturally, as technical progress continues, goods with advanced functions and materials that make life more convenient, such as plastics, are priced increasingly reasonably. Consumers are happy with those products, and their welfare seems to increase. As far as the arterial economy side is concerned, the situation appears positive, thanks to a market mechanism. That, however, is not the entire story. New products become end-of-life products (ELPs) eventually and must be treated by waste disposal firms or recyclers. As already noted, a market mechanism does not work perfectly in a venous market, and furthermore, the waste management system adopted so far has had problems with efficient disposal and recycling of waste. In these circumstances, the conventional venous business naturally cannot cope with a rapidly developing economy. The legal structure and policy for waste management and recycling should be overhauled. I now explain the problem from the viewpoint of economic incentives.

Under the Waste Management Act, municipal solid waste is supposed to be promptly collected from waste collection points and must be treated properly in waste-treatment facilities by municipalities. Municipal residents have long thought that municipal waste management employees would swiftly remove and dispose of waste if the residents put their waste in the appointed place at the appointed time and day. Swift removal and disposal of waste clearly provides benefits to municipal residents, although they may not be conscious of these benefits. This is because they do not have to express their willingness to pay for waste disposal – the costs of waste transportation and disposal are mainly covered by local taxes, and as a result, the residents are not charged for these costs. This situation eliminates motivation among residents to purchase manufactured goods that do not readily become waste at the post-consumption stage or to reduce the amount of waste they discharge.

On the producers' part, there is obviously no incentive to produce goods that do not readily become waste at the post-consumption stage. If they produce goods that easily become bads, these are properly disposed of by municipalities using taxation revenues. Therefore, producers need not consider the volumes of waste being created or disposed of. Moreover, they never pay attention to the costs involved in waste disposal. Regardless of the difficulty of disposing of their goods after use, it is expected that municipalities will cover the disposal costs through taxation. In these circumstances, producers have no motivation to create products that generate smaller volumes of waste at the post-consumption stage.

Because neither consumers nor manufacturers have any incentive to reduce the amount of waste and because neither side is concerned with the recyclability of products, products that easily become waste at the post-consumption stage or are not easily recyclable are sold in markets, so that the amount of difficult-to-process waste has continued to increase. Hence, although the Waste Management Act has contributed to the proper treatment of waste and the reduction of landfilled waste, it has failed to incorporate a mechanism that would prevent goods from being transformed into bads after consumption. This is the prime defect of the conventional waste disposal and recycling system: there is no incentive for both consumers and producers to choose products that do not readily become waste at the post-consumption stage and are easily recyclable.

A new institutional infrastructure must be introduced to solve the problem because a mere market mechanism cannot properly respond to the circumstances noted above. To reduce waste emissions and decrease waste disposal costs, various individual recycling-related laws were introduced pertaining to items such as containers, packaging, automobiles, and household appliances. However, recycling-related laws are not sufficient to avoid waste generation and promote cyclical use of resources.

To contribute to the cyclical use of resources in the overall production structure, the Act for the Promotion of Effective Utilization of Resources and the higher-ranked framework legislation, the Basic Act for Establishing a Sound Material-Cycle Society (hereinafter, the Material-Cycle Basic Act), were enacted (Figure 1.1). The Material-Cycle Basic Act is a basic law designed to promote the 3Rs (reduce, reuse, and recycle) and provide for the sound and smooth cyclical use of resources. The act requires the government to periodically formulate a Fundamental Plan for Establishing a Sound Material-Cycle Society (hereinafter, the Fundamental Plan).

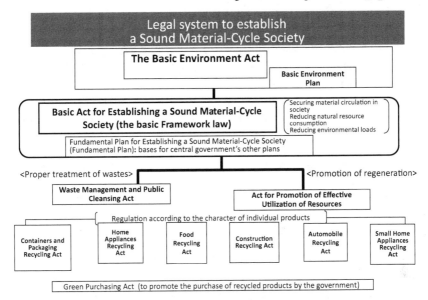

Figure 1.1 Legal system to establish a Sound Material-Cycle Society

Source: Ministry of Environment (2014). Some modifications are made.

Underlying the Material-Cycle Basic Act are a number of other laws that stipulate proper waste disposal and realization of the 3Rs. Under the Material-Cycle Basic Act is the law that has jurisdiction over proper disposal of waste, that is, the Waste Management Act. The law that is designated to promote the 3Rs is the Act for the Promotion of Effective Utilization of Resources. Beneath these two laws are other individual recycling-related laws.

I emphasize that the Material-Cycle Basic Act is a so-called framework act, which gives general principles for creating a circular economy but does not stipulate details nor regulate actors in the venous economy. Therefore, two pillars of the laws, namely the Waste Management Act and the Act for the Promotion of Effective Utilization of Resources, exist to support the Material-Cycle Basic Act for promoting proper disposal of waste and the 3Rs, and the individual recycling-related laws stipulate details for promoting sound and smooth recycling.

It is important to note that although the Waste Management Act is located under the Material-Cycle Basic Act, it takes the central role in the venous legal system noted above because it is the oldest law and it controlled waste disposal and recycling activities before other laws were introduced. First, the Waste Management Act defines and categorizes waste. Next, it is this law that gives permission for collecting, transporting, processing, and disposing of waste to venous actors. This fact has a significant meaning that must be carefully considered: it has the largest presence because none of the laws would have meaning or function without being linked to this overarching Act.

3.5 Evaluation of the individual recycling-related laws

Although I have noted that the Waste Management Act is situated at the center of the legal structure for waste disposal and recycling, the individual recycling-related laws have also contributed considerably to the promotion of the 3Rs since their enactment. It is interesting to explore their roles in the field of the 3Rs and what outcomes they have brought about.

First, through the implementation of the individual recycling-related laws, producers became responsible in some way for proper treatment of waste that was generated from their products. In the past, dischargers of waste, together with municipalities, waste disposal firms, and recyclers, were supposed to be responsible for proper treatment, and producers were exempted from responsibility. The circumstances have drastically changed since the individual recycling-related laws were enacted. Except for the Construction Recycling Act and the Small Home Appliances Recycling Act, the policy concept of EPR was introduced, making producers financially or physically responsible for their products at the post-consumption stage. Thanks to EPR, producers were given the motivation to produce products that are more easily recyclable than before and do not readily become waste, although the methods of EPR implementation differed depending on the item.

Second, whereas producers' responsibility came to be emphasized, all the actors in the same product chain (namely, the same arterial and venous chain) are encouraged by the laws to cooperate with one another to ensure sound and smooth waste disposal and recycling. The sound and smooth transaction of goods and bads (and so waste) in a visible product chain surely requires the cooperation of producers and businesses, such as waste collectors and transporters, demolition contractors, and recyclers, and the support of consumers and local governments is also needed. Otherwise, waste would be transacted in an invisible venous chain so that improper waste disposal or recycling and illegal dumping might occur. Proper waste disposal and recycling are guaranteed in a product chain only when the responsibilities of producers, dischargers, and waste disposal firms and recyclers are smoothly connected in a venous chain by cooperation.

Third, the money flow for recycling and the flow of ELPs are controlled, and collection schemes for recycling are stipulated, by the individual recycling-related laws, with the exception of the Food Recycling Act and the Small Home Appliance Recycling Act.[7] To transform bads into goods by recycling, charges should be collected and appropriately paid out for recycling activities. Those charges could not be collected by an ordinary market mechanism, and charge collection and payment mechanisms are stipulated in each recycling-related law, although the collection scheme for the charges differs with each law. I give some examples in the following.

Recycling charges are paid by users of products at the point of purchase in the cases of the Containers and Packaging Recycling Act and the Automobile Recycling Act. However, there is a subtle difference in the method of payment: the charges for recycling are incorporated into the product price in the former, whereas they are presented to users separately from the sales price in the latter.

Because users or dischargers need not pay those charges at the point of discharge, there is no incentive for them to dump ELPs illegally.

The Home Appliance Recycling Act adopts a different scheme for collecting recycling charges: users of home appliances (cathode ray tube (CRT) or liquid-crystal television sets, air-conditioners, refrigerators, and washing machines) are supposed to pay those charges at the point of discharge of ELPs. A similar method is applicable to the Construction Recycling Act: charges are paid by clients (owners of houses and buildings that are to be demolished) at the time of demolition and disposal.

Fourth, all the laws set numerical targets for recycling rates, although each law places the responsibility for achieving these targets with a different actor. Producers are responsible for achieving the targeted recycling rates in the case of the Home Appliance Recycling Act and the Automobile Recycling Act. In other recycling-related laws, certain actors related to the relevant ELPs are required to cooperate to achieve the given targets. I note that, in the case of the Small Home Appliance Recycling Act, the target is not for the recycling rate but rather for the number of small home appliances to be collected.

That being said, I now examine and evaluate the outcomes of the introduction of the individual recycling-related laws. EPR gives producers incentives to pay due attention to their products at the post-consumer stage of the life cycle. As expected in the implementation of EPR, Design for Environment (DfE) and Easy-to-Recycle plans for their products have been gradually realized. For example, in the fields of home appliances and automobiles, producers are motivated to design and sell products that are easy to recycle and dismantle so that advanced recycling is promoted, which is made possible by constant communication and cooperation between producers and recyclers. In the same way, producers are encouraged to disseminate refillable and lightweight containers.

DfE has also changed producers' attitudes toward choosing materials for their products. In the past, various materials, some of which are not easy to recycle, were used. After the individual recycling-related laws were enacted, however, producers began to choose limited numbers of recyclable materials. It is noteworthy that product labeling that shows the materials used in a product is becoming more popular among producers. Apparently, these considerations facilitate high-quality recycling and contribute to raising recycling rates.

Another advancement in the venous economy is the formalization of transacting actors along the venous chain. Generally, only qualified actors are allowed to make business transactions in the recycling fields that are regulated by the individual recycling-related laws. As a result, formal sectors increasingly dominate the venous economy, and the opportunity for adverse selection is narrowing. Furthermore, once-segmented actors in a venous chain have become linked with one another as formal actors. The linkage in the product chain, which implies cooperation among the actors in the chain, has facilitated the smooth flow of ELPs through the entire chain and, as a result, promoted smooth resource circulation.

The above-referenced advancement in a venous economy has brought about a tangible and remarkable result: the recycling rate targeted by each recycling related law was achieved, as already noted. As for end-of-life vehicles (ELVs), the target of a 95 percent recycling rate by 2015 was achieved in advance of the target year. I note that a 95 percent recycling rate is also the target of ELV recycling in the EU, although the definitions of recycling differ slightly between Japan and the EU. Similarly, for end-of-life electric appliances, the recycling rates for specific items in fiscal year 2013 were as follows: air conditioners (91 percent), CRT televisions (79 percent), LCD and plasma televisions (89 percent), refrigerators and freezers (80 percent) and washing machines and dryers (88 percent). All of these recycling rates exceeded the targeted recycling rates stipulated in the Home Appliance Recycling Act.

It is clear that each recycling-related law has contributed to increasing the recycling rates, reducing the amount of waste and therefore saving landfill space. I must note, however, that these results have been obtained by not only the individual recycling-related laws but also soft laws that I will explain in the next subsection.

3.6 The role of soft law in the institutional infrastructure

So far, I have emphasized the role of hard laws in raising recycling rates, reducing the amount of waste disposed of in landfill. Thanks to those laws, Japan has succeeded in promoting the 3Rs. However, that is only half of the story: we must not forget the role played by the other part of the institutional infrastructure, soft laws, which should not be overlooked in the advancement of waste disposal and recycling. In fact, the numerical targets for recycling of ELVs, home appliances, and other items were achieved by not only hard laws, represented by the recycling-related laws, but also soft laws. Furthermore, reduction of other waste not related to each recycling law was basically made possible by soft laws. I explain this through four examples.

Example 1: Recycling of ELVs

As noted, ELVs are recycled under the Automobile Recycling Act at present in Japan. Before the law was enacted, however, a voluntary action plan promoted more advanced recycling of ELVs. The plan was made by the cooperation of almost all the interested parties, and the government played a particularly important role in coordinating the plan's formation. Although the plan did not legally bind any actor, all the related parties respected and acted according to the plan. Under this plan, the actors concerned, including manufacturers, dealers, maintenance workshops, and scrap merchants, engaged in cooperation and implemented the appropriate recycling of ELVs. Thus, the plan is considered a typical example of a soft law. To develop the core idea of the plan and promote high-quality recycling, the government finally decided to pass a recycling law for ELVs based upon the plan. Therefore, the contents of the plan are now integrated in the law. Incidentally, a recycling ratio of 95 percent on a weight basis by 2015 was already targeted under the plan, and the target is still valid in the ELV recycling scheme set by the Automobile Recycling Act.

Example 2: Recycling of home appliances

We find a similar background with the Home Appliance Recycling Act. Before the act was introduced, used home appliances, such as CRT or liquid-crystal television sets, air-conditioners, refrigerators, and washing machines, were reused or recycled following a market mechanism or disposed of by municipalities; used home appliances that could be usable second-hand were transacted with positive prices by second-hand dealers or recycled by private recyclers with positive or negative prices, whereas most other used home appliances were disposed of by municipalities.

Municipalities had difficulty in treating large-sized electric appliances due to the limited capacity of their facilities. In response, the government designated refrigerators with a capacity in excess of 250 liters and televisions with a screen size above 25 inches under the Waste Management Act as items that are extremely difficult to process at the post-consumption stage.[8] Under the auspices of the designation, municipalities could request cooperation from the relevant producers to dispose of or recycle those appliances. In fact, most came to be properly disposed of or recycled by the producers. Although this was a request by municipalities to producers, under the Waste Management Act, which is a hard law, the cooperation of producers in disposing of these items was not compulsory but voluntary. Even so, producers acceded to the request.

In other words, the request and its granting were based upon a soft law in that the request asked appliance producers to promote the prompt and appropriate disposal or recycling of items that presented processing or disposal difficulties by implementing the manufacturers' own codes of conduct. This style of waste disposal and recycling is similar to EPR enforced by hard law.

Example 3: Recycling of motorcycles and small pleasure boats

I give other interesting examples that show the effectiveness of soft laws for waste disposal and recycling. Although there is a hard law for ELV recycling, there is no corresponding hard law for recycling of motorcycles. End-of-life motorcycles were disposed of or recycled following a market transaction, while some used parts were transacted with positive prices in a market. Currently, there is voluntary action by businesses to promote proper disposal or recycling of used motorcycles. Although the number of used motorcycles recycled under this scheme is low, those collected under the scheme are considered to be recycled properly.

A similar scheme exists for recycling small pleasure boats that are made of fiber-reinforced plastic (FRP). FRP is difficult to recycle, and users and municipalities had difficulty disposing of small FRP pleasure boats. Then, producers of small FRP pleasure boats, under the coordination of the government, devised a scheme to promote proper processing of those boats. So far, the scheme has worked well, and FRP from small pleasure boats is recycled in cement kilns.

Example 4: The Japan business federation's voluntary action to promote a circular economy

The Japan Business Federation has formulated a voluntary scheme to promote a circular economy and checks it periodically.[9] Member companies that participate in the program are required to reduce the amount of waste disposed of in landfill. They succeeded in reducing the amount of landfilled waste in fiscal year 2013 by 91.5 percent from that in 1990. The target reduction rate, a 65 percent reduction of landfilled waste from that in 2000, was already achieved in 2014. The actual rate was 73.5 percent.

The achievement of such a high reduction rate of landfilled waste is amazing, particularly when we consider that the scheme is voluntary and not at all compulsory. It should be almost impossible to achieve such a challenging target voluntarily without high consciousness of social norms and compliance.

Currently, soft laws represented by moral codes and social norms are respected and observed by business sectors and organizations and have sometimes played a crucial role in promoting the 3Rs, as I have shown by the above examples. Without soft laws, the 3Rs could not be fulfilled with high quality. This is partly because they are inherently flexible and adaptable to locally specific situations. Moreover, they may provide more room for maneuver than hard laws in responding to constantly changing circumstances.

However, in principle, soft laws would not function well without hard laws in place. The interrelationship and balance between hard and soft laws is also important. In this context, the example of used lead batteries is interesting. When the price of lead is so low that used lead batteries are bads, they must be handled as industrial waste that requires a special license under the Waste Management Act. However, once the price of lead rises high enough that used batteries become goods, they can be transacted in a market without any constraints, not being controlled by the Waste Management Act. Although there is a voluntary scheme by lead battery producers, the number of used batteries collected under the scheme is negligible and not effective for proper recycling of used lead batteries. Consequently, a large number of used lead batteries are considered to be transacted by informal sectors, and these are flowing out of Japan in an invisible flow of transaction. One might say that the hard and soft laws are not well balanced.

Finally, in this subsection, I reiterate the role of the government in the formation of soft laws. As I have shown in the cases of recycling of ELVs and home appliances, the government administration in many cases plays a coordinating role in the formation of soft laws. Clearly, there are conflicting interests among concerned actors in quite a few cases for promoting the 3Rs, and those interests must be harmonized. No actor other than the government can play this role. It is expected that the government will soon become even more important as a coordinator of soft laws.

4 The role of EPR in Japan

EPR, which was first proposed by Dr. Lindhqvist at Lund University, was defined and formulated in a practical form by OECD and has gradually been introduced in quite a few countries, although it is legally implemented in various ways. Although EPR may require a lengthy discussion, I focus only on the points necessary to address the present topics.

4.1 EPR: A definition and a few remarks

When I explained the individual recycling-related laws in the preceding section, I noted that the role of EPR is implemented in the recycling-related laws, such as the Containers and Packaging Recycling Act, the Home Appliances Recycling Act, and the Automobile Recycling Act. I explain EPR briefly in this section. OECD (2001) defines EPR as follows:

> OECD *defines* Extended Producer Responsibility (EPR) as an environmental policy approach in which a producer's responsibility, physical and/or financial, for a product is extended to the post-consumer stage of a product's life cycle. There are two related features of EPR policy: (1) the shifting of responsibility (physically and/or economically; fully or partially) upstream to the producer and away from municipalities; and (2) to provide incentives to producers to incorporate environmental considerations in the design of their products.

First, I emphasize that there are two types of responsibilities, "physical responsibility" and "financial responsibility". The former refers to the producer's responsibility to engage in the collection, disposal and recycling of products that have become waste. Recently, "organizational responsibility" has been used more often than "physical responsibility" (European Commission, 2014). Meanwhile, the latter refers to the case in which the producer may not have physical responsibility but does take responsibility for paying for disposal or recycling. Clearly, a mixture of the two types of responsibilities is possible.

Second, *logically*, EPR is nothing to do with the problem of internalization of external diseconomy. Suppose that household waste, such as used containers and packaging, is collected and disposed of by municipalities properly and that neither households' utility functions nor firms' production functions are adversely affected by the municipalities' treatment of those used containers and packaging. Thus, no external diseconomy is caused by the treatment. Even in this case, EPR can be applicable and effective because it may reduce the treatment costs by utilizing private waste disposal firms in the short run, and, moreover, DfE implemented by EPR will contribute to reduction of the treatment costs in the long run. EPR thus seeks to reduce social costs by reducing the burden placed on municipalities. However, it is not a tool of internalization of external diseconomy in this example.

In this context, we should recall why EPR has been introduced. Without EPR, there is no motivation for producers to consider how products come to the end of their life and how ELPs become waste. This circumstance results in increased waste disposal and recycling costs at the post-consumption stage of the life cycle, thus increasing social costs, even if there is no external diseconomy that is analyzed in an economic theory. Given this situation, the introduction of EPR provides producers with the motivation to design and manufacture products that do not readily become waste or those that are easily recycled, contributing to cyclical use of resources.

Third, there are various ways to introduce EPR as a waste management and recycling policy (European Commission, 2014). Industrial and transaction structures vary largely by country and are based on the character of the product. Similarly, the conditions for businesses engaged in waste disposal and recycling differ by country. Thus, the format of EPR in one country may not be applicable to other countries. Furthermore, the EPR format for one product may not apply to others; even within one country, EPR may be applied to each product differently because the nature of a product chain (an arterial chain and a venous chain) differs depending upon the product. I have already noted that EPR has been applied to ELVs and used home appliances in different ways in Japan.

4.2 How was EPR introduced in Japan?

When I discussed the characteristics of the individual recycling-related laws in Subsection 3.5, I briefly explained how EPR has been applied to some laws. I now explain the differences in EPR among the laws in more detail.

The Containers and Packaging Recycling Act is a typical example of financial EPR. Companies that engage in the production and use of containers and packaging do not bear any physical responsibility for the collection or recycling of containers and packaging at the post-consumption stage. Instead, they bear financial responsibility: all they must do is pay the Japan Containers and Packaging Recycling Association in advance for the recycling of containers and packaging that the companies produced or utilized.

Here, the role of this association as the Producer Responsibility Organization (PRO) must be emphasized. PRO generally refers to an organization that is commissioned by producers to manage the collection and recycling of ELPs. On behalf of producers, the association selects contractors to collect, transport, and recycle containers and packaging and manages recycling flows. In this way, producers are exempted from physical responsibility.

The Automobile Recycling Act is similar to the Home Appliances Recycling Act in that users (consumers) pay disposal and recycling charges whether the payment may be at the point of purchase (the Automobile Recycling Act) or the point of discharge (the Home Appliances Recycling Act). However, there is a major difference between the two laws: in the Automobile Recycling Act, users pay for the disposal and recycling of only three items, which are the fluorocarbons and other substances used in air-conditioners, air bags, and automobile shredder residue (ASR); in the Home Appliances Recycling Act, users pay for disposal and recycling of entire ELPs. This difference exists because EPR is applied only to these three items in the Automobile Recycling Act, and automobile manufacturers are required to dispose of and recycle only the items under their responsibility (physical responsibility). They are not responsible for the disposal and recycling of an entire ELV. Before the act was introduced, ELVs were 75 percent recycled by weight on a business basis. Even without a law in place, various parts were reused, and components and metals, such as steel and copper, found in ELVs were recycled in the market. That remains the case and is why only the three items, which are not recycled on a business basis, are targeted by EPR in the Automobile Recycling Act. Incidentally, the recycling rate has increased to more than 95 percent since the implementation of the law.

The money collected from users as disposal and recycling charges is managed by PROs known as a deposit management institution. This is also the case with the Containers and Packaging Recycling Act. However, here is a big difference from the Containers and Packaging Recycling Act: the collected money is saved by the PRO for over ten years and paid out to specialist businesses at the time the vehicle in question is disposed of and recycled. Because vehicles have a usable life from the time of purchase through scrapping in excess of 10 years, this deposit management institution manages sizeable funds. Additionally, it is difficult for manufacturers to precisely anticipate the amount of charges for disposal and recycling beyond ten years in the future. Therefore, manufacturers may profit or suffer a loss through these recycling activities.

The Home Appliance Recycling Act provides a contrasting example: users pay for disposal and recycling charges at the point of discharge of used home appliances rather than the point of purchase. The charges collected from users cover the costs of transportation from a discharge point (generally a store that sells home appliances because users are supposed to return used home appliances to stores) to a stockyard and costs of disposal and recycling.

Producers' responsibility is to transport used appliances from stockyards to recycling plants and to promote advanced recycling. Thus, producers are considered to bear physical responsibility. The recycling is largely supposed to take place at recycling plants designated by the producers. Basically, no other recycling facility is allowed to recycle the used home appliances targeted by the law. To achieve the recycling ratio stipulated by the law, the producers disburse the funds collected from users and implement recycling operations in either their own or contracted facilities. The money collected is spent on the disposal and recycling of used home appliances soon after the collection, and this vast amount of money is not accumulated at PROs, compared with the amount of money collected under the Automobile Recycling Act.

Apart from physical or financial responsibility, there are clear differences in EPR implementation among the three recycling laws cited above. The differences come mainly from the nature of products, industrial organization, and transaction style. In the case of automobiles, each vehicle is registered officially, and the owner of an automobile can be identified. Therefore, it is possible to manage costs for the recycling of vehicles on a per unit basis because vehicles are traceable and can be managed individually by the registration system. In contrast, there is no traceable system for containers, packaging, or home appliances; therefore, it is impossible to manage the collected money for their disposal and recycling on a per unit basis.

A question may arise regarding the Home Appliances Recycling Act. Why was an advance payment method not adopted for collection of the disposal and recycling charges? Because payment of the charges at the point of discharge seems to encourage illegal dumping, payment at the point of purchase (advance payment) seems preferable; prevention of illegal dumping is a positive aspect of an advance payment method. However, it is almost impossible to identify each home appliance without a registration system and trace it in a venous chain. Thus, it is not feasible to identify a one-to-one relationship between the money paid in advance and the home appliance discharged. There may then be a serious problem with how the money collected in advance should be allocated to used home appliances at the disposal stage, which is an apparent negative aspect of an advance payment method. Presumably, a comparative analysis of the negative aspects of advance payment versus the positive aspects led to the Home Appliance Recycling Act adopting a charge to be applied when the product is discharged.

4.3 PCC to connect arterial and venous chains smoothly

In this subsection, I present my own view about the method for promoting the 3Rs and creating a circular economy, that is, PCC (product chain control). PCC is characterized as follows: accountability, traceability, and transparency of the ELP flow are guaranteed in the product chain so that proper disposal and recycling is performed in a cost-effective manner with minimal environmental impact. Moreover, arterial and venous chains are connected soundly and smoothly, and cyclical use of resources is thus efficiently effected. The ultimate objective of waste disposal and recycling policy is to implement PCC to minimize social costs, promoting the cyclical use of resources and constructing a circular economy.

To promote PCC, three types of responsibilities must be joined in a product chain: extended producer responsibility (EPR), dischargers' responsibility, and disposal and recycling firms' responsibility. I have already demonstrated how EPR is required to control the flow of a product and ELP for promoting advanced recycling and reducing the amount of waste that goes to landfill. However, these are only the necessary conditions for implementation of the 3Rs.

Even if producers bear EPR and sell products that do not readily become waste at the post-consumption stage, the 3Rs will be incomplete if households do not buy those products or discharge ELPs without proper sorting. A key point of recycling is to sort venous resources at the point of discharge to the extent that efficient transportation and recycling can be accomplished in a venous chain. Hence, dischargers' responsibility is critical.

The same argument is true with disposal and recycling firms' responsibility. Suppose that EPR and dischargers' responsibility is fully implemented but that waste disposal and recycling firms improperly dispose of or recycle products in which DfE is embodied. This could occur particularly when financial EPR is introduced. In this case, EPR is implemented on the surface but is far from true realization.

Obviously, a market mechanism must be wisely utilized even when PCC is applied to a certain product. Without utilizing a market mechanism, the 3Rs cannot be promoted in a cost-effective way. I have shown that too-restrictive institutional infrastructure hinders efficient waste disposal and recycling. However, I have also noted that only a market mechanism does not promote sound and smooth waste disposal and recycling (and so also the 3Rs). Thus, we must introduce PCC, considering the balance between a market mechanism and institutional infrastructure.

Significantly, controlling venous chain flows also affects an arterial chain, that is, the chain of design of a product, procurement of resources, production, distribution, and sale. This control cannot be accomplished by a market mechanism, mainly due to the problem caused by double asymmetry of information between dischargers of waste and waste disposal or recycling firms (Hosoda, 2008). Whether in the physical or financial form, if responsibility for controlling venous chain flows is imposed on producers, possibly by EPR, they will be motivated to create products that do not readily become bads or products from which goods can be derived from bads by recycling. Furthermore, the methods of distribution and sale will change so that proper collection and recycling of ELPs will be promoted and waste will not be generated.

In other words, controlling venous chain flows also serves to regulate conditions in the arterial economy, shifting producers' practices in the direction of a circular economy. Hence, this control process uses the term *product chain control* or *PCC*: the arterial chain is soundly and smoothly connected to the venous chain.

Also important, PCC could be utilized to encourage producers to use secondary materials that are produced from venous resources. Not until producers input secondary materials to their production processes will arterial and venous chains be smoothly connected and a circular economy constructed. Unfortunately, at present, PCC is not well implemented; consequently, a circular economy is incomplete. I discuss this point further in the next section.

5 Toward a new circular economy

Under the Fundamental Plan and the individual recycling-related laws, the amount of waste landfilled and discharged has been reduced. While DfE has made some progress, recycling ratios of ELPs designated by the individual recycling-related laws have increased and the targeted recycling ratios have been achieved. These results show that PCC using Japanese-style EPR has exerted a certain effect. However, there remain some challenges to advancing a circular economy. In this section, I discuss those challenges and suggest how to address them.

5.1 Transaction of venous resources in an invisible flow

In 2004, an interesting story appeared in a newspaper: a number of used lead batteries were being exported from Japan to Vietnam. At that time, most people were not interested in this news, except for some who made a business of transaction of lead batteries, whether as producers or recyclers. They wondered how those used batteries were recycled in Vietnam, which lacked proper facilities for recycling used lead batteries.

During the mid-2000s, used PET bottles, which were supposed to be recycled domestically under the Containers and Packaging Recycling Act, were flowing out of Japan. Some of the used PET bottles that had been collected by municipalities were not passed to recycling businesses through a designated organization (a PRO, in EPR terms) but were channeled through other routes, resulting in a decrease in domestic recycling. From 2008 to 2010, more than half of the used PET bottles were recycled out of Japan.[10] It is thought that the majority of these missing PET bottles were exported to developing countries, such as China. Although the Ministry of Environment has encouraged municipalities to deliver collected PET bottles to the Japan Containers and Packaging Recycling Association, the designated PRO, this trend has continued.

In 2014, roughly a third of used lead batteries discharged in Japan were mainly considered to be exported to Korea. Because only two thirds of used batteries remained in Japan, firms functioning as secondary refineries of lead had difficulties in collecting used batteries. In fact, one recycler went bankrupt after it could not collect enough used lead batteries.

In the same year, the export of used aluminum cans began to increase, partly due to the devaluation of the yen. In particular, there was a remarkable increase in the amount of exports to Korea. Due to the rapid outflow, the recycling ratio of used aluminum cans in Japan decreased, albeit by only a few percentage points.

Before 2000, the amount of used paper exported was very small, less than 400,000 tons. Fifteen years later, it was ten times larger. Most was exported to China.[11] It is suspected that mainly used paper that is of good quality or well sorted is exported to China and that poor-quality used paper tends to remain in Japan.

These situations extend to other products, such as used electric and electronic products, other ELPs, and circuit boards. In other words, venous resources generated in Japan are flowing overseas in the form of *goods*. ELPs and other venous resources considered bads by the Japanese have turned out to be goods for people living in developing countries.

I emphasize that these venous resources were exported in an invisible flow of transaction. The uncontrolled outflow of venous resources in an invisible flow that are transacted as goods presents a serious problem. Because all venous resources have some pollution potential, improper disposal and recycling could cause contamination and environmental degradation through pollution (Hosoda, 2008), particularly in developing countries. For example, used electric and electronic appliances and circuit boards contain toxic substances, such as lead. If these venous resources are recycled improperly in developing countries, there is a high probability that contamination will occur. Indeed, examples of these cases have been reported (The Basel Action Network and Silicon Valley Toxics Coalition, 2002).

Although these exports are strictly regulated by the Basel Convention and the corresponding national law called the Act on Control of Export, Import and Others of Specified Hazardous Wastes and Other Wastes, these provisions tend to be ignored by informal businesses in a venous economy. These exports should be regarded as a variation of pollution exports.

There is another problem: some venous resources that are substitutable for natural resources are exported overseas and do not remain in Japan. Precious metals, such as gold, silver, platinum, and palladium, are exported in the form of venous resources. It is ironic that Japan is exporting valuable venous resources despite importing considerable amounts of natural resources.

Japan imports most of the metals contained in electric and electronic products, other ELPs, circuit boards, and other items, which are not obtained in natural forms in Japan. Japan will certainly continue to import those metals that are vital to the Japanese manufacturing industry. As the scarcity of these metals increases, their prices will certainly rise in the long run, and the volatility of their prices is also anticipated to increase. Consequently, stable procurement of those metals will become increasingly important. Clearly, then, recycled metals should be much more wisely utilized in the future, and Japan must now prepare for this situation.

Surprisingly, the current legal system for waste disposal and recycling contains no concept of using recycled resources (secondary materials) efficiently through the processing of venous resources that are generated in Japan. Venous resources are accumulating in the form of urban mines but are not utilized well at all. Although PCC by means of EPR has to date been successful in controlling waste generation and emissions and increasing the recycling ratio, it has failed to efficiently use resources that are extracted from urban mines.

5.2 Double resource constraints: peak-out of natural resources and exhaustion of landfill

Through examples, I have demonstrated that venous resources generated in Japan and recycled resources (secondary materials) attained from venous resources are not being effectively used domestically. Japan imports a huge amount of natural resources, while venous resources that have resource potential are increasingly flowing out to developing countries. This situation poses a serious challenge for Japan, which does not have any natural resources and is running out of landfill.

Because landfill space is regarded as a sort of resource, we may state that Japan faces double resource constraints: constraints on both natural resources and landfill space. These double resource constraints are likely to intensify in the coming years, and scarcities of those resources will increase in the long run. These two constraints are deeply and mutually interrelated.

Consider copper as an example. The fact that copper is being extracted from ever-lower grades of copper ore indicates that a single copper mine yields only low-grade, low-yield copper ore. This trend will surely continue in the future, further tightening the constraints on the supply of copper. Meanwhile, demand for copper will increase because economic development and growth of developing countries will require more copper as an input for production processes. Consequently, world competition for copper will surely intensify.

However, some ELPs that contain copper are not collected in a visible venous chain and are not recycled properly in Japan. The final destination of residuals of ELPs is developing countries or landfill. If copper and other potential resources contained in ELPs were extracted more efficiently and used inputs substitutable for copper and other resources obtained from the natural environment, we could save both natural copper and landfill space, clearing the double constraints. However, this is not the case at present.

This circumstance is almost the same as with other natural resources, and the two above-referenced constraints will only intensify for all resources, making both extraction of natural resources and disposal of waste at landfill sites all the more difficult. Accordingly, the scarcity of these natural resources and landfill will further increase in the future as will their market prices. Here, I note that market prices do not reflect all costs: although the costs of extraction, production, distribution, landfilling, and other processes are reflected in market prices, environmental costs, which accompany those economic activities, are not.

As noted, metals contained in natural ore grow thinner as they are extracted. Meanwhile, metals extracted from mines are accumulated in the form of urban ore in urban mines because metals that were extracted from mines have been transferred to the economic system. Urban mines will be richer with resources.

What is the implication of the above observation? The answer is clear: utilization of venous resources and secondary resources must be accelerated. As long as an economy continues to develop and grow, the resource stock in the economic system will surely increase but will never decrease. Venous resources are growing relatively richer than natural resources. For active use of venous resources, we should create a new system in which efficient collection and transportation of venous resources are organized on one hand and advanced technology for recycling is utilized as much as possible on the other. These goals could be accomplished by a well-designed institutional infrastructure.

5.3 A stumbling block to constructing a circular economy

While Japan was successful in reducing the amount of waste and promoting advanced recycling, it has not succeeded in creating a sound and smooth circular economy, as noted above: Japan is not well prepared to cope with the tightening of its double resource constraints. It is missing the opportunity to utilize venous resources domestically.

This might sound odd because Japan has enacted various laws to promote the 3Rs. One might think it possible to create a sound circular economy that takes into account the double resource constraints using the Fundamental Plan, which is based upon the Material-Cycle Basic Act. The Fundamental Plan was enacted for the purpose of creating a circular economy. Is there any problem with the conventional legal system for constructing a circular economy?

First, no law in the present legal system requires private firms to utilize secondary resources that are obtained by processing venous resources. Certainly, there is the Green Purchasing Act, which promotes the purchase of recycled products by the government and related public institutions. However, this act has no influence on private sectors, limiting its effect.

Accordingly, there are no means to collect venous resources efficiently or obtain recycled resources (secondary materials) that could be reused in Japan. Therefore, even if urban ore of a higher grade than natural ore flows out of Japan in the form of waste circuit boards, used lead batteries, and plastic, there are no effective means in place to staunch this flow.

It might be argued that the Fundamental Plan aims to achieve the cyclical use of resources by utilizing the index called resource productivity (GDP ÷ the amount of natural resource input) and that the resource productivity actually increased from 250,000yen/ton in 2000 to 380,000yen/ton in 2012 (Figure 1.2). However, there is neither a legal requirement nor a policy tool to increase the resource productivity, and the increase may have been partly due to increases in resource prices and partly due to the ceaseless exertion to save inputs of natural resources on the business side.

That being said, we see that the present legal system is insufficient for promoting further cyclical use of resources and that the target of resource efficiency

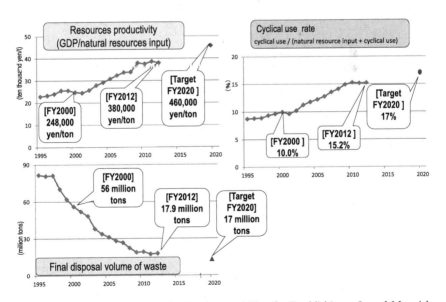

Figure 1.2 Three indices under the Fundamental Plan for Establishing a Sound Material-Cycle Society

Source: Ministry of Environment, Japan

of 460,000yen/ton in 2020 under the Fundamental Plan may not be achieved under the present system. The institutional infrastructure must be strengthened to accelerate domestic use of recycled resources in order to enhance cyclical use of resources.

Incidentally, there are other indices under the Fundamental Plan for the advancement of a circular economy: cyclical use rate as an index for the cyclical use of resources (the amount of cyclical resource input ÷ [the amount of natural resource input + the amount of cyclical resource input]) and amount of landfill (index of the quantity of material emitted from the economic system as waste). Resource productivity, cyclical use rate, and amount of landfill may be considered the input, throughput, and output indices of resources, respectively.

The above argument applies to the other indices, that is, a cyclical use rate and an amount of landfill: there is neither a legal requirement nor a concrete policy tool for achieving the targets of the indices. Although the indices have constantly improved, this improvement is *not* the direct result of the legal system.

I do not deny that the development of the present legal system for promoting the 3Rs contributed to improving the targets of the indices nor that the increase in the recycling ratio of various ELPs serves the objectives of the Fundamental Plan. However, there is no mechanism in place whereby the contents of the Fundamental Plan could be realized through implementing individual recycling-related laws. In other words, the contents of the Fundamental Plan are not functionally tied to the individual recycling-related laws. This is a stumbling block to constructing a sound circular economy. If the present circumstances remain unchanged, the realization of what is envisaged in the Fundamental Plan and creation of a circular economy do not seem feasible.

Finally, in this subsection, I emphasize that PCC supported by EPR alone cannot link arterial and venous chains smoothly because, as I have repeatedly emphasized, there is leakage of venous and recycled resources from visible flows to invisible flows. In addition to PCC, a demand network to collect and transport venous resources efficiently in a visible venous chain must be created. By doing so, various secondary or recycled resources obtained in Japan could be more effectively utilized domestically. In this way, the exit of venous resources could be linked to the entry point for the use of resources, so that cyclical use of resources would be complete. Unless strategic measures are launched for the express purpose of linking the exit point of venous resources to the entry point of secondary or recycled resources as inputs, it will be impossible to create a sound circular economy.

6 Conclusion: paving the way to a circular economy

As demonstrated in the introduction, Japan has a long tradition of waste disposal and recycling. The institutional infrastructure for sound waste disposal and recycling, although in a rudimentary form, had already been organized even in the Edo period. In the Meiji era, a formal legal system for waste disposal was gradually introduced to guarantee proper disposal of household waste (municipal solid waste), while the private sector was engaged in recycling on a business basis. We find such old traces in the modern system of waste disposal and recycling. For example, the incineration that was encouraged by the Meiji government is still the primary method for treating municipal solid waste,[12] whereas advanced recycling is pursued by private businesses.

However, it is clear that Japan should reconsider the conventional system of waste disposal and recycling to pave the way for a sound circular economy. Although finding the way to a sound circular economy is challenging, some guidelines exist. I have noted that, by utilizing PCC and creating a demand network, the exit of venous resources could be linked to the entry point for the use of resources so that cyclical use of resources will be complete. This is becoming reality.

In this context, the EU's strategy for constructing a circular economy is worth examining. The EU has recently announced two interesting policy measures called "end-of-waste" and "resource efficiency". By coupling these two measures, the EU is attempting to create a circular economy.

End-of-waste represents a measure by which the transformation of waste (bads) into recycled resources (goods) is controlled according to the format determined by the EU regulation. It requires venous companies to engage in a process control whereby waste ceases to be waste by a recycling operation and is transformed into a new resource. Insofar as venous resources are transformed into recycled resources following this measure, one can safely use those resources as inputs because the quality of the resources is controlled. In this sense, this measure is considered an exit policy for waste.

Resource efficiency requires companies and national governments to control natural resources and energy input volumes, for example, by utilizing recyclable resources and renewable energies more than at present, representing an entry measure for resource circulation.[13] Although specific measures have yet to be realized for resource efficiency, this is widely considered to be a further step toward realizing a resource circulation entry policy.

A policy for coupling a waste exit measure and resource circulation entry measure implies a grand strategy to close the loop of the resource cycle and construct a circular economy. Only when venous resources are properly processed and recycled or secondary resources produced by processing venous resources are actually inputted to production processes will the resource circulation loop be closed and a circular economy completed. Apparently, the EU's strategy is aimed toward this goal.

The EU's grand strategy for a circular economy indicates that Japan is proceeding in the right direction but is a little backward compared with the EU. Japan's PCC must be supported by the formation of venous resource collection networks through efficient transportation and logistics. The next step is the creation of a mechanism through which companies engage in the active utilization of recycled resources (secondary materials). Resource productivity defined under the Fundamental Plan must be a guiding principle for business sectors for cyclical use of resources. Whether by hard or soft law, enhancing resource productivity through utilization of recycled resources should be the obligation of business sectors. Needless to say, to open the path, cooperation among all the relevant actors is also indispensable.

Notes

1 The formal title was the "Basel Convention on the Control of Transboundary Movements of Hazardous Waste and Their Disposal".
2 For a more detailed explanation of arterial and venous economies, see Hosoda (2008).
3 Used batteries belong to a specific category of industrial waste called "specially controlled waste", and their transaction is strictly regulated when they are bads. However, they can be transacted without any constraint when they are goods.
4 I call residuals or by-products "residual so on".
5 There are some exceptions: for example, if plural municipalities treat waste jointly, waste is allowed to be transported beyond a municipality's border as long as the transportation is within those municipalities' borders.
6 For a more detailed explanation on the relationship between formal and informal sectors in a venous industry, see Hosoda (2008).
7 It is supposed that private businesses will successfully work for recycling under the Food Recycling Act and the Small Home Appliance Recycling Act even without charge collection stipulations; as a result, no stipulation is made and recycling charges are not collected.
8 Used tires and large-sized spring mattresses were also designated as such.
9 See http://www.keidanren.or.jp/policy/2015/023.html.
10 See http://www.petbottle-rec.gr.jp/data/calculate.html.
11 See http://www.jpa.gr.jp/states/used-paper/.
12 Nearly 80 percent of municipal solid waste is incinerated in Japan.
13 The EU's resource efficiency is a multi-dimensional concept that seeks to take a number of environmental and economic factors into account. Thus, not only utilization of recycled resources and renewable energies but also employment, economic growth, and other factors are considered parts of resource efficiency.

Bibliography

Ando, S. (1993) *Research Into History of Pollution in the Early Modern Period*, Yoshi-kawa Kobunkan, in Japanese.
Corbin, A. (1988) *The Foul and the Fragrant: Odor and the French Social Imagination*, Harvard University Press, Cambridge, US.
European Commission (2014) *Development of Guidance on Extended Producer Responsibility (EPR) Final Report*, European Commission – DG Environment.
Hosoda, E. (2008) "A New Regime for High Quality Recycling in the East Asian Region," in Makoto Yano, ed. *The Japanese Economy – A Market Quality Perspective*, pp. 267–280, Keio University Press, Tokyo.
Hosoda, E. (2012) *Economics of Goods and Bads*, Second Edition, Toyo Keizai, Inc, Tokyo.
Ishikawa, E. (2013) *The Edo Period had a Recycling Society*, Kodansha Publishing Company, in Japanese, Tokyo.
Ministry of Environment (2014) *History and Current State of Waste Management in Japan*, Ministry of Environment, Japan.

Mizoiri, S. (2007) *Waste Countermeasures in Meiji Japan*, Recycle-Bunkasha, in Japanese, Tokyo.

Morse, E.S. (1917) *Japan Day by Day*, Houghton Mifflin Company, Boston.

OECD (2001) *Extended Producer Responsibility: A Guidance Manual for Governments*, OECD, Paris.

Oishi, S. (1988) *The Edo Period*, Chuokoran-shinsha, Inc., in Japanese, Tokyo.

Schwartz, R. (1983) *Daily Life in Johnson's London*, University of Wisconsin Press, Madison.

The Basel Action Network and Silicon Valley Toxics Coalition (2002) *Exporting Harm, High-tech Trashing of Asia*. Retrieved from http://archive.ban.org/E-waste/tech notrashfinalcomp.pdf (accessed on 29 January 2016).

2 A survey of research on the theoretical economic approach to waste and recycling

Takashi Saito

1 Introduction

Many countries have introduced waste management and recycling legislation. Japan, for example, has enacted many recycling laws for containers and packaging, home electrical appliances, and automobiles, among other initiatives. Under these laws, recycling rates have risen for various items, and the amount of landfill waste has decreased.

These waste disposal and recycling activities have also expanded in developing countries such as China. Because of the growing market for used products and materials, many items are collected by individual collectors. Moreover, there are many disposal firms that separate and dismantle used items. Among them, there exist small individual firms that employ simple technologies such as hand dismantling, which may cause health and pollution problems.[1]

To prevent this type of situation, it is important not only to introduce proper recycling technologies but also to transport waste to the proper recycling facilities equipped with such technologies. In this sense, waste collection systems play an important role in solving these problems. In fact, China has enforced a recycling law for home electrical appliances and has put forth great effort to improve these problems.

This paper reviews the literature regarding economic models for waste management and recycling.[2] We focus especially on three issues: (1) the collection of the waste, (2) the construction of waste disposal and recycling facilities, and (3) the optimal policies for pollution associated with waste disposal and recycling activities.

The remainder of this chapter is organized as follows. Section 2 introduces two asymmetric characteristics of used materials: resource potential and pollution potential. These factors help us understand problems associated with proper/ improper waste disposal and recycling. Section 3 considers the collection of waste from two viewpoints. We will analyze households' emission behavior by using a theoretical economic model. We will also examine the introduction of the collection scheme in this section. In Section 4, we will analyze the optimal location and timing of the construction of waste disposal and recycling facilities. Section 5 provides optimal policies for controlling negative externalities associated with waste disposal and recycling. By taking the whole waste stream into consideration, we will discuss certain aspects of the above problems. Finally, Section 6 summarizes and concludes.

2 Waste management and recycling

2.1 Resource potential and pollution potential

In this section, we will consider problems of waste management and recycling from the viewpoint of negative externalities. To achieve this, we will begin with two characteristics of used goods, materials, and products: resource potential and pollution potential. These characteristics are explained by Hosoda (2007, 2008).

Used goods and product parts consist of various types of materials that can be extracted under certain economic conditions. For example, electrical and electronic equipment contains nonferrous metals such as gold, silver, and copper, among others. If a large quantity of the equipment is collected, it is possible to extract recycled metals from them. Interestingly, the amount of gold in a ton of this equipment is greater than that in natural ore.[3] The definition of resource potential is given as follows.

Resource potential[4]

Resource potential is defined as an attribute by which substances, after they are properly treated, contribute to production by positive marginal productivity. Resource potential may not be realized if substances with the potential are not treated in a proper way.

The degree of resource potential can change depending on economic conditions. If the demand for recycled materials grows, the market value of the used goods becomes higher and vice versa. Used goods or materials are sometimes traded internationally. In this case, whether the resource potential of the used goods or materials can be realized depends on international market prices. It might be possible that used goods have a negative value in domestic markets and a positive value in international markets.

We will next turn to pollution potential. Some used goods and product parts contain toxic substances such as lead. Improper disposal or recycling of these used goods may cause environmental pollution or health damage. In addition, harmful chemicals are used in some refining processes. For instance, mercury and cyanide are commonly used in the recovery process for gold. Although gold itself is not harmful, it is likely to lead to pollution as a consequence of incorrectly treating these chemicals. In this way, improper disposal or recycling may cause various problems. Pollution potential is defined as follows.

Pollution potential[5]

Pollution potential is an attribute by which substances degrade environmental quality if they are treated in an improper way. Pollution potential may not be realized if substances with the potential are treated in a proper way.

These two characteristics can help us understand the problem of electronic waste recycling. Because e-waste contains some nonferrous metals such as gold, the degree of resource potential is high. However, low-cost recycling practices such as hand dismantling may lead to environmental pollution or health damage. However, it should be noted that pollution potential cannot always be realized. With proper recycling technology, it is possible to realize only resource potential, not pollution potential. One of the reasons for e-waste problems in developing countries is the inability to secure proper recycling technology.

Next, we will turn to the realization of the resource potential of used goods or materials, drawing on the discussion by Hosoda (2008). In accordance with the literature, we will consider whether used goods or materials should be recycled. Define P as the market value that recyclers could obtain if used goods are recycled. In addition, P_R is the cost of recycling. The condition in which resource potential would be realized (in other words, the used goods would be recycled) is as follows:

$$P - P_R \geq 0 \tag{1}$$

This condition means that the profit from recycling does not take a negative value. Obviously, if the market price of recyclables is sufficiently large or if the recycling cost is sufficiently small, the above condition is satisfied.

Equation (1) can be viewed as a market-based condition under which recycling firms intend to realize resource potential without any waste management or recycling policy. In some situations, however, resource potential can be realized if condition (1) is not satisfied.

To observe this, let us define P_E as the cost of the proper disposal of waste. Under a waste management regime, used goods or materials should be disposed of without environmental damage. If the following condition holds, it is desirable to recycle while making a comparison to the disposal of waste.

$$P - P_R > -P_E \tag{2}$$

Condition (2) can be rewritten as $P_R - P < P_E$. This means that the net cost of recycling is smaller than that of proper disposal. Conditions (1) and (2) are helpful to examine waste management policies. We will refer to them later in this paper.

2.2 Controlling externalities associated with waste disposal and recycling

The problems associated with waste disposal and recycling possess unique features, unlike those of other environmental problems such as air pollution. For example, in waste disposal and recycling, it is necessary to collect and then treat the solid waste generated from economic activities.

In the case of air pollution, emitted waste (air pollutants) may cause various problems but cannot be collected after emission. Therefore, the environmental policy scheme controls the level of emission.

In contrast, waste may be collected and then disposed of or recycled, which may produce environmental or health damage. Therefore, the aim of environmental policy is not only to reduce the amount of waste generated but also to enforce proper treatment to avoid serious environmental damage.

To address waste management problems, it is necessary to consider how to control environmental damage through the whole waste stream of the production of goods, consumption, waste generation, disposal, and recycling. In addition, various policy instruments among the phases of waste streams can be used to address these problems. In Japan, for example, to address the lack of landfill space, Japan has promoted not only the recycling of various used goods but also the feasible reduction of waste generation in production and consumption.

The economic literature suggests several ways to consider externalities associated with waste problems. The accumulation of waste seems to be an externality in some studies. Wertz (1976), for example, incorporates disutility from waste accumulation into an economic model and analyzes household behavior regarding waste discharge, which is explained in detail in Section 3.1.

Other studies focus on the situation in which improper disposal and recycling cause environmental damage. As mentioned in the previous subsection, although pollution potential cannot always be realized, it becomes a serious problem with the lack of proper technology.

In case a negative externality associated with waste disposal occurs, directly controlling the behavior that generates this externality may help to achieve the socially optimal outcome. There is, however, another approach. Fullerton and Kinnaman (1995) reveal some policy schemes to achieve the first-best outcome, which is discussed in Section 5.1.

As implied in the literature, focusing on the whole waste stream could help us to consider various policy options that lead to the socially optimal outcome. From this point of view, the waste collection system plays an important role. We will address this topic in the next section.

3 Waste collection system

In this section, we will concentrate on the collection of waste. The first subsection analyzes household behavior, especially in terms of the generation and discharge of waste. We will introduce a household economic model and summarize the effects of the waste collection scheme on the amount of waste discharged. In the second subsection, we will discuss the introduction of a collection system (e.g., a deposit-refund system).

3.1 Household behavior with regard to waste generation

This subsection addresses the emission of waste from the household sector. Theoretical economic studies in this field include Wertz (1976), Dobbs (1991), Morris and Holthausen (1994), and Ferrara (2003), among others. We will provide a
brief description of the model used by Wertz (1976), who conducted one of the
earliest studies in this field.

The model considers an economy with n types of consumption goods. A part
of each good becomes waste after being consumed, for which the ratios are
assumed to be constant. In addition, a representative household gains utility from
the consumption of goods and disutility from waste accumulation. The utility
function is written as

$$U = U\left(x_1, \cdots, x_n, A\right),$$ (3)

Where $x_i (i=1,...,n)$ is the level of consumption goods i, and A is a variable that
represents an inconvenience due to accumulation of waste at home. A varies with
the level of waste discharge, the distance from the house to the collection point,
and the frequency of the collection service. The signs of the partial derivatives of
the utility function are $\dfrac{\partial U}{\partial x_i} > 0, \dfrac{\partial^2 U}{\partial x_i^2} < 0, \dfrac{\partial U}{\partial A} < 0,$ and $\dfrac{\partial^2 U}{\partial A^2} \leq 0$.

The total amount of waste consists of a part of each consumer good, and
the household pays a disposal fee in discharging the total amount of waste. The
budget constraint of the household is given by

$$\sum_{i=1}^{n} p_i x_i + tw - y = 0,$$

Where p_i is the price of the i-th consumption good, t is the disposal fee, w is the
amount of waste, and y is income. Under these assumptions, Wertz (1976) solves
the utility maximization problem and provides comparative statistics.

This model shows the effects of the variables on waste by using the Slutsky
Equation, which is expressed as follows:

$$\frac{\partial w}{\partial t} = \left(\frac{\partial w}{\partial t}\right)_{dU=0} - w\left(\frac{\partial w}{\partial y}\right)$$ (4)

In this equation, the first term on the right-hand side is a substitution effect, and
the second term is an income effect. In this model, the ratio of waste to consumption varies depending on the good. If the disposal fee rises, households choose a
good that generates less waste (substitution effect). On the other hand, a higher
disposal fee decreases a household's real income, which would also change the
demand for waste disposal services (income effect).

Based on Equation (4), Wertz (1976) derives the effects of other factors, such as the distance from the house to the collection point and the frequency of collection service, on household waste discharge behavior. For instance, the distance to the collection point can change the variable associated with waste accumulation, A in Equation (3), and can influence household disutility. If the distance increases, the household would have to exert more effort to bring the waste to the collection point, which leads to less waste generation through the substitution effect.

We can apply the same type of reasoning to the effect of the frequency of the collection service. If the collection service is conducted more frequently, the level of waste accumulation decreases. Given less inconvenience of accumulation, the household might make less effort to reduce waste.

Wertz's (1976) approach can be helpful to examine the optimal waste collection package. The next subsection addresses the introduction of the collection system.

3.2 Waste collection scheme

Waste collection schemes, including the deposit-refund system (DRS), play an important role in promoting the proper disposal of waste and the production of higher-quality recyclables. According to the DRS, consumers pay an extra deposit with the purchase of consumption goods that can be paid back after they return the used items, such as empty containers.

Massell and Parish (1968) conducted one of the first studies on the DRS; this study analyzes the collection of empty beverage bottles, dividing the market for bottles into two types – those to be collected and those not to be collected – and derives the optimal refund level by analyzing the effect of the intermarket.

Dobbs (1991) uses this type of model to consider waste in the form of litter and proposes a policy scheme to prevent litter: a tax imposed on those who litter. From a practical point of view, however, it is difficult to distinguish whether people intend to litter.

As Dobbs (1991) indicates, the DRS is thought to be effective in reducing littering and in promoting the collection of waste containing toxic substances. Many economic studies address this issues with empirical approaches, including Porter (1978), and Palmer et al. (1997), among others.

However, the aim of the DRS is not simply to restrain littering. Historically, the DRS was introduced to save on production costs. In a comprehensive study of DRS, Bohm (1981) classifies the system into two types: a market-generated system (or voluntary DRS) that the producer voluntarily initiates and a government-initiated system (or mandatory DRS) that is introduced for purposes of social efficiency.

Regarding the market-generated or voluntary DRS, we can apply the discussion in Section 2.1. Resource potential can be realized if the net recycling cost is smaller than the proper disposal cost, as given by Equation (2). Now, let P_E represent the production cost of a new beverage container and P_R includes both collection and recycling costs. Therefore, Equation (2) can be viewed as the condition for the introduction of voluntary DRS.

Because the introduction of DRS has many effects on producers and consumers, it is necessary to carefully examine whether the system should be initiated.[6] Numata (2011) investigates the optimal design of DRS considering the allocation of unrefunded deposits.

4 Construction of waste disposal and recycling facilities

Section 4 discusses an issue regarding the construction of waste disposal and recycling facilities. We will address two topics: the optimal location and timing of the construction of facilities. Although there are few studies on the topic, we will introduce an economic model for optimal location. Regarding the optimal timing of construction, studies on the optimal use of landfill and construction will be considered.

4.1 Optimal location of recycling facilities

This subsection examines a theoretical economic model by Highfill et al. (1994), who describe a model for the collection of waste from households and analyzes the optimal location for a recycling center. The authors consider an economy with households and a local government in the shape of a rectangle. Identical households are uniformly distributed over the area, $a \times b$, and each household generates waste.

Because the government is assumed to be responsible for waste management, it collects waste and transports it to a recycling center constructed at a point (x_1, y_1). At the recycling center, some or all of the waste is recycled, and the residuals are transported to a landfill, which is located at point $(0,0)$. An image of the area is shown in Figure 2.1.

In this model, two types of transportation are taken into consideration: transportation from the households to the recycling center and that from the recycling center to the landfill. It is assumed that all traffic is north-south or east-west, and an image of the transportation of waste and residuals is illustrated in Figure 2.2.

The average distance from the households to the recycling center is d_H, which is expressed by

$$d_H = \frac{1}{ab} \int_0^a \int_0^b |x - x_1| + |y - y_1| \, dy dx$$
$$= \frac{x_1^2}{a} + \frac{y_1^2}{b} + \frac{a+b}{2} - (x_1 + y_1).$$

On the other hand, the distance from the recycling center to the landfill is d_L, which is given by

$$d_L = |x_1 - 0| + |y_1 - 0| = x_1 + y_1$$

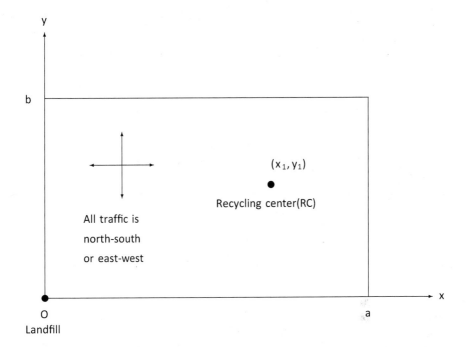

Figure 2.1 An image of the model by Highfill et al. (1994)

Note: This figure was illustrated by the author based on a description by Highfill et al. (1994).

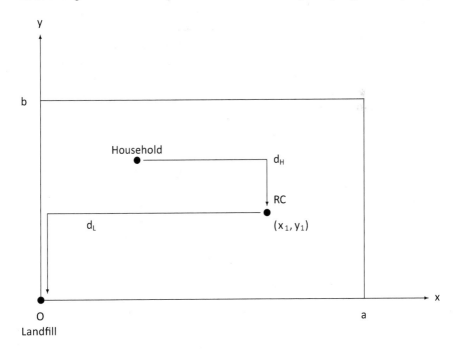

Figure 2.2 Transportation of waste and residuals

Note: This figure was illustrated by the author based on a description by Highfill et al. (1994).

The average transportation cost T can be written as the product of the distance, transportation cost, and weight of the waste or recyclables.

$$T = d_H \beta w + d_L (1 - \gamma) \beta w \tag{5}$$

In this equation, β is the per unit transportation cost, which is assumed to be constant, w is the amount of waste, and γ is the recycling rate. It should be noted that the transportation cost T depends on the amount of residual not recycled.

In Equation (5), we can derive the optimal location of the recycling center by minimizing the transportation cost, which can be expressed by

$$x_1 = \frac{a\gamma}{2}, \quad \text{and} \quad y_1 = \frac{b\gamma}{2}. \tag{6}$$

We can see that the optimal location depends on the recycling rate γ. For a higher recycling rate, the amount of residuals for transport to the landfill is small. Therefore, the optimal location would be close to the center of the area. For a lower recycling rate, on the other hand, the recycling center should be constructed close to the landfill at $(0,0)$ to save transportation costs.

In addition to the transportation cost, Highfill et al. (1994) consider other waste management costs, such as the recycling cost and sorting cost of separating recyclables from other waste. However, identical households consume goods and pay the same share of waste management and recycling costs. In addition, the utility of the household depends only on the level of consumption.

Addressing the optimization problem of households, we find interesting results. If the sorting cost is sufficiently large or if the per-unit transportation cost or the size of the area is sufficiently small, all waste will be landfilled. However, for a smaller sorting cost, a larger per-unit transportation cost, or a larger area, all waste will be recycled. In this special case, a recycling center should be located in the center of the area.

Although the model by Highfill et al. (1994) provides some interesting results, environmental pollution or other negative externalities are not taken into consideration. If externalities are produced in the recycling process, the optimal location would be affected under Equation (6). An expansion of this model could derive some important and attractive results.

4.2 *Optimal timing for construction of waste disposal facilities*

Another approach to the construction of waste and recycling facilities is optimal timing. This subsection focuses on the issue of the use of landfill sites, as addressed by Ready and Ready (1995), Highfill and McAsey (1997, 2001), and Hosoda (2000, 2001), among others. These studies view the landfill site as an exhaustible resource.

Ready and Ready (1995) examine the determination of the optimal landfilling fee by using a dynamic approach. From the viewpoint of resource economics, the level of the fee rises with the decrease in landfill capacity, the same result as that for the price of exhaustible resources, which is known as Hotelling's Rule.

In Ready and Ready's (1995) model, it is assumed that a new landfill site is constructed after an existing landfill is closed. The authors derive an optimal cycle of landfill sites and show that if the landfilling fee of the existing site is sufficiently high, a new landfill would be used. In this sense, the new landfill site could be viewed as a backstop technology.

Highfill and McAsey (1997) incorporate a recycling activity into the model and clarify the optimal timing of its introduction. According to the results, landfill capacity is gradually decreasing, and after a certain period, recycling begins. In other words, recycling is regarded as a backstop technology in this study.

The difference in the studies introduced above is their discussion of backstop technology. If there are a few waste disposal options, the rise in the landfilling fee leads to other options, such as recycling. However, it must be noted that these options are not necessarily desirable. It is likely that improper disposal is a potential backstop technology.

The issues of the optimal location and optimal timing of waste disposal and recycling facilities have many policy implications, when taking the possibility of improper disposal into consideration.

5 Optimal policies for controlling pollution associated with waste disposal and recycling

So far, we have examined the models that focus on a part of post-consumer waste streams. As mentioned in Section 2.2, it is important to consider the whole waste streams, including the production of goods, consumption, waste generation, disposal, and recycling.

This section provides an economic model of the whole waste stream and derives optimal policies for controlling the negative externalities associated with waste disposal and recycling.[7] The first subsection introduces the model by Fullerton and Kinnaman (1995), and the second subsection applies these discussions to the situation in developing countries.

5.1 Post-consumer waste stream

There have been many studies on the economic model of the whole waste stream since the 1990s, for example, Fullerton and Kinnaman (1995), Fullerton and Wu (1998), and Choe and Fraser (1999), among others. In this subsection, we will briefly summarize the model by Fullerton and Kinnaman (1995).

This model considers an economy with n identical households, a production sector of consumption goods, a garbage collection service, and virgin material extraction. The utility function of the representative household is as follows.

$$u = u[c, h, G, B, V]$$

Here, c is the consumption of goods, h is the use of leisure time, G is the total amount of garbage ($G = ng$), B is the total amount of illegal burning or other improper disposal ($B = nb$), and V is the total amount of natural resource use ($V = nv$).

In this model, the household gains satisfaction from consumption goods and leisure time, whereas the amount of garbage, improper disposal, and the use of natural resources bring disutility to the household.

After consuming goods, a user has three options: garbage collection (g), recycling (r), and improper disposal (b). The relationship among these options is given by

$$c = c(g, r, b)$$

As for the production sector, consumption goods are made by using recycled material (r), virgin material (v), and other production factors (k_c). The production function is as follows:

$$c = f(k_c, r, v)$$

In addition, resources are needed for virgin material extraction, garbage collection, leisure use, and improper disposal, which can be written by

$$v = \alpha k_v, g = \gamma k_g, h = k_h, \text{ and } k_b = \beta(b)$$

Finally, the resource constraint is expressed by

$$k = k_c + k_g + k_h + k_v + k_b$$

The abovementioned equations are the frameworks of the model.

Using these equations, we can derive the socially optimal conditions by maximizing the household utility function subject to the other equations. Because there are negative externalities generated from improper disposal, the socially optimal conditions cannot be achieved under a market mechanism without policy interventions. Fullerton and Kinnaman (1995) show the tax-subsidy schemes to achieve the first-best outcome.

Fullerton and Kinnaman (1995) also show that there are some cases for the first-best outcome. The improper disposal of waste could not always be punished and, sometimes, could not be found. Fullerton and Kinnaman (1995) consider the case in which improper disposal cannot be taxed and suggest schemes that include taxes on purchasing goods and subsidies for recycling. This scheme can be considered identical to the deposit-refund system.

From a more general point of view, this tax-subsidy scheme can be applied to different situations. In Fullerton and Kinnaman's model, the person who pays the tax is the same as the person who receives the subsidy because improper disposal, such as illegal burning or dumping, is performed by a household. However, there could be another situation in which waste disposal firms treat waste improperly. In this case, under the optimal tax-subsidy policies that Fullerton and Kinnaman's model implies, the disposal firm with the proper treatment of waste might obtain a subsidy, although the household still pays a tax for purchasing goods.

The optimal level of taxes for purchasing goods depends on the degree of marginal disutility from improper disposal. In other words, this taxation is used to control the level of consumption, which has the possibility of generating external costs for disposal. In that sense, this tax can be regarded as a Pigovian tax. However, a subsidy is used to promote proper disposal or recycling.

As mentioned above, by considering the whole waste stream from production to disposal, it is possible to work out the policy scheme to control negative externalities. There are various ways to achieve the first-best outcome. We will apply this scheme to another problem of improper disposal, which we can observe in developing countries.

5.2 Pollution emissions from informal sectors in the East Asia region

In developing countries, improper disposal or recycling remains a serious problem. In China, for example, there exist a large number of individual recyclers with small amounts to recycle. Some adopt low-cost recycling practices, such as hand dismantling in managing e-waste, which may lead to environmental pollution and health damage. China has made efforts to address this problem and has enforced a recycling law for home electrical appliances. However, there still exist informal recycling sectors with improper technology.

Under this recycling law, China has attempted to increase formal recycling facilities with proper technology through certification. In addition, a recycling firm with certification can obtain a subsidy for recycling. In the model by Fullerton and Kinnaman (1995), there are some policy options to achieve the socially optimal outcome. In China, because there are numerous recyclers with small amounts to recycle, it is difficult to regulate or monitor all of them. In this case, it would be reasonable to promote proper recycling through subsidies.

However, another problem seems to arise. Because the subsidy is not given for the collection of waste, individual collectors may sell used goods and materials to formal or informal recyclers who pay a higher price. Therefore, some formal recyclers cannot obtain a sufficient volume of used items.

If resource potential is sufficiently large, based on Equation (2) in Section 2.1 and the discussion in Section 3.2, the collection system of used products can be introduced voluntarily. If the government cannot regulate or monitor the system, an asymmetric information problem between consumers and collectors or between collectors and recyclers is likely to arise, promoting improper disposal or illegal dumping.

In China, there are many individual collectors of used goods and materials who lack certification. Therefore, the current waste collection system produces a great deal of uncertainty. Moreover, the degree of pollution potential in e-waste is also high. Therefore, it is necessary to build a transparent route for waste in which collectors and proper recyclers can grasp how to dispose or recycle. In other words, formalization not only of the recycling process but also of the collection system is needed.

China's recycling law for home electrical appliances includes the concept of extended producer responsibility (EPR), and the source of the subsidy is covered by producers.[8] EPR is expected to promote design for the environment (DfE), but it does not appear to offer sufficient incentives to promote DfE under the current recycling system.[9]

However, some other countries in the East Asia region have attempted to address the problems associated with e-waste disposal and recycling. Because e-waste has the characteristics of both high resource potential and pollution potential, it is necessary to consider how to collect it. In that sense, the collection system plays an important role in solving e-waste problems.

6 Concluding remarks

This paper reviews the literature on theoretical economic models for waste disposal and recycling. As mentioned in Section 2, both resource potential and pollution potential are important characteristics with which to understand the problems of improper disposal. A sufficiently high resource potential creates a possibility of introducing voluntary waste collection systems, which are sometimes accompanied by asymmetric information problems.

In developing countries in the East Asia region, recycling laws for e-waste have already been passed or are currently being deliberated. To make these recycling systems more effective, it is necessary to grasp the whole waste stream, including the production of goods, consumption, waste generation, disposal, and recycling. It is also important to examine the optimal design of the waste collection system, as discussed in Section 4.

Some recycling laws in developing countries include the concept of EPR. However, the EPR policies in developing countries are different from those in OECD countries, as these countries' various economic situations are different. The key factors to achieve the socially optimal outcome should be considered. This topic will be left for future research.

As mentioned in Section 5, informal recycling sectors and collectors exist in developing countries. The formalization of these informal sectors is a high-priority problem. However, there have been few economic studies on this issue, which will also be left for future research.

Notes

1 These problems are considered to be caused by informal recycling sectors that manage Waste Electrical and Electronic Equipment (WEEE or e-waste). See, for example, Chi et al. (2011).
2 An example of a study with a wide-ranging survey on waste management and recycling is Kinnaman and Fullerton (2000). In addition, Porter (2002) conducts a comprehensive study.

3 See Table 4 in Hosoda (2007) on p.145.
4 Cited from definition 1 in Hosoda (2007) on p.143.
5 Cited from definition 2 in Hosoda (2007) on p.143.
6 Onuma and Saito (2003) clarify the effects of DRS on producers and consumers.
7 There are many studies on improper disposal using partial equilibrium models without taking the whole waste stream into consideration. Sullivan (1987) examines the policy options for restraining pollution. In addition, Copeland (1991) considers improper disposal under the international trade of used goods.
8 Examples of studies on EPR or DfE include Fullerton and Wu (1998), Calcott and Walls (2000), Eichner and Pethig (2001, 2003), and Runkel (2003), among others.
9 This is noted by Hosoda and Someno (2014).

References

Bohm, Peter (1981) *Deposit-Refund Systems: Theory and Applications to Environmental, Conservation, and Consumer Policy*, Johns Hopkins University Press, Baltimore.

Calcott, Paul and Margaret Walls (2000) "Can down stream waste disposal policies encourage upstream 'design for environment'?," *American Economic Review*, Vol. 90, No. 2, pp. 233–237.

Chi, Xinwen, Martin Streicher-Porte, Mark Y.L. Wang, and Markus A. Reuter (2011) "Informal electronic waste recycling: A sector review with special focus on China," *Waste Management*, Vol. 31, pp. 731–742.

Choe, Chongwoo and Iain Fraser (1999) "An economic analysis of household waste management," *Journal of Environmental Economics and Management*, Vol. 38, No. 2, pp. 234–246.

Copeland, Brian R. (1991) "International trade in waste products in the presence of illegal disposal," *Journal of Environmental Economics and Management*, Vol. 20, No. 2, pp. 143–162.

Dobbs, Ian M. (1991) "Litter and waste management: Disposal taxes versus user charges," *Canadian Journal of Economics*, Vol. 24, No. 1, pp. 221–227.

Eichner, Thomas and Rüdiger Pethig (2001) "Product design and efficient management of recycling and waste treatment," *Journal of Environmental Economics and Management*, Vol. 41, No. 1, pp. 109–134.

Eichner, Thomas and Rüdiger Pethig (2003) "Corrective taxation for curbing pollution and promoting green product design and recycling," *Environmental and Resource Economics*, Vol. 25, No. 4, pp. 477–500.

Ferrara, Ida (2003) "Differential provision of solid waste collection services in the presence of heterogeneous households," *Environmental and Resource Economics*, Vol. 26, pp. 211–226.

Fullerton, Don and Thomas C. Kinnaman (1995) "Garbage, recycling, and illicit burning or dumping," *Journal of Environmental Economics and Management*, Vol. 29, No. 1, pp. 78–91.

Fullerton, Don and Wenbu Wu (1998) "Policies for green design," *Journal of Environmental Economics and Management*, Vol. 36, No. 2, pp. 131–148.

Highfill, Jannett and Michael McAsey (1997) "Municipal waste management: Recycling and landfill space constraints," *Journal of Urban Economics*, Vol. 41, No. 1, pp. 118–136.

Highfill, Jannett and Michael McAsey (2001) "Landfilling versus 'backstop' recycling when income is growing," *Environmental and Resource Economics*, Vol. 19, No. 1, pp. 37–52.

Highfill, Jannett, Michael McAsey, and Robert Weinstein (1994) "Optimality of recycling and the location of a recycling center," *Journal of Regional Science*, Vol. 34, No. 4, pp. 583–597.

Hosoda, Eiji (2000) "Material cycle, waste disposal, and recycling in a Leontief-Sraffa-von Neumann economy," *Journal of Material Cycles and Waste Management*, Vol. 2, pp. 1–9.

Hosoda, Eiji (2001) "Recycling and landfilling in a dynamic Sraffian model: Application of the Corn-Guano model to a waste treatment problem," *Metroeconomica*, Vol. 52, No. 3, pp. 268–281.

Hosoda, Eiji (2007) "International aspects of recycling of electrical and electronic equipment: Material circulation in the East Asian region," *Journal of Material Cycles and Waste Management*, Vol. 9, pp. 140–150.

Hosoda, Eiji (2008) *Shigen Junkan-gata Shakai (Resource Circulation Economy)*, Keio University Press, Tokyo (in Japanese).

Hosoda, Eiji and Kenji Someno (2014) "Chugoku jomyaku bizinesu no atarashii tenkai (New development of recycling business in China)," *Keizaigaku Kenkyu (Economic Research)*, Vol. 63, No. 2, pp. 159–173 (in Japanese).

Kinnaman, Thomas C. and Don Fullerton (2000) "The economics of residential solid waste management," in Tom Tietenberg and Henk Folmer, eds. *The International Yearbook of Environmental and Resource Economics 2000/2001*, Cheltenham, UK: Edward Elgar Publishing, pp. 100–147.

Massell, Benton F. and Ross M. Parish (1968) "Empty bottles," *Journal of Political Economy*, Vol. 76, No. 6, pp. 1224–1233.

Morris, Glenn E. and Duncan M. Holthausen, Jr. (1994) "The economics of household solid waste generation and disposal," *Journal of Environmental Economics and Management*, Vol. 26, No. 3, pp. 215–234.

Numata, Daisuke (2011) "Optimal design of deposit-refund systems considering allocation of unredeemed deposits," *Environmental Economics and Policy Studies*, Vol. 13, No. 4, pp. 303–321.

Onuma, Ayumi and Takashi Saito (2003) "Some effects of deposit-refund system on producers and consumers," *Keio Economic Society Discussion Paper Series*, KESDP No. 03–05, Keio University.

Palmer, Karen, Hilary A. Sigman, and Margaret Walls (1997) "The cost of reducing municipal solid waste," *Journal of Environmental Economics and Management*, Vol. 33, No. 2, pp. 128–150.

Palmer, Karen and Margaret Walls (1997) "Optimal policies for solid waste disposal: Taxes, subsidies, and standards," *Journal of Public Economics*, Vol. 65, No. 2, pp. 193–205.

Porter, Richard C. (1978) "A social benefit-cost analysis of mandatory deposits on beverage containers," *Journal of Environmental Economics and Management*, Vol. 5, No. 4, pp. 351–375.

Porter, Richard C. (2002) *The Economics of Waste*, Resources for the Future, Washington, DC.

Ready, Mark J. and Richard C. Ready (1995) "Optimal pricing of depletable, replaceable resources: The case of landfill tipping fees," *Journal of Environmental Economics and Management*, Vol. 28, No. 3, pp. 307–323.

Runkel, Marco (2003) "Product durability and extended producer responsibility in solid waste management," *Environmental and Resource Economics*, Vol. 24, No. 2, pp. 161–182.

Sullivan, Arthur M. (1987) "Policy options for toxics disposal: Laissez-faire, subsidization, and enforcement," *Journal of Environmental Economics and Management*, Vol. 14, No. 1, pp. 58–71.

Wertz, Kenneth L. (1976) "Economic factors influencing households' production of refuse," *Journal of Environmental Economics and Management*, Vol. 2, No. 4, pp. 263–272.

3 A survey of research on China's waste management system

Daisuke Ichinose

1 Introduction

Waste disposal is one of the world's most serious environmental problems, requiring a rapid and appropriate solution. According to the World Bank (2012), the world's total amount of municipal solid waste (hereafter MSW) is approximately 1.3 billion tons per year, and this total is expected to increase to approximately 2.2 billion tons per year by 2025. With the increasing amount of discharged MSW, the cost of solid waste management is presumed to increase substantially. In fact, according to the World Bank (2012), the total global cost of solid waste management is estimated to increase from 205.4 billion dollars in 2010 to 375 billion dollars in 2025. Further, the total amount of industrial waste has steadily increased, and considerable money has been spent in the public and private sectors to solve problems caused by industrial waste. Therefore, the issue of waste disposal is a serious threat from not only an environmental but also a financial perspective.

Waste represents a widespread problem among East Asian countries to varying degrees. In particular, China faces one of the most severe waste problems. Although rapid economic growth has greatly enriched China, this growth has been accompanied by a dramatic increase in the amount of waste, as might be expected. In fact, China is now the world's second largest MSW discharger and is expected to become the world's largest MSW discharger by 2025.[1] Thus, an examination of the worldwide waste disposal problem that does not include the case of China would be incomplete.

This chapter aims to describe the status of China's waste management system by focusing on three types of waste categories: MSW, industrial waste, and hazardous waste. For this purpose, this chapter surveys the contributions of previous studies on China's waste management system that are published in international academic journals. With the escalation of the waste management problem in China, this topic has become an active area of research, and several researchers have provided substantial contributions. However, to the knowledge of the author, there are no detailed overviews of the contributions of the previous literature on waste management in China. Reviewing the previous studies on this topic enables me to not only deepen the understanding of waste management in China but also identify topics that should be studied in the future.

This chapter is organized as follows. Section 2 briefly summarizes the current status of waste management in China. Subsequently, Section 3 summarizes the contributions of previous studies on China's MSW management system. Section 4 then discusses studies on industrial solid waste, and Section 5 reviews studies on hazardous waste. Finally, Section 6 provides a summary and conclusions.

2 Current status of waste management in China

In 1978, China changed its economic structure from a planned economy to a market-based economy. Since then, China has experienced extremely rapid economic growth, and in making use of its abundant labor force, and the country has become the "factory of the world". This economic expansion has greatly enhanced the standard of living in China. In fact, China's GDP per capita increased rapidly from 7,858 yuan in 2000 to 38,420 yuan in 2012 (see Figure 3.1). Moreover, given that China's population increased from 1267.4 million to 1354.0 million during the same period, China's economic expansion has occurred at an unprecedented speed.

However, with the economic benefits of economic expansion have come serious environmental problems related to waste, such as environmental contamination from toxic substances and shortages of landfill sites. As a preparatory step for further analysis, this section briefly describes the generating status of the three types of waste in China.

There are three categories of solid waste in China: MSW, industrial solid waste, and hazardous waste (Huang et al. (2006b)). As shown in Table 3.1, the amount of MSW in China has continued to increase, reaching 170,809 thousand tons in 2012. For comparison, this amount is approximately 3.8 times larger than that of Japan, the second largest discharger of MSW in East Asia, and approximately

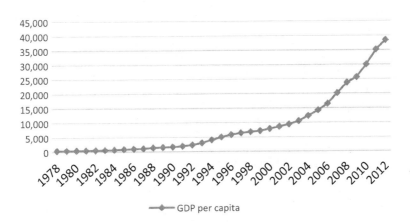

—◆— GDP per capita

Figure 3.1 Economic growth in China

Source: China statistical yearbook 2013

Table 3.1 The amount of waste in China[1]

Year	MSW	Industrial solid waste	Hazardous waste
2012	17080.9	329044.26	3465.24
2011	16395.3	322772.34	3431.22
2010	15804.8	–	–
2009	15733.7	–	–
2008	15437.7	–	–
2007	15214.5	–	–
2006	14841.3	–	–

Unit: 10,000 tons

Source: China statistical yearbook 2007 to 2013

[1]   For industrial solid waste and hazardous waste, Table 3.1 lists data only for 2011 and 2012 because the accounting method changed in 2011.

70 percent of the total for the United States, the world's largest discharger of MSW.[2] Currently, China is the world's second largest MSW discharger, and proper MSW disposal has become an urgent issue. Regarding industrial solid waste and hazardous waste, the former reached approximately 3290 million tons, and the latter approximately 34.7 million tons.

Official statistics provide relatively accurate data on MSW disposal methods. The China statistical yearbook (2013) shows that in 2012, 84.8 percent of total MSW was properly disposed of, of which 72 percent was disposed of by landfill, 25 percent by incineration, and 3 percent by other methods. Thus, the most widely used MSW disposal method in China is landfill.

In fact, the rate of landfill disposal in China is remarkably high relative to that of other countries in East Asia. For example, in 2012, landfill disposal accounted for only 3 percent of waste disposal in Japan and 36 percent in South Korea (World Bank, 2012). As noted in the following section, China's high rate of landfill disposal can be attributed to the content of its MSW. Because the major component of MSW in China is organic waste with high moisture content, it is hard to incinerate MSW, and a large portion of such waste is dumped into landfill sites without incineration.

China's annual generation of industrial solid waste reached 3,290,442.6 thousand tons in 2012. Although the definition of industrial waste differs somewhat between China and Japan, this value is approximately eight times larger than that of Japan. Further, the amount of hazardous waste was 34,652.4 thousand tons in 2012, which is larger than the total amount of MSW in Korea.[3]

3 Studies on MSW management in China

Although several types of studies examine the issue of MSW in China, the themes of these studies can be classified into two categories: those that attempt to present a comprehensive vision of China's MSW management system, and those that focus on MSW management in certain areas or on specific issues in MSW management.

3.1 An analysis of studies that provide an overview of MSW management in China

Compared with studies that focus on MSW management in certain areas or on specific issues, the number of studies that provide an overview of MSW management in China is relatively small. In addition, papers in international academic journals fully examined the problems of MSW management in China only recently. For instance, Suocheng et al. (2001) describe MSW production trends and analyze the problems with MSW management in China. In particular, they identify three specific problems: market mechanisms do not work well in MSW management, policy support is insufficient, and outdated technology is used in MSW disposal. The authors also discuss ways to improve MSW management in China. Wang and Nie (2001a) examine aspects of MSW management in China such as the amount of discharged waste, the properties of the waste disposal systems for MSW, legislation on MSW, and so on.[4] In addition, the authors conduct a regression analysis and show that urban population and GDP are the chief determinants of MSW generation in China. In response to the results of this study, Wang and Nie (2001b) identify the problems with MSW management in China and propose three types of remedial strategies: "institutional reform", "technology development", and "legislation and administrative improvement". Huang et al. (2006b) discuss the current status of the three types of solid waste management in China: industrial solid waste, MSW, and hazardous waste. Regarding the composition of MSW, they show that organic material accounts for approximately 60 percent of the total MSW discharged in China and that the water content ratio is above the 40 percent–50 percent range in many cases. More recently, Zhang et al. (2010) provide an overview of MSW management in China and discuss the present problems and opportunities associated with MSW management. Chen et al. (2010) provide an overview of MSW generation and disposal in China and examine the regulations and policies concerning MSW management and their related financial issues. The authors also consider the current challenges that China faces in MSW management, specifying four aspects as the major problems to be solved: the low rate of safe disposal, the ineffective enforcement of uniform solutions throughout the country, the need for precise research on waste properties and proper public consultations in waste management, and the promotion of MSW management commercialization. Further, based on a life cycle assessment analysis, Hong et al. (2010) calculate the impact of four waste disposal methods (landfill, incineration, composting plus landfill, and composting plus incineration) on the environment.

3.2 An analysis of the literature on specific issues

3.2.1 Studies on MSW in specific cities

Because China is a vast country and because the actual MSW management situation varies among different cities, a number of studies focus on the issue of MSW management in a specific city in China. In particular, a relatively large number of studies focus on Beijing, the capital of China. For example, Qu et al. (2009) conduct a survey on waste generation and its composition in Beijing based on data derived from samples obtained from 113 households. They find that the per capita amount of MSW is 0.23 kg per day and that the moisture content rate is approximately 50 percent. They also show that kitchen waste accounts for the greatest proportion of MSW at 69.3 percent. Zhen-Shan et al. (2009) and Xiao et al. (2007) also provide an overview of the current status of MSW management in Beijing. In particular, Zhen-Shan et al. (2009) show that daily MSW generation was 0.85 kg/capita and that food waste accounted for 63.39 percent of the total MSW generation in 2006. Xiao et al. (2007) further report that the amount of MSW generation reached 3,613.6 thousand tons and that food waste accounted for 48 percent of total MSW generation in 2003.

Conducting a life cycle assessment analysis of MSW management in Beijing, Zhao et al. (2011) consider three scenarios (i.e., the current scenario, a short-term planning scenario, and a long-term planning scenario) and conclude that in the preferred long-term planning scenario, landfills are replaced with integrated treatment facilities, and a method is introduced to separate food waste from other waste. The authors also describe the current status of MSW generation and content in Beijing. Among other findings, the authors report that the amount of MSW generation in Beijing in 2006 was 0.96 kg/day/capita and that the primary component of the MSW was food waste, which accounted for 63.4 percent of the total MSW. Wang and Wang (2012) examine the generation, content, and waste management system for MSW in Beijing and note that MSW generation reached 6.35 million tons in 2010. The main content of the MSW was food waste, which accounted for 65.98 percent of the total MSW, and the moisture content was 62.93 percent. Zhang and Wen (2014) focus on the consumption and recycling of polyethylene terephthalate (PET) bottles in Beijing and find that approximately 100,000 tons of bottles are disposed of annually, with more than half of that total collected by scavengers. The authors also examine individual characteristics affecting the amount of PET bottled-beverage consumption.

Several studies have focused on the issue of MSW in cities other than Beijing. For instance, Minghua et al. (2009) examine the MSW management system in Pudong New Area, Shanghai. In addition to describing the status of waste generation, such as the amount of MSW and its composition, the authors examine the current status of MSW collection and disposal in this area. For Hangzhou, Zhuang et al. (2008) focus on the source separation program implemented in the city and examine the program's effectiveness. To this end, they examine the status of waste generation and conduct a questionnaire survey on residents' response to this problem. The authors also perform a cost-benefit analysis of the program. Ma et al. (2014) also conduct a questionnaire survey in Hangzhou to determine citizens' attitudes toward the MSW management system in Hangzhou.

Chung and Lo (2004) conduct a questionnaire survey in two cities, Jiangmen city and Zhongshan city, and examine the waste collection system, a disposal fee, the possibility of waste reduction, citizens' behavior toward waste management, and citizens' environmental literacy. Applying a life-cycle assessment, Zhao et al. (2009b) evaluate the MSW management system in the city of Hangzhou and calculate the environmental impact of three scenarios: the scenario of the current waste management system, a scenario in which MSW is transported to the nearest incinerators, and a scenario in which free plastic shopping bags are banned. Tai et al. (2011) examine the status of MSW management and evaluate the performance of source-separated waste collection programs in eight cities: Beijing, Nanjing, Shanghai, Hangzhou, Xiamen, Guilin, Guangzhou, and Shenzhen. The authors evaluate the source-separated programs in Beijing and Shanghai as "excellent", Guangzhou as "adequate", and the other five cities as "limited". Studying the composition of waste and recyclables in Guangzhou, Chung and Poon (2001) show that the primary category of waste is putrescibles, which accounts for 58.1 percent of total MSW,[5] followed by plastics, ashes, sand, and unrecognizables. The analysis further shows that the yearly average moisture content of MSW is 47.4 percent and that the main recyclables are plastic bags, followed by paper and rags. Medina (2011) also reports on the status of waste generation, waste collection and transfer, recycling, and disposal in Guangzhou.

Wang et al. (2008) examine the community-based collection system for residential recyclables introduced in Haidian district in the city of Beijing. This system mainly consists of three actors – namely, residents, recycling service sites, and waste material collection companies – and it can be characterized by the inclusion of itinerant recyclable buyers as a formal actor. The authors analyze the system's efficacy based on survey research and conclude that the community-based collection system will be effective in improving resource recycling in China.

Focusing on waste management in Chongqing, Hui et al. (2006) examine waste generation, waste components, and MSW disposal methods in the city.

Table 3.2 Summary on the generation and components of MSW

Study area	MSW generation	Moisture content	The rate of kitchen waste[1]	Literature
Beijing (2003)	3,613.6 thousand tons/year		48%	Xiao et al. (2007)
Beijing (2008)	0.23 kg/day/ capita	50%	69.3%	Qu et al. (2009)
Beijing (2006)	0.85 kg/day/ capita		63.39%	Zhen-shan et al. (2009)
Beijing (2006)	0.96 kg/day/ capita	61%	63.4%	Zhao et al. (2011)
Beijing (2008)	1096.6 tons/year		66.19%	Tai et al. (2011)
Beijing (2011)	6.35 million tons/year	62.93%	65.98%	Wang and Wang (2012)
Chongqing (2001)	1.08 kg/day/ capita	64.1%	59%	Hui et al. (2006)
Pudong New Area, Shanghai (2006)	1.11 kg/day/ capita		55%[2]	Minghua et al. (2009)

(*Continued*)

Table 3.2 (Continued)

Study area	MSW generation	Moisture content	The rate of kitchen waste[1]	Literature
Shanghai (2008)	827.0 tons/year		71.14%	Tai et al. (2011)
Guangzhou (1999)		58.1%	47.4%	Chung and Poon (2001)
Guangzhou (2008)	516.9 tons/year		52%	Tai et al. (2011)
Shenzhen(2008)	587.6 tons/year		51.1%	Tai et al. (2011)
Hangzhou (2008)	245.0 tons/year		53%	Tai et al. (2011)
Hangzhou (2006)	0.92 kg/day/ capita	56.5%	64.48%	Zhuang et al. (2008)
Nanjing (2008)	195.0 tons/year		70.59%	Tai et al. (2011)
Xiamen (2008)	99.6 tons/year		74.63%	Tai et al. (2011)
Guilin (2008)	24.8 tons/year		61.31%	Tai et al. (2011)
Zhongshan (2001)	0.85 kg/day/ capita			Chung and Lo (2004)
Jiangmen (2001)	0.8 kg/day/ capita			Chung and Lo (2004)

[1] This study is based on the premise that the terms "kitchen waste", "food waste", and "organic waste" are synonymous.
[2] This value is the sum of the rate of food remnants and that of fruit. For details, see Minghua et al. (2009).

Their study shows that the daily per capita generation of MSW is 1.08 kg and that the predominant type of waste is food waste, which accounts for approximately 59 percent of the total MSW, followed by plastic waste and paper waste. Because food waste generally contains considerable moisture, the moisture content of MSW in Chongqing is 64.1 percent.

Table 3.2 summarizes the findings of previous studies on the generation and content of MSW. Regarding waste generation, most studies show that the amount of MSW in China's cities falls between 0.8 and 1.11 kg/day/capita, with the exception of Qu et al. (2009), who report that the MSW generation of Beijing is 0.23 kg/day/capita. As might be expected from these observations, the amount of discharged MSW in China's major cities is almost equal to that of developed countries. In fact, the amount of MSW generation in Japan is 1.188 kg/day/capita.[6] Further, in the major cities in China, kitchen waste accounts for the largest proportion of MSW. As shown in the fourth column in Table 3.2, almost all of the studies find that the proportion of kitchen waste to total MSW is greater than 50 percent in China's urban areas. This high ratio of kitchen waste is unique to developing countries. For example, as shown in Table 3.3, the World

Table 3.3 Income level and waste content

Income level	Organic	Paper	Plastic	Glass	Metal	Other
Low income	64	5	8	3	3	17
Lower middle income	59	9	12	3	2	15
Upper middle income	54	14	11	5	3	13
High income	28	31	11	7	6	17

Source: World Bank (2012)

Bank (2012) reports that the proportion of organic waste[7] in the total MSW generation in low income, lower middle income, upper middle income, and high income countries is 64 percent, 59 percent, 54 percent, and 28 percent, respectively. Because food waste contains high moisture content, the rate of moisture content in MSW is also high in China.

In addition, as shown in Table 3.2, most previous studies focus on cases in specific cities, such as Beijing. Thus, more research on the status of MSW management systems in other cities in needed.

Some studies have focused on forecasting the future of MSW generation. For instance, Xu et al. (2013) describe a method that can be applied to forecast future MSW generation and to provide an estimate for Xiamen city. They combine the seasonal autoregressive integrated moving average (SARIMA) model and grey system theory and develop a forecasting method to estimate MSW generation at multiple time scales without the need to consider demographic and socioeconomic factors. The study estimates MSW generation in Xiamen city at three time scales: monthly MSW generation from 2011 to 2015, annual MSW generation from 2011 to 2015, and annual MSW generation from 2016 to 2020.

3.2.2 E-waste

In recent years, the use of a variety of electric appliances, such as televisions, washing machines, personal computers, and mobile phones, has become widespread, as these products make our lives incredibly convenient. With the increased consumption of electric appliances, the amount of obsolete electric appliances (so-called e-waste) has also increased. Because e-waste contains valuable metals such as gold and copper, the recycling of e-waste has the potential to provide substantial economic benefits. However, because e-waste also contains several toxic substances, recycling this type of waste can be very dangerous for humans and the environment.

Thus, a proper treatment method is a crucial need for e-waste recycling. China's income growth dramatically increased the demand for electronic products. In fact, as shown in Table 3.4, the number of color television sets owned per 100 households increased in urban areas from 59.04 in 1990 to 136.07 in 2012, and in rural areas from 4.72 to 116.9. Similar trends are observed for other home electric appliances. Currently, each urban household possesses more than one

Table 3.4 Number of home electric appliances owned per household

Item	Per 100 urban households						Per 100 rural households					
	1990	1995	2000	2005	2011	2012	1990	1995	2000	2005	2011	2012
Washing machine	78.41	88.97	90.5	95.51	97.05	98.02	9.12	16.9	28.58	40.2	62.57	67.22
Refrigerator	42.33	66.22	80.1	90.72	97.23	98.48	1.22	5.15	12.31	20.1	61.54	67.32
Color television set	59.04	89.79	116.6	134.8	135.15	136.07	4.72	16.92	48.74	84.08	115.46	116.9
Black-and-white TV set	–	–	–	–	–	–	39.72	63.81	52.97	21.77	1.66	1.44
Air conditioner	0.34	8.09	30.8	80.67	122	126.81	–	0.18	1.32	6.4	22.58	25.36
Computer	–	–	9.7	41.52	81.88	87.03	–	–	0.47	2.1	17.96	21.36

Unit: sets per 100 households

Source: China statistical yearbook (2013)

color television and air conditioner, and nearly every urban household possesses one washing machine and one refrigerator. In the case of rural areas, each household possesses more than one color television; however, the adoption rate for washing machines, refrigerators, air conditioners, and PCs is still relatively low. In other words, the data show that there is further room for the number of home electric appliances to increase, especially in rural areas. Thus, rural areas in China could become a huge source of obsolete home electric appliances.

However, the diffusion of home electric appliances has brought not only improvements in quality of life but also negative impacts on living quality owing to the increase in waste electrical and electronic equipment (WEEE). The amount of WEEE in China is estimated to increase at a rate of 5–10 percent per year (Huang et al., 2009). In addition, China has now become the world's largest importer of e-waste (Ni and Zeng, 2009). Because WEEE contains valuable metals such as gold and platinum, the great majority of WEEE is recycled in China. However, to reduce recycling costs, improper methods are often used, causing serious environmental contamination. Thus, WEEE disposal has become one of the most serious waste-related problems in China, and many studies have begun to focus on the issue.

One major aim of studies on WEEE is to estimate the amount of WEEE and to examine the level of environmental contamination caused by informal WEEE recycling. Within this literature, Liu et al. (2006) generate predictions about the amount of five types of waste home electric appliances (i.e., television sets, refrigerators, washing machines, air conditioners, and personal computers; hereafter, for simplicity, we call these simply home electric appliances) and examine the flow of this waste into the city of Beijing. They conclude that the number of discarded home electric appliances totaled 885,354 units in 2005, and this amount is expected to increase to 2,620,000 by 2020. In addition, Chung et al. (2011) estimate that 80,443 tons of obsolete home electric appliances are disposed of each year in Hong Kong.

While the above studies focus on WEEE disposal in a specific city, Li et al. (2006) calculate the amount of obsolete home electric appliances in all of China from 2004 to 2015. Their estimations show that the total number of obsolete home electronic appliances will increase from 33.2 million units in 2004 to 918.4 million units in 2015. Moreover, focusing on the flow of home electric appliances and recycling systems for home electric appliances, Yang et al. (2008) show that the total number of waste home electric appliances would increase from approximately 56 million units in 2003 to 105 million units in 2010. The authors also examine policies on WEEE in China. Further, Veenstra et al. (2010) calculate the total number of obsolete home electric appliances from 2001 to 2012, which reached approximately 230 million units in 2012. Applying a stocks-based model to predict the total number of discarded home electric appliances in all of China, Zhang et al. (2012) show that the amount of home electric appliance waste will increase from 130 million units in 2010 to 216 to 221 million units in 2020 and further to 259 to 282 million units in 2030. More recently, Habuer et al. (2014) use time-series product flow analysis and substance flow analysis to estimate the total number of home electric appliances owned by households and the total number of discarded electric appliances. According to their calculations, the total number of discarded electric appliances will reach approximately 314 million units in 2030.

The results of these studies are summarized in Table 3.5. Regarding the number of obsolete home electric appliances in 2010 in all of China, the predictions range from 105 million to 163.8 million units.

Wong et al. (2007) examine the trace metal contamination caused by improper WEEE recycling in Guiyu. Their findings reveal that some river sediments are contaminated by metals such as cadmium and copper. Because Guiyu is one of the most notorious villages damaged by environmental pollution caused by inappropriate WEEE recycling, a number of studies, including Leung et al. (2007) and Xing et al. (2009), examine the pollution problems in this village.

While these studies mainly focus on measuring the level of contamination caused by improper WEEE recycling or estimating the amount of WEEE, several studies discuss the specific recycling system for WEEE or legislation on WEEE recycling. For instance, Hicks et al. (2005) describe the current status of WEEE recycling and disposal in China and the associated effects on the environment and human health. In addition, they provide an overview of legislation aimed at preventing WEEE problems and examine market responses to the introduction of WEEE policies. He et al. (2006) also provide an overview of the current status of WEEE recycling and the policy responses to the issue in China. Further, in the context of reviewing the research on e-waste and describing the status of e-waste management in Asia in general, Terazono et al. (2006) examine the

Table 3.5 Predicted number of obsolete home electric appliances

Predicted number (year)[1]	Area	Source
1.75 (2010)	Beijing	Liu et al. (2006)
2.31 (2015)		
2.82 (2020)		
2.95 (2012)	Hong Kong	Cung et al. (2011)
33.2 (2004)	All of China	Li et al. (2006)
163.8 (2010)		
918.4 (2015)		
56 (2003)	All of China	Yang et al. (2008)
105 (2010)		
33 (2001)	All of China	Veenstra et al. (2010)
132 (2010)		
230 (2012)		
130 (2010)	All of China	Zhang et al. (2012)
216–221 (2020)		
259–282 (2030)		
314 (2030)	All of China	Habuer et al. (2014)

Unit: million units

[1] The value listed in this column is extracted from the results of each study.

e-waste management and regulation scheme in China. More recently, based on the idea of extended producer responsibility (EPR), Kojima et al. (2009) examine the current status of WEEE recycling and obstacles to the implementation of WEEE policies in developing Asian countries. For this purpose, they review and compare legislation on WEEE in China and Thailand.

Furthermore, Zeng et al. (2013) discuss legislation on electronic products and WEEE in China by comparing it with such legislation in the EU, and Wang et al. (2010) examine the effect of laws and regulations on the recycling, disposal, and trade of obsolete home electric appliances. In providing an overview of the policies and pilot projects relating to the management of WEEE, Yu et al. (2010) discuss the problem of e-waste management in China and propose two alternative polices: one aims to provide an incentive for consumers to use the formal recycling system, and the other is designed to integrate the formal and informal recycling sectors.

In addition to the above-mentioned studies, other studies focus on citizens' disposal methods of WEEE. For instance, Huang et al. (2006a) conduct a questionnaire survey among citizens in Ningbo to examine consumer behavior concerning five types of home electric appliances: color television sets, refrigerators, air conditioners, personal computers, and mobile phones. The survey includes questions regarding the replacement cycle of home electric appliances, the reason for replacement, and the method of disposal for WEEE. Streicher-Porte and Geering (2010) use a questionnaire survey to examine how citizens in Jiaojiang city dispose of WEEE, and they find that the disposal method varies depending on the type of WEEE.[8] The study also includes information on the average price paid by junk buyers to the WEEE discharger.

3.2.3 Informal sector

The informal sector plays an important role in MSW management in China because informal waste pickers collect a large portion of household recyclables. In this respect, the informal sector may contribute to increasing the recycling ratio but may constitute an underlying cause of environmental contamination. Moreover, numerous people earn a living from informal waste picking, so simply imposing a severe punishment for informal waste picking might not solve the problem. Thus, the informal recycling collection system is a complex problem for China that needs to be solved.

Examining the issue of the informal sector is actually a fairly demanding task because the available data on informal waste pickers' behavior are very limited. However, several studies address this topic.

To examine the current status of recycling conducted by informal junk buyers, Li (2002) conducts a survey on three actors involved in MSW recycling in Wuhan, the capital of Hubei Province: households, junk buyers, and redemption depots. The authors examine the scale of the redemption depots, the relationship between waste dischargers and junk buyers, and the extent of the territory where junk buyers collect recyclables, among other issues. Chi et al. (2011) discuss the similarities and differences between the formal and informal sectors of WEEE recycling and identify the reasons for the informal sector's substantial influence on WEEE recycling. Examining the role of the informal sector in recycling in Guangzhou, Medina (2011) finds that over 100,000 scavengers are present in Guangzhou and that their earnings of 1,800 to 2,000 yuan per month are higher than sanitation workers' earnings of 1,100 to 1,200 yuan per month. In addition, the authors report that scavengers collect approximately 1,200 metric tons/day of paper.

Linzner and Salhofer (2014) conduct a survey of previous studies on the informal sector in MSW management in China. Examining the impact of the informal sector on the collection of recyclables by estimating the number of people involved in informal waste collection and the volume of recyclables collected by the informal sector, the authors find that the number of informal waste collectors is approximately 3.4 to 5.6 million in urban China, including 151,900 to 182,280 in Beijing. In addition, they estimate that the rate of informally recycled materials accounts for approximately 17 to 38 percent of the total recycled products. Zhang and Wen (2014) also examine the role of scavengers in the recycling of PET bottles in Beijing, and they find that over half of the PET bottles in Beijing are collected by scavengers.

4 Studies on industrial solid waste

While the number of studies on MSW management is relatively large, the number of studies focusing on industrial solid waste is rather small. As previously noted, Huang et al. (2006b) discuss the status of not only MSW management but also industrial solid waste management in China by using Chinese statistical data to examine the generation, components, and stockpiles of industrial solid waste. Geng et al. (2007) also examine data on industrial solid waste in their study of an integrated solid waste management system introduced in the industrial park in Tianjin, the Tianjin Economic Development Area (TEDA). They show that in the TEDA, 35,000 tons of industrial waste is sent to landfills, 60,000 tons is reused or recycled, and 4,000 tons is collected by scavengers. To calculate the effective reduction target for industrial solid waste in 30 regions of China, Hu and Lee (2008) apply data envelopment analysis (DEA) and develop a model where the capital stock, the number of employees, and the volumes of industrial solid waste, industrial waste water, and industrial waste gas are used as inputs, while GDP is used as an output.

Several studies focus on the relationship between industrial solid waste generation and income levels. For example, De Groot et al. (2004) examine this relationship by applying the Environmental Kuznets Curve theory, and they find an N-shaped relationship between the amount of industrial solid waste and gross regional product per capita (GRP per capita). In other words, the amount of industrial waste increases as GRP per capita increases when the GRP level is relatively low or high, whereas the amount of waste decreases as GRP per capita increases when the GRP level falls in the middle of the range.

Diao et al. (2009) also examine the relationship between the amount of industrial solid waste and GDP per capita. Using data from Jiaxing city in Zhejiang province, they find a weak N-shaped relationship between the two variables: the amount of industrial solid waste increases as GDP per capita increases when the level of GDP per capita is relatively low; however, the positive relationship between industrial solid waste and GDP per capita becomes weak when the level of GDP per capita is in the middle of the range; finally, when the level of GDP per capita is relatively high, then the positive relationship between industrial solid waste and GDP per capita again becomes relatively strong.

While these studies examine all types of industrial solid waste, several other studies focus on specific types of industrial waste. For instance, examining coal mining waste, Haibin and Zhenling (2010) find that China produced 2,716 Mtons of raw coal in 2008 and generated approximately 315 million tons of coal mining waste, such as coal gangue, fly ash, coal slime, and coal mine drainage. In addition to summarizing traditional methods for treating coal mining waste, the authors discuss the waste management scheme of the Jincheng Anthracite Mining Group in Shanxi Province, which can be considered a company that is taking a progressive approach to coal mining waste recycling.

5 Studies on hazardous waste

Waste generation is a complex problem, as the generation of waste causes a shortage of landfill sites and the generated waste may contain hazardous substances that can negatively affect human health or the environment. Indeed, current products contain a wide variety of hazardous substances. For instance, fluorescents contain mercury, and some types of dry-cell batteries include mercury and cadmium. There are also countless other examples of products that contain hazardous substances. If these products are not properly disposed of, they can cause serious harm to society.

In China, hazardous waste is categorized into three types: industrial hazardous waste, medical waste, and household hazardous waste (Duan et al., 2008). Duan et al. (2008) examine all three types of hazardous waste and discuss the status of the generation and management of these types of waste. Using official statistics, they show that the amount of industrial hazardous waste is approximately 11.62 million tons, of which 0.6 percent is not properly disposed of. Regarding medical waste and household hazardous waste, the authors find a dearth of detailed data on the management of these types of waste. However, in the case of medical waste, they estimate that the amount was approximately 740,000 tons in 2005 by using medical-related data such as the number of hospitals.

Among the three types of hazardous waste, medical waste seems to attract particular attention among researchers. In 2003, China was hit by an outbreak of Severe Acute Respiratory Syndrome (SARS), and this epidemic induced many scholars to acknowledge the necessity of proper medical waste disposal.[9]

Examining the status of health care waste (HCW) generation, disposal methods for HCW, and the legislative framework for HCW, Yang et al. (2009) report that the annual amount of discharged HCW reaches 650,000 tons and that incineration is the major disposal method for HCW. Although there are 149 facilities for HCW disposal in China, the authors find that nearly none of the existing HCW disposal facilities can fulfill the criteria for the proper HCW disposal. In analyzing the general status of medical waste management in China, Geng et al. (2013) specifically study the methods of medical waste management in Shenyang, the capital city of Liaoning province. At the national level, the authors report that the amount of discharged medical waste is 0.45 million tons, the number of medical waste facilities in China is 184, and the amount of safely disposed medical waste is 0.39 million tons. Hence, according to their findings, approximately 13 percent of the medical waste in China is improperly disposed of. They also examine the components of medical waste in China. As shown in Figure 3.2, the most common medical waste is glass, followed by paper. In the case of Shenyang, the authors summarize the current situation and describe the challenges of medical waste management in Shenyang.

Gai et al. (2009) discuss the current status of the medical waste management systems in hospitals in Shandong Province. Based on a survey of 23 hospitals of three different types (i.e., tertiary hospitals, secondary hospitals, and county hospitals), the authors estimate that the daily amount of medical waste discharged by tertiary, secondary, and county hospitals is 1,309.69 kg, 381.44 kg, and 292.46 kg, respectively. Regarding the components of medical waste, the authors report that the main types of waste discharged from tertiary and secondary hospitals are infectious waste, sharps waste, and pathological waste, whereas infectious waste, sharps waste, and pharmaceutical waste are the major types of wastes discharged from county hospitals. In addition, the authors find that general county hospitals more often fail to take sufficient measures to address medical waste problems compared with tertiary and secondary hospitals. Yang et al. (2009) conduct similar research in the case of Nanjing, the capital of Jiangsu province. Their study shows that the weighted average amount of discharged medical waste was 0.68 kg/bed per day and that the total amount of medical waste was approximately 3,771 tons in 2006. Regarding waste collection methods, the authors find that the system of segregated collection for all types of medical waste has

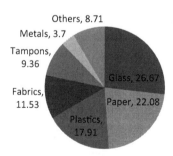

Figure 3.2 Components of medical waste in China

Source: Geng et al. (2013)

been introduced in 73 percent of hospitals, while 27 percent of them have not yet adopted this system. In addition, the authors analyze the storage of medical waste, training and education programs for handling medical waste in hospitals, the current status of medical waste disposal, and the public perception of medical waste. Meanwhile, Ruoyan et al. (2010) focus on the medical waste management of health care facilities (HCF) in Binzhou District, Shandong Province. Similar to Gai et al. (2009), the authors examine the status of medical waste management in HCFs and find that the status varies according to the size of the HCF (tertiary, secondary, or primary HCF). Their results reveal that the amount of discharged health care waste in tertiary, secondary, and primary HCFs is 1.22, 0.77, and 1.17 kg/bed/day, respectively. In addition, the authors examine the medical staff's knowledge of health care waste management and the precautionary method introduced to protect waste cleaning staff from contamination caused by health care waste.

Because the primary disposal method for health care waste is incineration, a large amount of ash is generated from health care waste disposal facilities. In this vein, Zhao et al. (2009a) focus on the ash produced from health care waste incineration and examine its chemical properties. They show that ash from health care waste contains a high proportion of heavy metals relative to ash from MSW incineration. The authors also examine the leachability of toxic metals and find that in the case of Cd, Cu and Pb, the amount of leaching exceeds the allowable limit set by the US Environmental Protection Agency.

As noted above, while several studies examine the issue of medical waste, a limited number of studies analyze household hazardous waste and industrial hazardous waste. One exception is the study by Gu et al. (2014), which focuses on household hazardous waste in Suzhou. By applying factor analysis and a regression model, the authors examine the status of the generation and content of household hazardous waste and analyze the factors that determine the amount of household hazardous waste generation. The results show that the amount of household hazardous waste generation is 6.16 g/capita/day and that the primary component of household hazardous waste is home cleaning products, which account for 21.33 percent of the waste, followed by medicines and personal care products. In addition, the authors find that the educational status of the household financial manager has the strongest influence on the amount of household hazardous waste generation.

6 Summary and conclusions

This chapter provides an overview of the current status of waste management in China by reviewing extant studies on this issue. With the increase in waste generation in China, the number of studies on waste management in the country has also increased. Although these studies play an important role in elucidating the status of waste management in China, considerable room remains for future research. First, while the literature on the status of the generation or content of waste in China is relatively abundant, few studies examine the mechanisms of waste generation. In fact, an understanding of the factors that affect the level of MSW generation in China is crucially important to inform efficient waste management policy.

Second, the role of the informal sector in waste management systems should be more closely analyzed. As previously mentioned, the informal sector collects a large portion of household recyclables and plays an important role in resource recycling in China. In addition, the informal recycling sector is regarded as a cause of serious environmental contamination. Thus, an analysis of the informal sector is crucially important to address waste management issues in China. However, the number of studies that focus on this issue remains relatively small, and further research will surely contribute to a better understanding of waste management in China. In particular, while several studies examine informal waste recycling, the number of studies on the role of the informal sector in recyclable collection is quite limited.

China is certainly becoming one of the highest waste-generating countries in the world, and efficient waste management policies are a crucial need. Expanding studies on waste management in China and accumulating knowledge on this topic will contribute to the development of an efficient policy scheme for waste management.

Notes

1 See World Bank (2012) for details.
2 In 2012, the amount of MSW in Japan was 45,234,000 tons, and the total for the United States was 250.9 million tons. See Japanese Ministry of Environment (2012) and US EPA (2012) for details.
3 See OECD Stat Extracts for details.
4 The authors find that low calorific value and high moisture content characterize MSW in China.
5 This value was the yearly average in 1999.
6 See the Japanese Ministry of Environment (2012) for details.
7 The definition of organic waste is essentially same as that of food waste.
8 For example, more than 60 percent of obsolete laptop computers are sold to junk buyers, while in the case of obsolete stereo units, less than 10 percent of units are sold to junk buyers and more than 40 percent are stored. For details, see Figure 1 of Streicher-Porte and Geering (2010).
9 For details, see Yang et al. (2009) or Gai et al. (2009).

References

Chen, X., Y. Geng, and T. Fujita (2010) "An overview of municipal solid waste management in China," *Waste Management*, Vol. 30, pp. 716–724.
Chi, X., M. Streicher-Porte, M.Y.L. Wang, and M.A. Reuter (2011) "Informal electronic waste recycling: A sector review with special focus on China," *Waste Management*, Vol. 31, pp. 731–742.
Chung, S., K. Lau, and C. Zhang (2011) "Generation of and control measures for, e-waste in Hong Kong," *Waste Management*, Vol. 31, pp. 544–554.

Chung, S.S. and C.W.H. Lo (2004) "Waste management in Guangdong cities: The waste management literacy and waste reduction preferences of domestic waste generators," *Environmental Management*, Vol. 33, pp. 692–711.

Chung, S.S. and C.S. Poon (2001) "Characterisation of municipal solid waste and its recyclable contents of Guangzhou," *Waste Management & Research*, Vol. 19, pp. 473–485.

De Groot, H.L.F., C.A. Withagen, and Z. Minliang (2004) "Dynamics of China's regional development and pollution: An investigation into the Environmental Kuznets Curve," *Environment and Development Economics*, Vol. 9, pp. 507–537.

Diao, X.D., S.X. Zeng, C.M. Tam, and V.W.Y. Tam (2009) "EKC analysis for studying economic growth and environmental quality: A case study in China," *Journal of Cleaner Production*, Vol. 17, pp. 541–548.

Duan, H., Q. Huang, Q. Wang, B. Zhou, and J. Li (2008) "Hazardous waste generation and management in China: A review," *Journal of Hazardous Materials*, Vol. 158, pp. 221–227.

Gai, R., L. Xu, X. Wang, Y. Zhang, H. Li, C. Zhou, J. He, W. Tang, and C. Kuroiwa (2009) "Hospital medical waste management in Shandong Province, China," *Waste Management & Research*, Vol. 27, pp. 336–342.

Geng, Y., W. Ren, B. Xue, T. Fujita, F. Xi, Y. Liu, and M. Wang (2013) "Regional medical waste management in China: A case study of Shenyang," *Journal of Material Cycles and Waste Management*, Vol. 15, pp. 310–320.

Geng, Y., Q. Zhu, and M. Haight (2007) "Planning for integrated solid waste management at the industrial Park level: A case of Tianjin, China," *Waste Management*, Vol. 27, pp. 141–150.

Gu, B., W. Zhu, H. Wang, R. Zhang, M. Liu, Y. Chen, and Y. Wu (2014) "Household hazardous waste quantification, characterization and management in China's cities: A case study of Suzhou," *Waste Management*, Vol. 34, pp. 2414–2423.

Habuer, J. Nakatani, and Y. Moriguchi (2014) "Time-series product and substance flow analyses of end-of-life electrical and electronic equipment in China," *Waste Management*, Vol. 34, pp. 489–497.

Haibin, L. and L. Zhenling (2010) "Recycling utilization patterns of coal mining waste in China," *Resources, Conservation and Recycling*, Vol. 54, pp. 1331–1340.

He, W., G. Li, X. Ma, H. Wang, J. Huang, and M. Xu (2006) "WEEE recovery strategies and the WEEE treatment status in China," *Journal of Hazardous Materials*, Vol. 136, pp. 502–512.

Hicks, C., R. Dietmar, and M. Eugster (2005) "The recycling and disposal of electrical and electronic waste in China – Legislative and market responses," *Environmental and Social Impacts of Electronic Waste Recycling*, Vol. 25, pp. 459–471.

Hong, J., X. Li, and C. Zhaojie (2010) "Life cycle assessment of four municipal solid waste management scenarios in China," *Waste Management*, Vol. 30, pp. 2362–2369.

Hu, J.L. and Y.C. Lee (2008) "Efficient three industrial waste abatement for regions in China," *The International Journal of Sustainable Development and World Ecology*, Vol. 15, pp. 132–144.

Huang, K., J. Guo, and Z. Xu (2009) "Recycling of waste printed circuit boards: A review of current technologies and treatment status in China," *Journal of Hazardous Materials*, Vol. 164, pp. 399–408.

Huang, P., X. Zhang, and X. Deng (2006a) "Survey and analysis of public environmental awareness and performance in Ningbo, China: A case study on household electrical and electronic equipment," *Journal of Cleaner Production*, Vol. 14, pp. 1635–1643.

Huang, Q., Q. Wang, L. Dong, B. Xi, and B. Zhou (2006b) "The current situation of solid waste management in China," *Journal of Material Cycles and Waste Management*, Vol. 8, pp. 63–69.

Hui, Y., W. Li'ao, S. Fenwei, and H. Gang (2006) "Urban solid waste management in Chongqing: Challenges and opportunities," *Waste Management*, Vol. 26, pp. 1052–1062.

Japanese Ministry of Environment (2012) Nihon no Haikibutsu Shori in FY 2012. Retrieved from http://www.env.go.jp/recycle/waste_tech/ippan/h25/index.html (accessed on 30 January 2016).

Kojima, M., A. Yoshida, and S. Sasaki (2009) "Difficulties in applying extended producer responsibility policies in developing countries: Case studies in e-waste recycling in China and Thailand," *Journal of Material Cycles and Waste Management*, Vol. 11, pp. 263–269.

Leung, A.O.W., W.J. Luksemburg, A.S. Wong, and M.H. Wong (2007) "Spatial distribution of Polybrominated Diphenyl Ethers and Polychlorinated Dibenzo-p-dioxins and Dibenzofurans in soil and combusted residue at Guiyu, an electronic waste recycling site in Southeast China," *Environmental Science & Technology*, Vol. 41, pp. 2730–2737.

Li, S. (2002) "Junk-buyers as the linkage between waste sources and redemption depots in urban China: The case of Wuhan," *Resources, Conservation and Recycling*, Vol. 36, pp. 319–335.

Linzner, R. and S. Salhofer (2014) "Municipal solid waste recycling and the significance of informal sector in urban China," *Waste Management & Research*, Vol. 32, pp. 896–907.

Li, J., B. Tian, T. Liu, H. Liu, X. Wen and S. Honda (2006) "Status quo of e-waste management in mainland China," *Journal of Material Cycles and Waste Management*, Vol. 8, pp. 13–20.

Liu, X., M. Tanaka, and Y. Matsui (2006) "Generation amount prediction and material flow analysis of electronic waste: A case study in Beijing, China," *Waste Management & Research*, Vol. 24, pp. 434–445.

Ma, J.Y., J.Y. Zhan, and Y.J. Zhang (2014) "Municipal solid waste management practice in China-a case study in Hangzhou," *Advanced Materials Research*, Vol. 878, pp. 23–29.

Medina, M. (2011) "Integrated solid waste management in Guangzhou," *Biocycle*, Vol. 52, pp. 50–51.

Minghua, Z., F. Xiumin, A. Rovetta, H. Qichang, F. Vicentinic, L. Bingkaia, A. Giustic, and L. Yid (2009) Municipal solid waste management in Pudong new area, China," *Waste Management*, Vol. 29, pp. 1227–1233.

National Bureau of Statistics of China (2013) China statistical year book 2013. Retrieved from http://www.stats.gov.cn/tjsj/ndsj/2013/indexeh.htm (accessed on 30 January 2016).

Ni, H.G. and E.Y. Zeng (2009) "Law enforcement and global collaboration are the keys to containing e-waste tsunami in China," *Environmental Science & Technology*, Vol. 43, pp. 3991–3994.

Qu, X., Z. Li, X. Xie, Y. Sui, L. Yang, and Y. Chen (2009) "Survey of composition and generation rate of household wastes in Beijing, China," *Waste Management*, Vol. 29, pp. 2618–2624.

Ruoyan, G., X. Lingzhong, L. Huijuan, Z. Chengchao, H. Jiangjiang, S. Yoshihisa, T. Wei, and K. Chushi (2010) "Investigation of health care waste management in Binzhou District, China," *Waste Management*, Vol. 30, pp. 246–250.

Streicher-Porte, M. and A.C. Geering (2010) "Opportunities and threats of current e-waste collection system in China: A case study from Taizhou with a focus on refrigerators, washing machines, and televisions," *Environmental Engineering Science*, Vol. 27, pp. 29–36.

Suocheng, D., K.W. Tong, and W. Yuping (2001) "Municipal solid waste management in China: Using commercial management to solve a growing problem," *Utilities Policy*, Vol. 10, pp. 7–11.

Tai, J., W. Zhang, Y. Che, and D. Feng (2011) "Municipal solid waste source-separated collection in China: A comparative analysis," *Waste Management*, Vol. 31, pp. 1673–1682.

Terazono, A., S. Murakami, N. Abe, B. Inanc, Y. Moriguchi, S. Sakai, M. Kojima, A. Yoshida, J. Li, J. Yang, M.H. Wong, A. Jain, In-Suk Kim, G.L. Peralta, C. Lin, and T. Mungcharoen (2006) "Current status and research on E-waste issues in Asia," *Journal of Material Cycles and Waste Management*, Vol. 8, pp. 1–12.

US EPA (2012) Municipal Solid Waste (MSW) in the United States: Facts and Figures. Retrieved from http://www.epa.gov/solidwaste/nonhaz/municipal/msw99.htm

Veenstra, A., C. Wang, W. Fan, and Y. Ru (2010) "An analysis of E-waste flows in China," *The International Journal of Advanced Manufacturing Technology*, Vol. 47, pp. 449–459.

Wang, J., L. Han, and S. Li (2008) "The collection system for residential recyclables in communities in Haidian District, Beijing: A possible approach for China recycling," *Waste Management*, Vol. 28, pp. 1672–1680.

Wang, H. and Y. Nie (2001a) "Municipal solid waste characteristics and management in China," *Journal of the Air & Waste Management Association*, Vol. 51, pp. 250–263.

Wang, H. and Y. Nie (2001b) "Remedial strategies for municipal solid waste management in China," *Journal of the Air & Waste Management Association*, Vol. 51, pp. 264–272.

Wang, Y., Y. Ru, A. Veenstra, R. Wang, and Y. Wang (2010) "Recent developments in waste electrical and electronics equipment legislation in China," *The International Journal of Advanced Manufacturing Technology*, Vol. 47, pp. 437–448.

Wang, H. and C. Wang (2012) "Municipal solid waste management in Beijing: Characteristics and challenges," *Waste Management & Research*, Vol. 31, pp. 67–72.

Wong, C.S.C., S.C. Wu, N.S. Duzgoren-Aydin, A. Aydin, and M.H. Wong (2007) "Trace metal contamination of sediments in an e-waste processing village in China," *Environmental Pollution*, Vol. 145, pp. 434–442.

World Bank (2012) What a waste: A global review of solid waste management. Retrieved from http://go.worldbank.org/BCQEP0TMO0 (accessed on 30 January 2016).

Xiao, Y., X. Bai, Z. Ouyang, H. Zheng, and F. Xing (2007) "The composition, trend and impact of urban solid waste in Beijing," *Environmental Monitoring and Assessment*, Vol. 135, pp. 21–30.

Xing, G.H., J.K.Y. Chan, A.O.W. Leung, S.C. Wu, and M.H. Wong (2009) "Environmental impact and human exposure to PCBs in Guiyu, an electronic waste recycling site in China," *Environment International*, Vol. 35, pp. 76–82.

Xu, L., P. Gao, S. Cui, and C. Liu (2013) "A hybrid procedure for MSW generation forecasting at multiple time scales in Xiamen City, China," *Waste Management*, Vol. 33, pp. 1324–1331.

Yang, C., L. Peijun, C. Lupi, S. Yangzhao, X. Diandou, F. Qian, and F. Shasha (2009) "Sustainable management measures for healthcare waste in China," *Waste Management*, Vol. 29, pp. 1996–2004.

Yang, J., B. Lu, and C. Xu (2008) "WEEE flow and mitigating measures in China," *Waste Managemen*, Vol. 28, pp. 1589–1597.

Yu, J., E. Williams, M. Ju, and C. Shao (2010) "Managing e-waste in China: Policies, pilot projects and alternative approaches," *Resources, Conservation and Recycling*, Vol. 54, pp. 991–999.

Zeng, X., J. Lia, A.L.N. Stevels, and L. Liua (2013) "Perspective of electronic waste management in China based on a legislation comparison between China and the EU," *Journal of Cleaner Production*, Vol. 51, pp. 80–87.

Zhang, D.Q., S.K. Tan, and R.M. Gersberg (2010) "Municipal solid waste management in China: Status, problems and challenges," *Journal of Environmental Management*, Vol. 91, pp. 1623–1633.

Zhang, H. and Z.G. Wen (2014) "The consumption and recycling collection system of PET bottles: A case study of Beijing, China," *Waste Management*, Vol. 34, pp. 987–998.

Zhang, L., Z. Yuan, J. Bi, and L. Huang (2012) "Estimating future generation of obsolete household appliances in China," *Waste Management & Research*, Vol. 30, pp. 1160–1168.

Zhao, L., F.S. Zhang, K. Wang, and J. Zhu (2009a) "Chemical properties of heavy metals in typical hospital waste incinerator ashes in China," *Waste Management*, Vol. 29, pp. 1114–1121.

Zhao, Y., T.H. Christensen, W. Lu, H. Wu, and H. Wang (2011) "Environmental impact assessment of solid waste management in Beijing City, China," *Waste Management*, Vol. 31, pp. 793–799.

Zhao, Y., A. Damgaard, H. Wang, W. Lu, and T.H. Christensen (2009b) "Life cycle assessment of the municipal solid waste management system in Hangzhou, China (EASEWASTE)," *Waste Management & Research*, Vol. 27, pp. 399–406.

Zhen-Shan, L., Y. Lei, Q. Xiao-Yan, and S. Yu-Mei (2009) "Municipal solid waste management in Beijing City," *Waste Management*, Vol. 29, pp. 2596–2599.

Zhuang, Y., S.W. Wu, Y.L. Wang, W.X. Wu, and Y.X. Chen (2008) "Source separation of household waste: A case study in China," *Waste Management*, Vol. 28, pp. 2022–2030.

Part II

Waste management policy in East Asia

4 Circular economy policy and regulation and the venous industry in China

Kenji Someno and Chang Miao

1 Current status of waste and recycled resources

1.1 Definitions and categories of waste

In China, the definition of waste is stipulated in the Law of the People's Republic of China on the Prevention and Control of Environmental Pollution by Solid Waste enacted in 1995 (enforced in 1996). A partial revision was made to this law in December 2004, also involving changes to the definition for waste. Thus, the stipulation defining solid waste as "solid or semi solid waste materials that are produced during production or construction activities, daily life, or other activities, and which pollute the environment" (Article 74 (1)) was revised to "articles and substances in solid, semi-solid state or gaseity in containers that are produced in the production, living and other activities and have lost their original use values or are discarded or abandoned though haven't yet lost use values, and articles and substances that are included into the management of solid wastes upon the strength of laws and administrative regulations" (Article 88 (1) of the revised law). Clearly, the revision broadened the scope of waste, adding 1) articles or substances that are discarded or abandoned regardless of whether or not they pollute the environment or retain use value, 2) articles and substances in solid, semi-solid state or gaseity in containers, and 3) articles and substances determined by specific laws and administrative regulations.

This solid waste can then be divided into industrial solid waste and urban house refuse. The revised law defines industrial solid waste as "solid waste discharged in industrial production activities" and urban house refuse as "solid waste discharged from daily life or services provided in daily life, as well as solid waste regarded as urban house refuse according to the provisions of laws and administrative regulations" (Article 88 (2) and (3)).

Moreover, the statistics regarding industrial solid waste and urban house refuse in this paper are according to the China Statistical Yearbook (edited by the National Bureau of Statistics of China), which categorizes industrial solid waste as "solid, semisolid, and high concentration liquid residues produced by industrial enterprises from production processes, including hazardous wastes, slag, coal ash, gangue, tailings, radioactive residues and other wastes, but excluding stones stripped or dug out in mining – gangue and acid or alkaline stones not included" and urban house refuse (consumption wastes) as "solid wastes produced from urban households or from service activities for urban households, and solid wastes regarded by laws and regulations as urban consumption wastes, including those from households, commercial activities, markets, cleaning of streets, public sites, offices, schools, factories, mining units and other sources."

1.2 State of industrial solid waste

The volume of industrial solid waste generated in China has increased rapidly in recent years, reaching approximately 3.3 billion tons in 2013. Since it used to be approximately 0.6 billion tons in 1993 and 1 billion tons in 2003, this means the amount has grown to less than twice the amount in the decade from 1993, but more than tripled in the decade from 2003. Even in terms of absolute amounts, China's solid waste amount is more than eight times the size of Japan's industrial waste amount of FY2011 (approximately 0.38 billion tons), and since the GDP figures for both countries are roughly the same, it can be assumed that there is much room for improvement in terms of China's resource efficiency.[1]

No correlation may be observed between the relationship of industrial solid waste and gross regional product (GRP) for China's 31 provinces, autonomous regions, and direct-controlled municipalities. Looking at the sources that generate industrial solid waste, the industries of electric/thermal energy, metals (ferrous/non-ferrous), and coal account for a large proportion, and thus it is inferred that the types of main industries in the region do influence the amount of waste generated.

The ratio of industrial solid wastes utilized was 62.8 percent for 2013, with 829.69 million tons of industrial solid waste ultimately going to landfill. (See Figures 4.1 and 4.2.) Since the ratio for 2003 was 55.8 percent, with 177.51 million tons in landfill, the increase in the ratio for this decade remains around 7 percent, but the landfill amount has increased more than four times, exceeding the increase rate for the generated amount of waste.

1.3 State of urban house refuse

The volume of urban house refuse is also increasing steadily along with the population rise or economic growth, but the increase rate is milder compared to that of industrial solid waste, with the FY2013 amount at approximately 172.39 million tons. Since the figures were 87.91 million tons for 1993 and approximately 148.57 million tons for 2003, China's generated waste is nearly four times Japan's FY2012 figure for common waste (approximately 45 million tons).

The per capita waste generated per day is approximately 350 grams, which is much less compared to the Japanese figure of approximately 960 grams. However, an examination by region reveals that Beijing marks the highest figure at 858 grams, with Shanghai following at 824 grams, and there is practically no difference compared to the Japanese amount. (See Figure 4.3.)

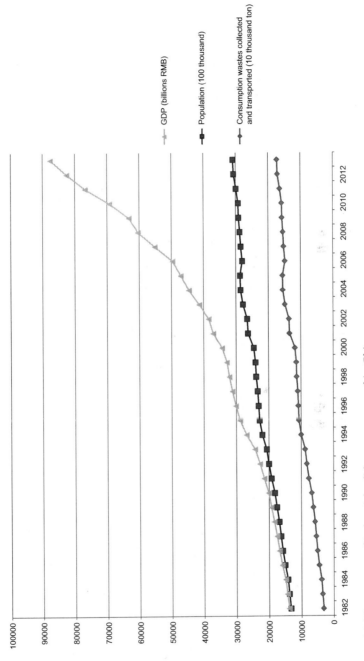

Figure 4.1 The amount of industrial solid waste generated in China

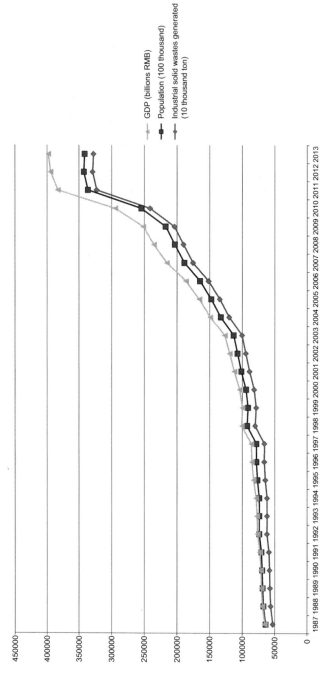

Figure 4.2 The amount of industrial solid waste generated and GRP in China (2013)

Legend:
- GDP (billions RMB)
- Population (100 thousand)
- Industrial solid wastes generated (10 thousand ton)

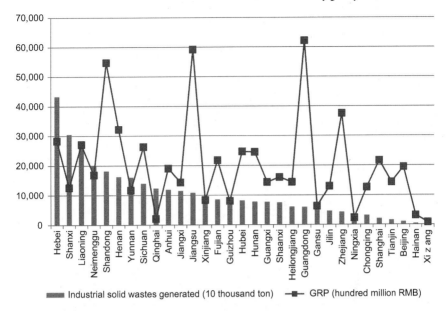

Figure 4.3 Amount of consumption wastes in China

1.4 State of recycled resources

The products being thrown away as waste in China are also changing with the rise in living standards. According to China National Resources Recycling Association (CRRA), supposedly as many as 1.35 million cars and 0.53 million motorcycles were collected in 2013, while 38.5 million televisions, 12.79 million refrigerators, 12.65 million washing machines, 18.3 million air-conditioners, and 32.06 million personal computers were thrown away.[2]

Looking at the present state of China, the appropriate legislation and law enforcement for the collection/processing of such generated waste or used products/parts/material, etc. (hereinafter referred to as "venous resources") needs to catch up with the actual situation. In April 2014, the Environmental Protection Law of the People's Republic of China was revised, stipulating the government's promotion of cleaner production and resource recycling (Article 40), and the duty of local governments to sort and collect waste (Article 37). It is anticipated that the revised law will prompt the legal system to develop in the future, but so far only three laws address venous resources – the Law of the People's Republic of China on the Prevention and Control of Environmental Pollution by Solid Waste, promulgated in 1995; the Cleaner Production Promotion Law of the People's Republic of China, promulgated in 2002; and the Circular Economy Promotion Law of the People's Republic of China, promulgated in 2008 – and the lower level administrative regulations and ministerial regulations for these laws are yet to be organized.

2 Circular economy policy

2.1 Background and definitions towards a circular economy

In China, the "circular economy" refers to the recycling-based economy of "resource -> product -> waste -> recycled resource" (3R principle of "reduce, reuse, and recycle"), in contrast to the traditional one-way economy of "resource -> product -> waste" (mass production, mass consumption, and mass disposal).

In Japan, the term "Sound Material-Cycle Society" is used to describe a society that promotes 3R initiatives, but the Chinese "circular economy" refers to the means, and hence the society that is achieved through the means is called a "resource-saving society". (For example, state leaders have said in speeches, "develop the circular economy to construct a resource-saving society".)

The Chinese circular economy is not only about environmental problems, but also involves the issues of resources, trade, and other economic policies. Initially, the word had often been used in the context of the efficient use of resources and recycling of waste, but now it is also being applied to the contexts of saving energy (saving coal/petroleum oil/electricity, etc.), water (saving water, reuse of water for miscellaneous use, use of sea water, etc.), and land resources (housing construction, factory location, underground development, etc.), as well as promoting service industries, etc., and thus it is becoming a concept closer to the idea of "sustainable society".

2.2 The 12th 5-year plan for national economic and social development of the People's Republic of China

The 12th 5-Year Plan for National Economic and Social Development of the People's Republic of China, promulgated on March 16, 2011, sets out specific chapters on the venous industry and circular economy policies.[3]

Part 3, Chapter 10 ("Foster and develop strategic emerging sectors") names seven industries, including the energy-saving/environment-friendly industry and biotechnology industry, as emerging strategic industries and points out advanced environmental protection and the industrialization of resource recycling as processes to develop an energy-saving/environmental industry.

Regarding circular economy policies, Chapter 23 of Part 6 ("Green development and construction of a resource-saving/environmentally friendly society") sets the goal of developing and strengthening the circular economy. This chapter is comprised of four sections: i) promotion of circular production methods, ii) healthy system for resource recycling, iii) promotion of the green consumption model, and iv) stronger policies and technology support. The first section states the goals of increasing the ratio of industrial solid wastes utilized to 72 percent, constructing/renovating industrial parks according to circular economy regulations, and enhancing the resource production rate (GDP/resource input) by 15 percent. The second section outlines the construction of a collection network comprised of the three elements of resource collection stations, waste sorting stations, and recycled resource markets in city residential areas and rural villages, as well as the establishment of a system for the separate collection of waste. The third section describes the purchase and use of energy-/water-saving products, energy-saving environmental automobiles, and energy-/land-saving residences, as well as the reduction of throwaway products, restrictions on excessive packaging, reduction of unreasonable consumption, green procurement by the government, and increased percentage of energy-/water-saving products and recycled products, in order to form a green lifestyle and consumption model that suits the state of affairs in China. The fourth section explains the support for monetary/tax/finance policies, establishment of laws and standards, implementation of extended producer responsibility (EPR), and establishment of a labeling system for renewed products and a system for evaluating circular economy statistics, as well as the deepening of the "state circular economy model", implementation of the circular economy Thousand-Hundred-Ten project, and promotion of circular economy trial projects (to be mentioned later).[4]

An aspect that should be noted here is the introduction of the resource production rate as a new indicator. The resource calculation rate (resource productivity) in China, which had been 1,428 RMB/ton in 1990, increased over the next 15 years by 66 percent to 2,370 RMB/ton in 2005. However, the amount peaked in 2001 at 2,473 RMB/ton before slipping into a gradual decline thereafter. This is due to the fact that China's economic growth in the 21st century has been led by heavy industrialization and urbanization, involving many high-input, high-consumption, and high-pollution projects. Thus, it is assumed that this target setting is also intended to adjust the structure of the industries leading the Chinese economy.

The 12th 5-Year Plan also has a column touching on the seven key processes for the circular economy.

The first is the comprehensive use of resources; the second is a model system for collecting used products, establishing 80 network bases; the third is the construction of 50 "urban mining demonstration bases" with advanced technology; the fourth is the promotion of remanufacturing industries, constructing districts for state-level remanufacturing industries of automotive parts, etc.; the fifth is the use of food waste as resources, constructing facilities to recycle food waste in 100 cities (districts); the sixth is the incorporation of recycling in industrial parks; and the seventh is the promotion of technology models of resource recycling.

2.3 Laws

2.3.1 System

The legal system regarding the circular economy in China can be divided into two types of laws: one that involves the appropriate processing of waste (from the point of view of environmental conservation), and the other involving the 3Rs of venous resources (from the point of view of saving resources). An example of the former, deliberated at the National People's Congress (NPC), is the Law of the People's Republic of China on the Prevention and Control of Environmental Pollution by Solid Waste enacted in 1995; the waste subject to this law can be divided into industrial solid waste, urban house refuse, and hazardous waste. Examples of the latter include the Cleaner Production Promotion Law of the People's Republic of China, enacted in 2002, and the Circular Economy Promotion Law of the People's Republic of China, enacted in 2008.

Under these laws are State Council orders (set by the State Council), and those related to the appropriate processing of waste include the "Regulations on city appearance and environmental sanitation management" (1992) for urban house refuse, "Regulations on the safety management of hazardous chemicals" (2002), "Regulations on the management of medical waste" (2003), and "Administrative measure of management for hazardous waste businesses license" (2004) for hazardous waste.[5] Beneath these State Council orders for household and hazardous waste are ministerial regulations (set by the State Council's related ministries), including the "Ordinance on the management of city urban house refuse" and "Ordinance on the prevention and control of environmental pollution by waste hazardous chemicals", as well as notices (technology policies, management regulations, etc.) that are administrative guidance in nature.[6] Furthermore, just as the "Regulations on city appearance and environmental sanitation management" was enacted before the Law of the People's Republic of China on the Prevention

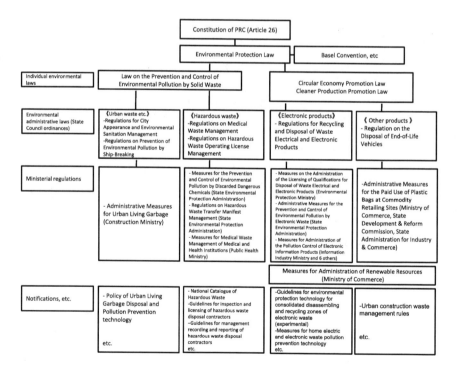

Figure 4.4 Legal system of the circular economy in China

and Control of Environmental Pollution by Solid Waste, there are many cases in China where the lower regulations, which are easier to enact, precede laws to address actual problems.

Examples of State Council orders for the 3Rs of venous resources are the "Regulations on the management of recycling and disposal of waste electrical and electronic equipment" (2009) and "Ordinance on the management of the recycling of scrap cars" (2001).[7],[8] There is a clear difference between these regulations. With the waste electrical and electronic products, the regulations are already in effect and progress is being made in ministerial regulations, etc., regarding the collection, reuse, and prevention of pollution of home appliances to ensure that the regulations are enforced; however, with scrap cars, a gap remains between the law enforcement and reality, and little progress is being made in organizing the lower regulations.

Furthermore, the Ministry of Commerce has enacted the "Ordinance on the management of the recycling of renewable resources" (2007), which focuses on the process of resource collection instead of specific items.[9]

2.3.2 *Law of the People's Republic of China on the prevention and control of environmental pollution by solid waste*

The prevention of pollution by solid waste in China used to be regulated within the series of laws that included the 1956 "Factory safety and sanitation regulations", "Proposed regulations on the protection of mining resources" (1973), "Guidance on environmental protection and improvement (proposed draft)" (1973), "Regulations on city appearance and environmental sanitation management" (1982), "Regulations on the management of ocean dumping" (1985), and "Law on the protection and control of communicable diseases" (1989). In 1979, the "Environmental Protection Law (proposed)" was promulgated, stipulating the prevention of environmental pollution by waste or residue from industry/mining and urban life (besides what is regulated in the recycling regulations of mining resources), as well as the adoption of technology to recycle waste and process pollutants in industrial companies. Laws, such as the Law on Marine Environment Protection, Law on the Prevention and Control of Water Pollution, and Law on the Prevention and Control of Atmospheric Pollution, also stipulate regulations to reduce emissions and prevent pollution by solid waste via the restrictions on the "three wastes" (atmospheric pollution, water pollution, and solid waste) discharged by industrial companies, the system of collecting fines for emitting pollutants, and sanitation standards of industrial companies.

The State Environmental Protection Administration (SEPA) started preparing a draft for a law on the prevention and control of environmental pollution by solid waste in 1984. After a decade of exchanges and discussions with experts, the Law of the People's Republic of China on the Prevention and Control of Environmental Pollution by Solid Waste was passed at the 16th Meeting of the Eighth NPC Standing Committee on October 30, 1995, and enforced on April 1, 1996. This was then revised at the 13th Meeting of the Tenth NPC Standing Committee on December 29, 2004, and enforced on April 1, 2005, increasing the provisions of Chapter Six from 77 to 91 articles to reinforce the government's responsibility in preventing environmental pollution by solid waste, increase regulations for pollution by packed waste, and enhance focus on the prevention of pollution by solid waste in rural villages.

2.3.3 *Cleaner production promotion law of the People's Republic of China*

Cleaner production is a concept proposed by the United Nations Environment Program (UNEP) in 1989, attracting global attention as with its incorporation into Agenda 21, which was established by the United Nations Conference on Environment and Development (UNCED) in 1992.

In China, the National Environmental Protection Agency (NEPA) issued the "Guidance on the promotion of cleaner production" in 1997, and the State Economic and Trade Commission (SETC) issued the "Notice on the implementation of the cleaner production model plan" in 1999, and it was decided to implement cleaner production model programs in petrochemical, chemical, metallurgical, light manufacturing, and shipping industries in the 10 cities of Beijing, Tianjin, Shanghai, Chongqing, Shenyang, Taiyuan, Jinan, Kunming, Lanzhou, and Fuyang.

Cleaner Production Promotion Law of the People's Republic of China was then passed at the 28th Meeting of the Ninth NPC Standing Committee on June 29, 2002, and enforced on January 1, 2003. This was revised at the 25th Meeting of the 11th NPC Standing Committee on February 29, 2012, and put into effect on July 1, 2012, reorganizing the provisions of Chapter Six from 42 to 40 articles.

2.3.4 *Circular economy promotion law of the People's Republic of China*

At the opening ceremony of the Second Global Environment Facility (GEF) Assembly on October 16, 2002, President Jiang Zemin stated that only by proceeding down the path of a circular economy, based on the effective use of resources and environmental protection, will it be possible to achieve sustainable development. This is considered to have been the first time a Chinese leader stated the words "circular economy". Since then, "circular economy" has appeared several times in statements by government leaders and senior officials in various meetings, as in President Hu Jintao's statement at the Central Population Resources Environment Meeting of 2003. In terms of policy papers, the State Council announced the "Guidance on the development of a circular economy" in July 2005, outlining the government goals and benchmarks for promoting the circular economy.[10] The 11th 5-Year Plan for National Economic and Social Development of the People's Republic of China, promulgated in March 2006, then outlined a chapter for the development of a circular economy, clarifying the general rules and specific measures for development.

The "Eleventh Five-Year Plan for national environmental protection regulations", promulgated by the SEPA in November 2005, stated the necessity to establish related rules and regulations, such as the Circular Economy Promotion Law, to build a resource-saving, environmentally friendly society. At the end of 2005, the legislative project for the circular economy was officially incorporated into the legislative plans of the Tenth NPC Standing Committee, and a draft was deliberated at the NPC Standing Committee in 2007. This law had initially been considered within the scope of environmental policies by the Ministry of Environmental Protection, but the National Development and Reform Commission (NDRC) took over the leading role along the way. Since the NDRC also regarded the circular economy as an economic policy to find a solution to the issue of resource restrictions, the law thus became more than just an environmental policy. The Circular Economy Promotion Law of the People's Republic of China was passed at the 4th Meeting of the 11th NPC Standing Committee on August 29, 2008, and put into effect on January 1, 2009.

2.3.5 Regulations regarding waste electrical and electronic products

Serious consideration has been given to the recycling of waste electrical and electronic products since around 2002. The "Tenth Five-Year Plan for the collection and use of renewable resources", promulgated by the SETC in January 2002, outlined the prompt establishment of the "Regulations on the management of the collection and use of renewable resources" and related regulations, including the "Ordinance on the management of the collection and use of used household electrical appliances" and "Ordinance on the management of the collection and use of used personal computers and other electronic waste".[11] The SETC also started model programs to collect waste home appliances in Zhejiang province and Qingdao of Shandong province in 2003.

When the SETC was dismantled in 2003, its operations were transferred to the NDRC, Ministry of Commerce, and other entities. The NDRC disclosed the draft for the "Regulations on the management of the collection and disposal of used household appliances and electronic equipment" in September 2004, and asked for public comments. It then added the cities of Beijing and Tianjin as areas to implement the model program of collecting waste home appliances. The NDRC then continued to work on the draft, and the "Regulations on the management of the collection and disposal of used electrical and electronic equipment" was passed at the State Council 23rd Standing Committee Meeting on August 20, 2008, and put into effect on January 1, 2011.[12] These regulations apply to the five items of televisions, refrigerators, washing machines, air conditioners, and personal computers, stipulating the collection and recycling by designated resource recycling companies and the provision of grants. Article 4 of these regulations stipulates the responsibilities of each State Council ministry, and the regulations themselves are jointly managed by the Ministry of Environmental Protection, NDRC, and Ministry of Industry and Information Technology (with the primary responsibility belonging to the Ministry of Environmental

Protection in terms of execution). The Ministry of Commerce only jointly manages the part regarding the collection of used electrical and electronic equipment, and the Ministry of Finance; State Administration of Taxation; General Administration of Quality Supervision, Inspection and Quarantine; and others are regarded as related agencies.

Meanwhile, the SEPA proceeded to consider the issue in terms of preventing environmental pollution by waste electrical and electronic equipment. It announced the "Notice on strengthening the management of the environmental sanitation of waste electrical and electronic equipment" on August 26, 2003, and enforced the "Technical specifications for the environmental protection of centralized disassembly and disposal areas of waste electromechanical equipment (proposed)" (HJ/T181–2005) on September 1, 2005. It also established the "Technology policy to prevent and control pollution by waste household electrical and electronic equipment" with the Ministry of Science and Technology, Ministry of Information Industry, and Ministry of Commerce on April 27, 2006, the "Ordinance on the management of the prevention and control of pollution by electronic waste" on February 1, 2008, and "Technical specifications for controlling pollution from processing waste electrical and electronic equipment" (HJ527–2010) on April 1, 2010.

On June 28, 2009 (after the promulgation and before the enforcement of the "Regulations on the management of the collection and disposal of used electrical and electronic equipment"), seven ministries, including the NDRC, Ministry of Finance, Ministry of Commerce, and Ministry of Environmental Protection, announced the "Ordinance on the old-for-new household appliance replacement scheme".[13] This "Old-for-New" scheme was implemented to stimulate domestic consumption along with the "Rural household appliance subsidy program" (started in 2008 to spread home appliances to rural areas), and was applied to the nine areas of Beijing city, Tianjin city, Shanghai city, Jiangsu province, Zhejiang province, Shandong province, Guangdong province, Fuzhou city, and Changsha city from June 1, 2009 to May 31, 2010. The subject area was then expanded to 19 provinces and cities, including Hebei province, Shanxi province, Liaoning province, Dalian city, and Jilin province, from June 1, 2010 to the end of December 2011, providing a 10 percent price subsidy for newly purchased televisions, refrigerators, washing machines, air conditioners, and personal computers on condition that the used products were traded in.[14] Since the main objective of these regulations was to stimulate consumption, the initiative was led by the Ministry of Commerce.

Meanwhile, the "Regulations on the management of the collection and disposal of used electrical and electronic equipment" was supposed to be put into effect on January 1, 2011, but was delayed by the protracted discussions between the government and the business community regarding the amount that should be borne by the home appliance manufacturers, and was finally enforced on July 1, 2012. The Old-for-New scheme also seems to have served as a test case for enforcing these regulations. For example, the "Regulations on the management of the collection and disposal of used electrical and electronic equipment" sets a stricter screening process to address the problem of inappropriate subsidy applications, which troubled the Old-for-New scheme; however, because the Old-for-New scheme was mainly led by the Ministry of Commerce and the "Regulations on the management of the collection and disposal of used electrical and electronic equipment" was led by the Ministry of Environmental Protection, the Ministry of Environmental Protection did not possess the Ministry of Commerce's practical experience of the Old-for-New scheme, and practically had no choice but to build the operational structure from the ground up. This indicates how short-term changes in jurisdiction in a complex system can result in major drawbacks.

The Ministry of Environmental Protection and Ministry of Industry and Information Technology announced the "Guidelines on the process of dismantling waste electrical and electronic equipment and optimization of production management (2015 edition)" on December 5, 2014. These guidelines stipulate the detailed requirements for the dismantling process and production management at companies that have acquired grants from the waste electorical and electronic equipment processing fund, such as details on management regulations, data management, establishment of video surveillance measures, processing facilities and equipment, optimization of the dismantling process, and use/processing of the dismantled result. These guidelines can be used as a reference document in terms of supervision management and grant eligibility screening for related companies by the dapartment responsible for environmental issues at each level.

Moreover, entities including the NDRC and Ministry of Finance started planning the second electrical and electronic waste processing index in June 2013, studying electrical and electronic waste that could potentially be subject to subsidies besides the five items of televisions, refrigerators, washing machines, air conditioners, and personal computers. Small home appliances such as cell phones, copy machines, and printers are expected to be next on the list.

On December 15, 2013, the NDRC Department of Resource Conservation and Environmental Protection announced the "Adjustments to the electrical and electronic waste equipment processing index (public comment edition)". The main adjustments are shown in Table 4.1. However, the fact that the second index has not been announced as of January 2015 suggests that they are having difficulty narrowing down the subject products.

Table 4.1 Adjustments to the electrical and electronic waste equipment processing index (public comment edition)

No.	Large category	Middle category	Small category
01	Products including regulated gases (ozone-depleting or greenhouse gases)	Coolers Air-conditioning apparatus Cleaning and hygiene devices Water and beverage heating devices	Refrigerators Air-conditioning apparatus Household electric water heaters Cooling / heating water servers

(Continued)

Table 4.1 (Continued)

No.	Large category	Middle category	Small category
02	Products including a display of 100cm² or larger	Video equipment Information media equipment Computers	Television sets Surveillance cameras Displays
03	Electric light source	Electric light source	Fluorescent lights
04	Batteries	Storage batteries	Lead-acid batteries Lithium batteries
05	IT and Communication devices	Computers and peripheral equipment	Microcomputers Printers Printer consumables Copy machines Copy machine consumables Scanners
		Mobile communication terminals	Mobile communication terminals
		Communication end devices	Fixed-line phones Fax machines
06	Others	Electric appliances for home or similar use	Washing machines Electric fans Kitchen ventilating fans Rice cookers Electric pressure cookers Microwave ovens Soy milk makers Juicers Household gas water heaters

2.3.6 Issues

One of the issues of the legal system supporting the circular economy in China is its complexity, caused by the insufficient cooperation between State Council ministries, or compartmentalization. For example, by type of waste, industrial solid waste is managed by the environmental division and macroeconomic division, urban house refuse is managed by the construction division, hazardous waste is managed by the environmental division, and venous resources (3R) are managed by the macroeconomic division.[15] In terms of process, from the generation to collection and recycling/processing of venous resources, in addition to the aforementioned three divisions, the commerce division is involved with the collection process, the customs division and export/import inspection division are involved with exports and imports, the industry division is involved with the waste processing and venous resource collection at production companies, and the science and technology division is involved with research/technology development. There are also cases where these responsibilities are intertwined and in conflict with each other.

The other issue is the inadequacy of the legal system. There are only two laws that are equivalent to the specific recycling laws in Japan – for home appliances and cars – and although there is a law for cars, the lower level laws are inadequate and practically non-existent. Instructions for plans to consider the legislation for items such as waste batteries, used paper, and waste tires can be observed as early as in the "Tenth Five-Year Plan for the collection and use of renewable resources" of 2002, but more than a decade later there is still no legislation.

2.4 Designation of cities and regions

In China, there are several types of what are known as environmental model cities, and the main ones related to the circular economy are as follows.

2.4.1 Eco-provinces, eco-cities, eco-counties, and eco-industrial parks

To prevent pollution, enhance the efficiency of environmental protection, and promote sustainable development, the SEPA started designating trial areas as eco-provinces, eco-cities, and eco-counties in 2002. Based on the existing 389 eco-construction model districts, eight eco-construction model provinces (Hainan, Jilin, Heilongjiang, Zhejiang, Shandong, Anhui, Jiangsu, and Fujian provinces) and 11 eco-construction model cities and counties (districts) were designated.

The SEPA also started building an eco-industrial park in Guigang of Guangxi Zhuang Autonomous Region in 1999. After approving the construction of the National Eco-Industrial (Sugar Industry) Demonstration Park in Guigang of Guangxi Zhuang Autonomous Region as the first national eco-industrial demonstration park in August 2001, the National Eco-Industrial Demonstration Park in Suzhou Industrial Park, National Eco-Industrial Demonstration Park in Suzhou National New & Hi-tech Industrial Development Zone, and National Eco-Industrial Demonstration Park in Tianjin Economic-technological Development Area were certified as national eco-industrial demonstration parks by March 2008, and the construction of 27 demonstration parks have been approved since Guigang of August 2001 for the Kunming Hi-tech Industries Development Zone of August 2008.

There are three types of eco-industrial development parks – comprehensive, business type, and venous industry – and the Qingdao New World Eco-industrial Park is the only location to be approved as a venous industry type eco-industrial development park (approved on September 11, 2006).

2.4.2 Circular economy trial points

While designating eco-construction model provinces and eco-industrial demonstration parks, the SEPA also designated the two provinces of Liaoning and

Jiangsu, as well as the six cities of Panjin, Rizhao, Yiwu, Hebi, Guiyang, and Wuwei, as locations for circular economy trial points from 2002 to 2004, with the objective to save and achieve the high efficiency of resources, reduce waste, encourage recycling, and process waste in a safe manner, although these initiatives are in actual fact essentially the same as those with the aforementioned eco-construction model provinces.

Based on the above, the six entities of the NDRC, SEPA, Ministry of Science and Technology, Ministry of Finance, Ministry of Commerce, and National Bureau of Statistics designated 10 provinces and cities, 13 industrial parks, 17 companies and regional governments in 4 focus areas, and 42 companies of 7 focus business categories (total of 82 trial projects) as the first circular economy trial points in October 2005. At the same time, the NDRC, SEPA, and other related ministries established circular economy trial points work leader groups and expert groups, promoting initiatives and instructing skills in the trial points.

By December 2007, the 6 entities designated 17 provinces and cities, 20 industrial parks, nine companies in 3 areas, and 50 companies in 12 business categories (total of 96 trial projects) as second circular economy trial points. Since the 11th 5-Year Plan started the initiative of saving energy and reducing pollution, there were expectations for the second circular economy trial points to help save energy and reduce pollution in addition to achieving elements of resource recycling.

Thus, of the 178 trial points approved as the first and second national circular economy trial points, 26 provinces/autonomous regions/direct-controlled municipalities have also implemented province-level circular economy trial points, resulting in 133 cities/districts/counties, 256 industrial parks, and 1,352 companies designated as trial points.

2.4.3 Urban mining demonstration bases

In May 2010, the NDRC and Ministry of Finance announced the construction of 30 urban mining demonstration bases in 5 years to collect electronic waste and other resources. The first group of designations consists of the seven locations of Anhui Jieshou Tianying Circular Economy Industrial Park, Tianjin Ziya Circular Economy Industrial Park, Ningxia Jintian Industrial Park, Hunan Guluo Industrial Park, Guangdong Qingyuan Renewable Resources Industrial Park, Qingdao New World Recycling Park, and Sichuan Southwest Neijiang Recycling Park, aiming to construct recycling facilities capable of processing 1.9 million tons of copper, 0.8 million tons of aluminum, 0.35 million tons of lead, and 1.8 million tons of plastic by 2015. An additional 37 locations were also designated by July 2014 (15 locations in the second round, 6 in the third round, 10 in the fourth round, and 6 in the fifth round), resulting in 44 locations designated as urban mining demonstration bases so far.

2.4.4 Low-carbon model areas

On February 9, 2011, the NDRC announced the designation of five provinces (Guangdong, Liaoning, Hubei, Shaanxi, and Yunnan) and eight cities (Tianjin,

Chongqing, Shenzhen, Xiamen, Hangzhou, Nanchang, Guiyang, and Baoding) as model areas to realize a low-carbon society, instructing them to incorporate low-carbon plans into the 12th 5-Year Plan for each area. The low-carbon economy is centered on encouraging the use of natural energy, energy-saving, and energy efficiency, but since the effective use of resources also helps, the circular economy initiatives are also expected to be included. Later in 2012, the second group of designations followed with an additional 29 provinces/cities/districts including Beijing city, Shanghai city, Hainan province, and Shijiazhuang city.

3 Venous industry

3.1 History

When the Chinese communist party became the ruling party in 1949, two divisions were responsible for managing the collection and use of venous resources. Since one responsibility accompanied production activities, this was managed by the supply of goods division (materials and equipment administration under the State Council, and the later Ministry of Materials and Equipment), in charge of the logistics of industrial commodities and production materials; the other, accompanying daily life, was managed by the commercial business division (purchase and sales cooperatives: sub-level organizations of the Ministry of Commerce). For example, the materials management division organized the system for collecting used metal resources in provinces/autonomous regions/ direct-controlled municipalities, lower-level cities, counties, and even towns. In the 1970s, management authorities were established to collect material in the six national regions of North, Northeast, East, South Central, Southwest, and Northwest China. They were given a certain level of administrative authority and collected huge amounts of venous resources each year.

The transition from the planned economy to market economy since 1984 also impacted the collection and use of venous resources. As the logistics system was restructured, and the venous resources collection industries were also gradually privatized, the Ministry of Materials and Equipment and Ministry of Commerce were terminated at the first meeting of the Eighth NPC in 1993. In 1994, the Ministry of Public Security promulgated the "Ordinance on the management of the public security of used metal purchasers", sorting used metals into production and urban house refuse, and established the special industry administrative registration system for production waste metals. However, the trend of market liberalization and privatization continued, and by 1996, the registration and prioritization conditions for state-owned companies and private companies were reconciled so they could be managed in a uniform manner. The government also terminated the special industry management approval system for venous resources in 2002, fully opening up the collection market for venous resources.

As above, the venous resource collection in China has developed in stages. In the first stage of the 1950s, residents sold venous resources to small companies, who then sold the venous resources in the distribution market to small manual industry factories, who used them to produce products. In the second stage of the 1960s to 1990s, venous resources were collected by state-owned companies and gathered at purchase stations, where they were sorted and processed to be used to manufacture products in factories. In the third stage from the 1990s, venous resources are collected by collection companies via fixed stations and door-to-door visits, and through distribution trade markets the resource processing companies recycle them into resources that can be utilized in companies using recycled resources.

The present Chinese market is in the third stage in general, but in some regions, resources are collected by small companies, including part-time farmers, as in the first stage. Meanwhile, the "*Guo jin min tui*" phenomenon (the situation where state-owned companies develop and private companies are on the decline), seen in various industries in China, is also observed in the venous resources industry, with state-owned companies increasing their presence as in the second stage.[16]

The resource collection methods are also becoming more diversified. From around 2010, in particular, some developed areas have actively promoted the online collection method. One notable example is the city of Shanghai taking advantage of internet technology in building its electronic waste recycling system. The process enables the citizens of Shanghai to have easy access to the Shanghai new Jinhua Group's waste online collection site, the Jinqiao recycled resources platform "Ala environmental protection network" or other special online collection platforms, where they are only a click away from having waste operators come to collect electronic waste at their home.

3.2 Present status

According to the industry group research regarding the scale of venous industries in China, the amount of resources collected in 2013 was approximately 160 million to 164 million tons, nearly double that of 2005; the total value of collected resources amounted to 481.71 billion to 571.6 billion yuan, with 200,000 to 300,000 collection points nationwide.[17]

Of the 100,000 to 137,000 collection companies registered at administration for industry and commerce nationwide, 10,000 to 12,000 companies are medium-sized or larger collection companies, while 18 million to 18.5 million people work in collection, of which 11 million are supposedly unauthorized individual proprietors. Eighty percent of companies are private companies, 75 percent of employees work for private companies, and approximately 80 percent of the nationwide collection companies are concentrated in East China (Shanghai city, Shandong province, Anhui province, etc.), South China (Guangdong province, etc.), and Southwest China (Sichuan province, Chongqing city, etc.).

3.3 Issues

Many problems exist with the venous industries in China.

Firstly, since most of the collectors are unauthorized individual proprietors, collection work lacks order in terms of legal structure and business practices.

Conversely, this has also resulted in qualified major companies being unable to collect sufficient amounts of resources. Secondly, the medium-sized and larger companies only account for roughly 10 percent of the total, which means most businesses are small and the amounts they handle are small, resulting in low collection efficiency. Thirdly, the generally low level of processing and recycling technology means it is only possible to produce low-standard recycled products and renewed resources, even with good quality venous resources. Furthermore, the unauthorized small companies not only lack the technology but are also without environmental measures. As they process circular resources, including heavy metal waste such as electrical and electronic products and chemical substances, they pile waste outdoors, engage in crude dismantlement, and extract parts using liquid solutions, resulting in cases of severe environmental pollution. Fourthly, the intermediary distributors are also spreading and increasing pollution by making speculative sales reselling the resources and transporting the resources to multiple regions and collection bases. To develop venous industries, it is first of all crucial to organize the system for collecting and using recycled resources. The question is whether it is possible to formalize the venous industries by organizing the legal structure and other measures.

Moreover, the venous industries have been consolidated in recent years in China, and companies are growing larger. These large companies with financial power install the latest equipment and facilities from Europe and other countries, achieving processing and recycling technology levels comparable to those of developed countries. They are also making progress in the division of labor as they absorb and entrust the collection of venous resources to smaller collection operators with mobility, while they perform the processing in their own factories equipped with environmental measures.[18]

Since it is usual to collect venous resources as valuables in China, the profits of recycling businesses are limited to revenue from selling recycled resources. Thus, for instance, Japanese affiliated companies construct plants of a size that suits the revenue, making efforts to increase the operational efficiency within the restraints. Meanwhile, the large Chinese companies have plants with large buildings on huge sites, equipped with state-of-the-art equipment and facilities, but it is often the case that vast spaces are vacant, occupied by just one operation line. Since it is generally extremely difficult for operations to rely solely on revenue from selling recycled resources, operations in Japan rely on gaining fees for processing waste, and businesses in China anticipate grant revenue such as with the present recycling of home appliances. Although it depends on the items handled as venous resources, it is assumed that formal companies, which give consideration to the environment, will find it difficult to earn large margins in a market where the informal sector remains. Despite this, it seems the Chinese companies are making investments in excess of anticipated profits.

This is probably because the larger companies with stamina are focused on market share (securing the amount of collected circular resources) rather than profit rates, aiming to dominate the market. Although, putting the well-financed state-owned companies aside, it is unclear how the large private companies are securing their funding, and this lack of clarity of their revenue structure is also blurring the future of the Chinese venous industry market.

4 Observations

Since the economic reforms, the Chinese society has been changing at a dramatic pace. The country has produced huge amounts of steel and cement as "the world's factory" and has become the second largest economic giant in the world. However, the pace has been so rapid that the environmental measures have been unable to keep up with the production scale, causing serious environmental problems of atmospheric and water pollution.

Although the venous industry in China has changed in stages, the present venous industry market is a mix of small manual industry companies and resource collection companies, medium-sized companies and Japanese affiliated companies engaged in local resource recycling, well-financed state-owned companies that hope to run operations nationwide, and large private companies that are increasing their market share although their revenue structure is unclear. It is an era of vicious competition as each player aims to survive. If this were pure economic competition, things would be left to the market, and the market would not be distorted by unnecessary laws and regulations. However, it is necessary to reinforce the laws and regulations – more specifically, environmental regulations – to lay out the conditions so that the competition is not in favor of informal companies without environmental measures. Looking at the whole legal system supporting the circular economy in China from this point of view, regulations regarding infectious medical waste, toxic chemical substances, and other hazardous waste are in place, but areas requiring stronger regulations including enforcement also remain, such as the logistical processes of resource collection and standards for recycling facilities.

Moreover, although the effective use of recycled resources should be encouraged to increase resource efficiency, because much of the circular resources in China are currently transacted as valuables, little progress has been made in the organization of recycling laws for individual items except for waste electrical and electronic products. However, although items may seem to have value at first glance, there are cases where only the metal parts are recycled and much of the remainder ends up as residue. Since it is also believed that there will be an increase in circular resources that are collected for a fee in China in future, it is desirable to organize individual recycling laws.

At present, the legal regulations are trying to catch up with the actual changes in reality, and ministries have been announcing plans (such as the "Circular economy development strategy and short-term action plan" of January 23, 2013), guidelines, and model projects in rapid succession.[19] This is a pragmatic way to address the matter, but relying on ministerial regulations, notices, and other administrative guidance, which are of lower level than laws or State Council orders, does raise concerns that it will lead to overlapping ministerial policies, etc., and inefficiency. For example, as mentioned, even the designation of cities and areas in relation to the circular economy are congested, with "eco-provinces/cities/counties/industrial parks", "circular economy trial areas", and "urban mining demonstration parks".

To develop a healthy venous industry, it is also important for new companies entering the market to be able to engage in fair competition. Allowing large companies with revenue streams besides income from venous businesses, or state-owned companies that find it easy to acquire government approvals and licenses to enter the market and engage in activities focused on gaining market share rather than profits, creating a monopolistic or oligopolistic market, would be setting back the clock that moved forward from the planned economy to open market, with the possibility of unexpected repercussions in circular resource logistics. It is also necessary to implement appropriate competition policies or disclose company management information, transcending the realm of environmental law regulations.

The above issues are mainly related to hard law, but there are also soft law issues: the need to enhance the government's law-enforcement capabilities for environmental regulations (governance), and to raise environmental awareness of companies and citizens. With regard to governance, specifically, it is necessary to organize/consolidate responsibilities and reinforce the organization of the national government ministries, and to make sure the local governments are able to enforce the state-ruled laws and regulations (eliminating actions that look as though they are obeying the rules but not at heart), and thus, there are issues that on reflection can also be considered as hard law issues.

At first glance, the legal system for environmental law in China is making progress, and thus, some people have praised the environmental policies in China. However, the legal system cannot be separated from the actual state of the society or economy, and true evaluation cannot be made without examining the actual situation of the market and law enforcement. For the venous industry to develop further in China, and for the healthy and smooth use of recycled resources, there must be increased initiatives towards organizing the regulatory infrastructure.

Based on the above issues, it would be necessary to improve the following points in the circular economy policies in China. It will be interesting to see how the circular economy policies and venous industry in China will develop in future.

i) The waste management policies and legal system, including the introduction of extended producer responsibility and recycling regulations for individual items, must be reinforced and be complete; measures to prevent environmental pollution and control environmental risks in all processes must be strengthened;

ii) The coordination between the central and local government ministries, as well as the organization including manpower and budget of the environmental division must be reinforced;

iii) The main ministries responsible must organize the law enforcement and management system, use the best management means, and increase the efficiency of supervision and management;

iv) The economic policies, including grants and tax benefits, must be organized; research and development of related technologies must be encouraged to support the sustainable development of the venous industry; and

v) Efforts must be made to raise the awareness of companies and residents regarding environmental issues, clarify the mechanism of participation, and encourage the participation and supervision by the whole society.

Notes

1 When the nominal GDP is converted at a rate of JPY1=USD$0.013 (as of October 2011).
2 CRRA, "Industry development of recycled resources of China (2013–2014)," *China Fortune Press* (2014), pp. 61 and 77, in Chinese.
3 Government of China website, "Outline of the 12th Five-Year Plan for the national economic and social development of the people's republic of China (full text)," 16 March 2011, in Chinese. http://www.gov.cn/2011lh/content_1825838_2.htm
4 The Thousand-Hundred-Ten project is an initiative led by the NDRC to develop a circular economy by promoting 10 major circular economy projects, and developing 100 circular economy cities and 1,000 circular economy companies.
5 Ministry of Housing and Urban-Rural Development HP, "State council regulations on the city appearance and environmental sanitation management," *State Council Order* (1992) No. 101, 28 June 1992, in Chinese. http://www.mohurd.gov.cn/zcfg/xzfg/200611/t20061101_158934.html
6 Government of China website, "Ordinance on the management of city household waste," *Ministry of Construction Order* (2007) No. 157, 28 April 2007, in Chinese. http://www.gov.cn/ziliao/flfg/2007-06/05/content_636413.htm
7 Government of China website, "Regulations on the management of recycling and disposal of waste electrical and electronic equipment," *State Council Order* (2009) No. 551, 25 February 2009, in Chinese. http://www.gov.cn/flfg/2009–03/04/content_1250844.htm
8 Government of China website, "Ordinance on the management of the recycling of scrap cars," *State Council Order* (2001) No. 307, 16 June 2001, in Chinese. http://www.gov.cn/gongbao/content/2001/content_60919.htm
9 Government of China website, "Ordinance on the management of the recycling of renewable resources," *Joint Order of Ministry of Commerce and Five Other Ministries* (2007) No. 8, 27 March 2007, in Chinese. http://www.gov.cn/ziliao/flfg/2007–06/05/content_636413.htm
10 Government of China website, "State Council Guidance on promoting the development of a circular economy," *State Council Order* (2005) No. 22, 2 July 2005, in Chinese. http://www.gov.cn/gongbao/content/2005/content_64318.htm
11 Government of China website, "Regulations on the management of the collection and use of renewable resources," (2002) No. 9, January 10, 2002, in Chinese. http://www.gov.cn/gongbao/content/2002/content_61730.htm
12 Government of China website, "Ordinance on the management of recycling and disposal of used electrical and electronic equipment," *State Council Order* (2009) No. 551, 25, February 2009, in Chinese. http://www.gov.cn/gongbao/content/2009/content_1257453.htm
13 Government of China website, "Notice on the home appliance old for new rebate program," *Ministry of Finance, Ministry of Construction* (2009) No. 298, 28

June 2009, in Chinese. http://www.gov.cn/zwgk/2009-07/02/content_1355598.htm

14 Government of China website, "Notice on the home appliance old for new rebate program (revised version)," *Ministry of Commerce, Ministry of Foreign Trade and Economic Co-operation* (2010) No. 231, 21 June 2010, in Chinese. http://www.gov.cn/zwgk/2010–06/23/content_1634925.htm

15 For the 3R also at the time of formulating the law, the SETC was mainly responsible for the Law on the Promotion of Cleaner Production and the NDRC was mainly responsible for the Circular Economy Promotion Law. When SETA was dismantled and absorbed into the NDRC, etc., in 2003, both laws fell under the NDRC.

16 The China Recycling Development Co., Ltd. is not a central state-owned company (113 central companies owned by the State Council State-owned Assets Supervision and Administration Commission), but is approved by the State Council, and is one of the top Chinese domestic recycling companies, under the China CO-OP, established in Beijing in May 1989. It has bases nationwide, including Neijian of Sichuan province, Qingyuan of Guangdong province, Luoyang of Henan province, Changzhou of Jiangsu province, Linyi of Shandong province, Yinchuan Lingwu of the Ningxia Hui Autonomous Region, Tangshan of Hebei province, Xi'an of Shaanxi province, Heilongjiang province, and Jiangxi province.

17 160 million tons for the eight categories of waste steel, waste non-ferrous metals, waste plastic, waste paper, waste tires, waste electrical and electronic products, waste ships, and scrap cars, according to the CRRA. The figure is 164 million tons for nine categories (adding waste glass to the aforementioned eight), according to the China Resource Recycling Association.

18 Kenji Someno (2014) "Economic changes in China's Interior produced by the arterial and venous sectors," *Tokyo Foundation, Views on China.* http://www.tkfd.or.jp/research/project/news.php?id=1240

19 Government of China website, "Circular economy development strategy and short-term action plan," (2013) No. 5, January 23, 2013, in Chinese. http://www.gov.cn/gongbao/content/2013/content_2339517.htm

Reference

China National Resources Recycling Association (CRRA) (2014) *Industry Development of Recycled Resources of China (2013–2014)*, China Fortune Press, Beijing, in Chinese.

5 Municipal solid waste management and recycling businesses in Thailand

Current situation and future possibilities

Janya Sang-Arun, Piya Wanpen, Simon Gilby and Matthew Hengesbaugh

Introduction

Thailand is an upper middle income country with population of 67 million (World Bank, 2015) with a population density as of 2014 of 132 person/ km², lower than China (145) and Japan (349) (World Bank, 2015). In 1999, Thailand passed the Decentralization Act giving self-governing powers to the provincial and local levels. As a result, currently Thailand has 7,853 local authorities, including special administrative areas (Bangkok and Pattaya), provincial administrative organizations (PAO), municipalities, and sub-district (Tambon) administrative organizations (TAO). These local authorities are autonomous in policy formulation, administration, finance, and personnel management (Cabinet Secretariat, 1999). Local authorities are also directly responsible for municipal solid waste (MSW) management for waste generated in their jurisdictions.

In general, each local authority is responsible for a small area especially those in the high population density zones. Therefore, it is difficult for local authorities to secure sufficient space for waste treatment and disposal sites and there is a need to request cooperation from other local authorities to access land. Moreover, the establishment of waste treatment facilities is leading to resistance from locals due to the unpleasant smell and fear of long term health and environmental impacts. Hence, promotion of the 3Rs (reduce, reuse, recycle) is an alternative solution for governments that can both minimize waste disposal to the collection system and create a good environmental reputation for the cities.

This paper provides an overview of the national policy on MSW management and recycling, which is aligned to the country sufficiency economic policy and the 3Rs. It summarizes the current actual waste management and recycling situations, which are still very much behind national targets. In addition, this chapter provides examples of local initiatives to promote recycling as well as estimating the potential economic value of recycling businesses before finally discussing the future of recycling businesses in Thailand.

National policy and law on MSW management and recycling

Overall, Thailand promotes the 3Rs (reduce, reuse, recycle) and waste-to-energy to enhance resource efficiency and a green economy under its national strategy of sufficiency economy. Sufficiency economy is "philosophy that stresses the middle path as an overriding principle for appropriate conduct by the populace at all levels. This applies to conduct starting from the level of the families, communities, as well as the level of national in development and administration so as to modernize in line with the forces of globalisation" (NESDB, 1999). This concept was advanced by His Majesty King Bhumibol Adulyadej to promote a balanced approach to development in line with principles of moderation and restraint, aimed at guiding a harmonious relationship among individuals, households, communities, projects, businesses, institutions, polities, societies, nation states, regions, humanity and the biosphere (NESDB, 1999). This philosophy is a cornerstone of Thailand's development strategy at all levels, including, but not limited to, the "Policy and Prospective Plan for Enhancement and Conservation of National Environmental Quality B.E.2540–2559 (1997–2016) (ECNEQ)" (ONEP, no date a).

To guide the adoption of the concept of sustainable development, the Ministry of Natural Resources and Environment (MONRE), the responsible authority, as defined by the ECNEQ policy, formulated the national "Environmental Quality Management Plan (EQM)", covering a 5-year period. The current EQM plan (2012–2016) is also working towards the effective implementation of the Green Economy concept, which includes reducing the environmental load through improved resource recovery practices (ONEP, no date b). Intended to be used as a guideline for all agencies to follow in connection with the current 11th National Economic and Social Development Plan (NESD), the EQM plan has been designed to prevent pollution, to address the country's pollution problems more effectively, and to keep pace with global trends. It also aims to encourage all sectors of society to take part in pollution management with a view towards enhancing and maintaining the country's environmental quality at an acceptable standard.

For waste management, the EQM plan is being introduced with a target of increasing the reuse and recycling rate to at least 30 percent by 2016 and proposes recommendations to introduce the Polluter Pays Principle (PPP), including the utilization of economic instruments such as a deposit refund system and incentive measures to reduce pollution and promote pollution-free production processes. Furthermore, the plan emphasizes the importance of developing environmental friendly services, implementing cleaner production, and changing consumer behavior (ONEP, no date b).

However, it is likely that the government cannot achieve the target set by the EQM. Therefore, in August 2014, the Government of Thailand announced the national roadmap for waste management with the aim of handling 80 percent of the accumulated untreated waste, building at least 15 waste-to-energy plants, introducing the separation of general and hazardous waste, and creating specific laws for waste management. The government has ordered all provinces, especially the prioritized provinces, to improve waste management with cessation of open dumping, regulation of waste separation at source, and construction of provincial waste management centers (PCD, 2014a).

Currently, there is no specific law for MSW management and recycling. However, waste management has been included in the Public Health Act, 1992 (revised 2007), which stated that local authorities are responsible for waste collection, treatment, and disposal of municipal solid waste, but are permitted to outsource this duty to a third party. For industrial hazardous waste, the waste generator is responsible for the collection, treatment, and disposal of its waste but is also permitted to outsource to third parties. It must also report activities to the local authorities. This law also included residential waste fee collection, mandated not to be higher than a set ceiling, but did not include the duty of residents to pay. This being the case, most local authorities cannot collect sufficient fees for proper waste management and must allocate budget from other sources. Additionally, the law does not include any obligation on the part of residents to cooperate with local authorities. Therefore, most local authorities are confronted with a lack of cooperation from residents who believe that waste management is the duty of the local authorities.

In order to increase efficiency of waste management, local authorities are allowed to announce local ordinances to regulate waste management. But as the mayor of each authority is elected by vote of residents, mayors are frequently reluctant to announce local ordinance that may have a negative impact on their re-election chances.

Current status of waste management in Thailand

Before 2010, waste generation in Thailand continuously increased in line with GDP, but it has fluctuated in the past few years due to various factors, including an economic downturn, natural disasters (e.g., typhoon and flooding), and political instability. In 2008, waste generation was approximately 24 million tonnes (metric tons) per year (PCD, 2014b), increasing to 26 million tonnes per year by 2014 (8 percent increase; PCD, 2015) (Figure 5.1). Based on this data, waste generation rate in Thailand is higher than Japan (0.98 kg/capita/day; MOEJ, 2014), but lower than China (1.2 kg/capita/day; WMW, 2012). Nevertheless, it is worth noting that such data fluctuations could also be influenced by poor data records and reporting by local authorities, especially where waste management service are not currently established.

Only 4,422 local authorities (out of 7,853; 56 percent) have waste collection services, covering 57 percent of the total waste generation (PCD, 2015). Most local authorities provide waste collection services, but some outsource this task to private companies. Unfortunately, only 53 percent of the collected waste is treated properly with the remainder being disposed in open dumps (PCD, 2015). Many local authorities promote composting and separated waste for sale, but

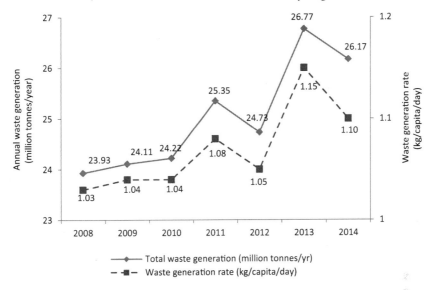

Figure 5.1 Annual waste generation in Thailand during 2008–2014 (extracted from PCD, 2014b and PCD, 2015)

such efforts are still at a small, community level scale. A few large-scale anaerobic digestion and composting facilities exist, but other local authorities are frequently uninterested in replicating because of reports of high investment and operation cost, insufficient food waste input, and the frequent need to shut down facilities for maintenance.

In order to decrease fossil-fuel dependence for energy, the government is promoting waste-to-energy, but as only 1.5 percent of waste generated is delivered to incineration plants for electricity generation (PCD, 2015), the government has tried to allocate more funds for waste-to-energy projects. However, there is uncertainty regarding whether this strategy will succeed because local residents are frequently concerned regarding health and environmental impacts, which may lead governments and investors facing strong social resistance during the siting, construction, and/or operation, an issue which is already happening in many places.

Current status of recycling in Thailand

Thai MSW comprises approximately 30 percent recyclables: 17 percent plastic, 8 percent paper, 3 percent glass, and 2 percent metals (including aluminum) (PCD, 2011). However, 18 percent of municipal solid waste generated or 60 percent of recyclable waste is recycled (mainly by the private sector) (PCD, 2015). There is some room for the government to increase this rate but it may need active cooperation from residents to create an economical, viable opportunity for businesses.

Given the promotion by the government, the recycling rate should be continuously increasing, but Figure 5.2 illustrates that the recycling rate during the last 3 years has slightly decreased (PCD, 2014b and PCD, 2015). The amount of waste recycling has decreased by 380,000 tonnes per year between 2012 and 2014 while the prices of recyclables have fluctuated (Figure 5.3). Some increased and some decreased, depending on the global and domestic market demand. In term of time and transportation efficiency, recyclable waste collectors and buyers will pay less attention to recyclables that have lower prices because they will

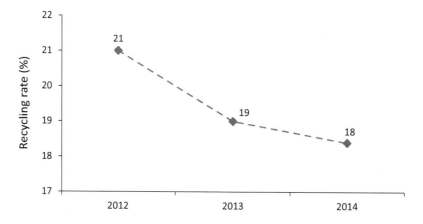

Figure 5.2 Recycling rate of Thailand during 2012–2014 (extracted from PCD, 2014b and PCD, 2015)

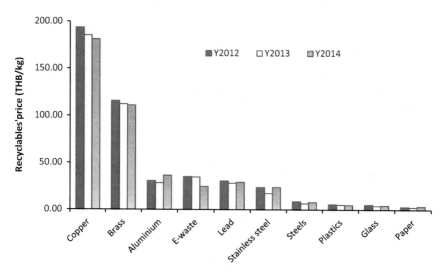

Figure 5.3 Changes of recyclables' price during 2012–2014 (extracted from Wong-panit, 2014)

provide less monetary benefits – especially plastic, the major recyclable in the waste stream, which is very bulky and costly for transport and pre-processing. Hence, it is hypothesized that the economic value of recyclables is a key factor for the growth of recycling in Thailand and that it will be difficult to increase the recycling rate without government intervention to enable business investment in recycling, such as mandatory waste separation at source.

Principally, the recycling business is carried out by the private sector (including waste pickers), without a subsidy from the government, based on the assumption that recycling is economically viable by itself. Therefore, recycling in Thailand is a free market where sellers can sell recyclables to any buyers who offer better prices and services. It is observed that recycling business practice in Thailand is very much similar to conventional recycling business operations of China, and most enterprises in this business are ethnic Chinese-Thai. Therefore, specific terms used in the recycling business still remain the same as those in use in China.

As recycling is run by the private sector for profit, most investors pay little attention to investing in environmental countermeasures. The PCD is aware of this problem and has initiated the "green junk shop" project in 2009. Waste buyer shops that pass standard criteria will receive a certificate to display at their shop to demonstrate their attitude on social and environmental responsibility.

Local initiatives to promote recycling

To address challenges associated with waste collection and disposal, many local authorities in Thailand have introduced 3R (reduce, reuse, recycle) principles, focusing on waste separation and the sale of recyclable materials. This initiative has been shown to generate income as well as reduce the financial burden shouldered by local governments. Examples of local initiatives include waste banks, waste-to-points, waste-to-eggs, and waste donation programs.

- *Waste bank*

  The waste bank initiative involves the collection and sale of recyclable waste. Waste banks accumulate recyclables from student households, as students are instructed to bring these materials to school on designated days (usually once a week). Profits made from the sale of recyclables are deposited in individual savings accounts from which students are allowed to withdraw on specified days. Benefits include increasing the access of waste buyers to a large volume of recyclables, generating income for students' families, and providing life skills training for students both in terms of working and saving.

  The waste bank concept has been operational since 1998 in Phitsanulok Municipality, Thailand, and has been supported by collaboration between the Municipality and Wongpanit (a recyclable waste buyer company). Currently, this initiative is being replicated nationwide in the form of 'school waste banks' and 'community waste banks' (Figure 5.4).

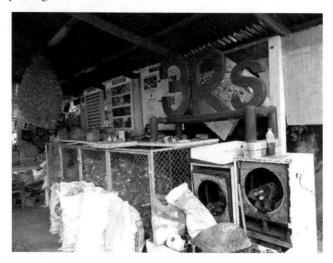

Figure 5.4 Example of a community waste bank

- *'Waste to points' and 'waste to eggs' programs*

  This initiative is similar to the waste bank program, however, rather than monetary transactions, it follows a points-based incentive system. Partic- ipants accumulate points on the basis of the trade of recyclables, which in turn can be used to obtain household equipment, such as electric fans, rice cookers, etc. These types of programs are generally operated by municipalities and/or communities. A similar program is the "waste- for-eggs" initiative, whereby participants trade waste for eggs.

- *Waste donation*

  Waste donation events involve waste buyers collaborating with Buddhist temples to collect recyclables from local residents, from which proceeds are donated for temple activities. This type of event is attractive for all income groups because it also serves as a form of religious merit making.

- *Waste separation at source for sale*

  Unlike Japan, waste separation at source is not generally practiced in Thai- land. Currently, many cities work in cooperation with waste buyers to promote community-based waste management, including separated waste for sale. This presents a win-win business model where local gov- ernments can reduce costs associated with waste management, waste buyers can access a wider source of recyclables, and residents can earn from selling their waste, which in turn can be allocated for the payment of municipal waste fees. This model is currently being replicated nation- wide through a Low Carbon Cities project promoted by the Thailand Municipal League.

- *Zero Baht Shop*

    This initiative is supported by the Thailand Institute of Packaging and Recycling Management for Sustainable Environment (TIPMSE). Zero Baht Shop operates as a community cooperative, wherein customers can barter for certain goods with recyclables. Revenue generated from the sale of recyclables to waste buyers is collectively shared among members every 6 months. This initiative has been successfully implemented in low-income neighborhoods such as slum areas and progressively replicated in many communities across Thailand.

Economic value of recycling business in Thailand

The recycling business is highly labor intensive. For instance, one company in Ayudhaya has expanded its business operations and currently employs more than 20 people in the area to work in its waste sorting facility (Figure 5.5). It has been estimated that in Thailand the recycling process chain may generate as many as 675 skilled local employment opportunities at various levels, ranging from waste collectors to managing directors or equivalent, generating USD$94 of income per tonne of recyclables (Menikpura et al., 2012). Based on this assumption, the economic value of recycling business in Thailand would be as high as USD$443 million in 2014.

Recycling businesses can therefore also reduce the financial burden of local authorities on waste collection, transport, treatment and disposal. Expenditure on waste management of each area is different depending on various factors, including types of vehicles and fuel use, distance, technologies, etc. For example, Phitsanulok municipality spent about USD$35 on processing costs per tonne of waste in 2013 (Phitsanulok Municipality, 2014). If this rate is applied as an average cost of local governments for waste management in Thailand, the recycling

Figure 5.5 Green job creation for local residents in recyclable sorting facilities

of 4.7 million tonnes in 2014 can save the government budget USD$165 million per year. The contribution of the recycling business can be considered much higher if the cost for land and infrastructure development is included.

The future of recycling businesses in Thailand

Considering the current recycling rate of 60 percent of recyclables, this rate is relatively high and would be difficult to increase without government intervention. The majority of remaining recyclables in final disposal sites are plastics, which require considerable efforts to separate, clean, shred, and pre-process prior to recycling. Plastic recycling could boom again if oil prices increase with positive knock on effects for recycling rates.

Even though the amount of recyclables in the markets is decreasing, more investors are interested in this business, making it very competitive. Wongpanit Group, a big recyclable waste dealer in Thailand, has also witnessed phenomenal growth in recent years, increasing its franchise base to nearly 1,000 shops and aiming to increase its franchise coverage to all sub-districts of Thailand. Additionally, Wongpanit has provided formal training courses and facilitates establishment of new waste buyer shops across Thailand (Wongpanit, 2012).

Waste buyers will need to apply various strategies to secure large volumes of recyclable waste, and some have already started doing so, such as offering higher prices, providing door-to-door collection services, cooperating with cities to promote waste separated at source for sale, etc.

In addition, some waste buyers try to increase profitability by investing in pre-processing to reduce transportation costs, especially for plastics and glasses (e.g., cleaning, shredding, and compacting), and to obtain higher prices compared with non-processed recyclables. Some have even upgraded to become small-scale recyclers. Increased mechanization will minimize the use of workers. This not only lowers costs but also lowers the amount of competition because experienced workers frequently leave in order to establish their own small-scale businesses as barriers to entry are low.

As the recycling rate is relatively high, efforts to improve the recycling business in Thailand should not only concentrate on increasing the recycling rate but also improve the reputation of the business through promoting the public relationship between waste buyers and residents and improving the environmental practices and social responsibility of investors, especially in competitive areas. The government may accelerate this movement by providing tax incentives to enterprises that employ environmental countermeasures that meet certain standards.

Several non-profit organizations (NPO) have been established to promote recycling, such as the TIPMSE and 3R Foundation, and it is expected that more NPOs will become engaged in the recycling business. TIPMSE, founded in 2005, is primarily funded by members of the Federation of Thai Industries and private enterprises who are manufacturers and producers of packaging and consumer products. One stated goal of TIPMSE is to jointly promote industrial activities that assist in increasing the country's annual recycling rate to 25 percent by 2016, with an emphasis on the packaging recycling industry. TIPMSE also operates as a database center, concentrating on used packaging and recycling materials management. TIPMSE has been working with more than 24 municipalities to promote recycling, including the Bangkok Metropolitan Administration (TIPMSE, 2015).

3R Foundation is working closely with TIPMSE to promote 3R practices in municipalities and industrial estates. For example, Amata Corporation Public Company Limited, a large industrial estate in Thailand, signed a Memorandum of Understanding to implement the 3Rs among its subsidiary companies. It is expected that, in time, more municipalities and enterprises will implement the 3Rs in support of sustainable resource management goals. In addition, many manufacturers, offices, and organizations understand the economic benefits associated with separating recyclable waste, both in terms of reducing waste management costs and promoting an environmentally responsible image among the wider public. Accordingly, many companies have started to sort recyclables for sale with contracted waste buyers, which in turn has supported the creation of local green job opportunities.

In terms of Thailand's recycling industry, the aggregate number of recycling facilities has increased. As of 2012, more than 150 facilities with an operating capacity of more than 50 tonnes per day were registered to the Department of Industrial Work (Chulalongkorn University, 2012). New investors are also seeking opportunities to capitalize on the recycling business. These include well-recognized international companies such as Panasonic-Thailand and Toshiba-Thailand. For instance, Panasonic is currently researching the feasibility of establishing a recycling facility in Thailand. Toshiba applies the 3Rs and promotes green innovation through its business practices (TDP, 2015).

Conclusions

Thailand has promoted the 3Rs (reduce, reuse, recycle) with a view towards supporting sustainable development under its national sufficiency economy approach. However, at present there is no regulation that mandates 3Rs practices. In addition, there is no government-provided subsidy for recycling activities. As a result, recycling businesses in Thailand are scaling-up based on private investors who are attracted to the sector's earnings potential. Many waste buyer shops and recycling facilities have been established with monetary benefits, even though prices are fluctuating.

Although the government has introduced relevant policies and there is an increase in interest by the private sector, recycling rates have dropped recently. The government may need to bring in further measures to combat these issues. These could include mandatory waste separation at source and incentives for minimizing environmental impacts from recycling, such as tax reduction for enterprises whose activities meet environmental standards.

References

Cabinet Secretariat (1999) Decentralization Act 1999. PTT. 15P.

Chulalongkorn University (2012) Project on lists of waste to resources. Retrieved from http://recycle.dpim.go.th/wastelist/download_files/D/factory_105_106. pdf (accessed on 10 February 2015).

Menikpura, S.N.M., S.H. Gheewala, S. Bonnet, and C. Chiemchaisri (2012) "Evaluation of the effect of recycling on sustainability of municipal solid waste management in Thailand," *Waste Biomass Valorization*, No. 4, pp. 237–257.

Ministry of Environment, Japan (2014) Status quo of waste management km in Japan in 2012, 25P (in Japanese). Retrieved from https://www.env.go.jp/recycle/waste/ (accessed on 30 January 2016).

National Economic and Social Development Board (NESDB) (1999) An Introductory Note on Sufficiency Economy. Referred by Yuwasatirakun Foundation. Retrieved from http://www.sufficiencyeconomy.org/old/en/files/4.pdf (access on 13 February 2015).

Office of Natural Resources and Environmental Policy and Planning, Thailand (ONEP) (no date a) Policy and Prospective Plan for Enhancement and Conservation of National Environmental Quality B.E.2540–2559.

ONEP (no date b) Executive Summary of Environmental Quality Management Plan 2012–2016. Retrieved from http://www.onep.go.th/download/EXE_EQM_Plan 2012_2016.pdf (accessed on 7 July 2015).

PCD (Pollution Control Department) (2011) Reduction, separation and utilisation of waste. PPT. Retrieved from http://infofile.pcd.go.th/waste/23Jul2011_waste_1.pdf? CFID=9491985&CFTOKEN=58744544 (accessed on 18 November 2014), in Thai.

PCD (Pollution Control Department) (2014a) Approved roadmap of solid and hazardous waste on 26th August 2014. Retrieved from http://infofile.pcd.go.th/ mgt/Roadmap_Aug262014.pdf?CFID=20298892&CFTOKEN=82925674 (accessed on 3 July 2015), in Thai.

PCD (Pollution Control Department) (2014b) *Status Quo of Waste Management in Thailand 2013*, in Thai.

PCD (Pollution Control Department) (2015) Survey data of municipal solid waste in 77 provinces in 2014 (1st draft), in Thai.

Phitsanulok Municipality (2014) *2013 Phitsanulok Municipality Expenditure*, unpublished data.

Thai Department Stores Pool (TDP) (2015) Recycle: Business for the future. TDP's New, 10 February 2015. Retrieved from http://www.tdpthailand.com/admin/ show_news.php?show=26 (accessed on 10 February 2015).

Thailand Institute of Packaging and Recycling Management for Sustainable Environment (TIPMSE) (2015) About TIPMSE. Retrieved from http://www.tipmse. or.th/2012/en/about/vision.asp (accessed on 10 February 2015).

Waste Management World (WMW) (2012) China set to produce twice as much waste as US by 2030. Retrieved from http://www.waste-management-world.com/articles/ 2012/06/china-set-to-produce-twice-as-much-waste-as-us-by-2030.html (accessed on 10 February 2015).

Wongpanit (2012) Wongpanit business strategies (personal communication with CEO).

Wongpanit (2014) Price of recyclables. Retrieved from www.wongpanit.com (accessed on 10 February 2015), in Thai.

World Bank (2015) Databank: Population density (people per sq. km of land area) during 2010–2014. Retrieved from http://data.worldbank.org/indicator/EN. POP.DNST (accessed on 3 July 2015).

6 An introduction to Taiwan's waste management and recycling policy

Shou-Chien Lee

1 Laws

Taiwan formulated the Waste Disposal Act (WDA) in 1974 for the effective clearance and disposal of waste, improvement of environmental sanitation, and maintenance of public health. The Act is the first special law for waste management in Taiwan. The WDA defines classification of waste and the responsibility of clearance and disposal of wastes, specifies the authority and responsibility of competent authorities, and regulates the collection, storage, clearance, and disposal of wastes. Taiwan also formulated the Resource Recycling Act (RRA) in 2002 to conserve natural resources, reduce waste, promote recycling and reuse of materials, mitigate environmental loading, and build a society in which resources are used in a sustainable manner. The RRA specifies the hierarchy of waste management, the responsibility of the competent authorities, enterprises and citizens, and the rules of waste reduction and resource reuse and recycling. The WDA and the RRA are the two major laws for waste management and recycling in Taiwan.

2 Categories of wastes and responsibility for clearance, treatment and disposal

Wastes are divided into two categories, general waste and industrial waste, according to their generators. General wastes refer to the garbage generated by households or non-industrial sources. The Environmental Protection Bureaus (EPB) of city or county government and the municipal government (enforcement authorities hereafter) are responsible for the collection and clearance of general wastes. The EPB of city or county government is responsible for the treatment or disposal of general wastes. When necessary, the city or county can commission townships to perform such work. Industrial wastes are those generated by farms; factories; mining sites; construction enterprises; medical institutions; waste clearance, treatment or disposal companies; laboratories; and other enterprises designated by the Taiwan Environmental Protection Administration (TEPA). Industrial wastes are further categorized into hazardous industrial wastes and general industrial wastes, according to the characteristics of the wastes.

3 Management of general wastes

3.1 Clearance, treatment, and disposal of general wastes

People should hand general wastes to the enforcement authority for clearance and disposal in accordance with the time, location, and waste classification set by the authorities. "Garbage Off the Ground Policy" is enforced in most part of Taiwan. The policy requires citizens to separate wastes into garbage, recyclables, and food wastes and hand them to the hauling trucks of the enforcement authorities. Discarding the wastes or storing the wastes in bins on the roads before the arrival of the hauling trucks is not allowed except in a few non-urban areas. For bulky wastes like furniture, appliances, and branches, citizens need to make appointments with the enforcement authority for pick-up.

Garbage collected by the enforcement authorities is shipped to incinerators or landfills for treatment or disposal. The composition of general wastes in 2013 is listed in Table 6.1. There are 24 general waste incineration plants in Taiwan with a total capacity of 24,650 metric tons per day. In 2013, the incinerators as a whole treated 6,349,912 metric tons of wastes, two thirds of which were general wastes and the rest of which were general industrial wastes, generating about 3.1 billion kilowatt hours of electricity. In 2013, 104 sanitary landfills in Taiwan disposed of 91,355 metric tons of wastes. In addition, 130,851 metric tons of bulky wastes were cleared, 64 percent of which were recycled. Another 795,213 metric tons of food wastes were cleared, of which 71 percent were used for pig feeds and 28 percent for composts. Recyclables collected for recycling amounted to 3,273,188 metric tons in 2013.

3.2 General waste clearance and disposal fee

The enforcement authorities levy the general waste clearance and disposal fees in accordance with the costs incurred. As of December 2013, Taipei City, New

Table 6.1 Composition of general waste in 2013 (percent)

Physical composition (wet basis)	Combustible	Paper	41.71
		Textile	2.35
		Wood, leaves, and alike	1.32
		Food waste	35.07
		Plastics	16.57
		Leather, rubber	0.36
		Others (including debris below 5 mm)	0.52
		Subtotal	97.88
	Non-combustible	Ferrous-metal	0.27
		Non-ferrous metal	0.21
		Glass	0.68
		Other non-combustible material (ceramics, sand)	0.96
		Subtotal	2.12

Table 6.2 Rates of volume-based general waste clearance and disposal fee (NT$/liter)

Taipei City	New Taipei City	Shi-Gang District of Taichung City
0.36	0.4	0.3

Taipei City and Shi-Gang District of Taichung City levied the fee based on the volume of the special garbage bag in which citizens must put garbage to hand to the garbage hauling trucks of the enforcement authorities. Table 6.2 lists the fee rates of the special garbage bags. Other areas levied the fee based on water bill or household. The water bill-based fee rate varies from NT$2.9 to NT$4.1 per cubic meter of water by areas. The household-based fee rate for Taichung City, for example, is NT$1,200 per year. Enforcement authorities collect recyclable, food waste, and bulky waste free of charge. The relevant costs are included in the general waste clearance treatment and disposal fees.

3.3 Source reduction

Article 21 of the WDA authorizes the TEPA to ban or restrict the manufacturing, import, sale, or use of articles or their containers or packaging that have the potential to severely pollute the environment. Article 22 of the WDA authorizes the TEPA to designate articles to be collected by means of monetary rewards. In addition, Article 13 of the RRA authorizes the TEPA to ban or restrict the use of articles or their containers or packaging. To prevent excessive packaging, Article 14 of the RRA authorizes the TEPA to restrict the packaging volume ratio, number of packaging layers, and the types or quantity of materials used in packaging. According to the above-mentioned laws, the TEPA promulgated the following regulations for waste reduction.

Year	Regulation	Requirements
2002	Restrict the use of plastic shopping bags and disposable tableware	Governments, schools, department stores, shopping centers, hypermarkets, supermarkets, chain convenience stores, and chain fast food restaurants shall not provide plastic shopping bags thinner than 0.06 mm, or plastic disposable tableware. Nor can they provide free of charge plastic shopping bags thicker than 0.06 mm. Restaurants or drink shops shall not use plastic disposable tableware.
2006	Restriction of excessive packaging	Restrict number of packaging layers and packaging volume ratio of packaging of software disks and the gift boxes of pastries, cosmetics, wine, and processed foods.

(Continued)

Year	Regulation	Requirements
2006	Restriction of manufacturing and import of general dry batteries	General dry batteries shall not contain more than 5 ppm of mercury.
2007	Restriction of the use of plastic trays and packaging boxes	Hypermarket and supermarket shall cut the use of plastic trays or packaging boxes of eggs, bread, cakes, fresh foods, and deli by 15% in 2007, rising year by year to 40% in 2012. Reduction target for plastic trays or packaging boxes of eggs, bread, cakes, fruit, and vegetables is 80% starting 2013. Selling products without packaging, cutting down the weight of plastic packaging, or using alternative packaging can be counted in calculating reduction percentage.
2008	Restriction of the import and sales of mercury-containing thermometers	
2011	Source reduction and monetary rewards for returning disposable cups of take-out drinks	Chain drink stores, convenience stores, and fast food stores shall pay monetary rewards of NT$1 for every two disposable cups returned by consumers, unless the stores offer discounts, coupons, or extra drinks for consumers who use their own cups.

Besides these regulations, the TEPA also promoted voluntary reduction measures, such as (1) governments providing no disposable paper cups; (2) restaurants cutting the use of disposable tableware; (3) industrial packaging reduction.

3.4 Reuse

The TEPA has been implementing bulky waste reuse and recycling program since 2003, which provides grants to enforcement authorities for fixing and refurbishing waste bicycles and furniture for resale. In 2013, the enforcement authorities collected 85,378 metric tons of waste bicycles and furniture, 4,366 metric tons of which were fixed or refurbished for reuse. To promote reuse of secondhand objects, the TEPA established an information exchange platform "i2so5". Starting January 2014, citizens can search secondhand objects for exchange or sale and find information of opening hours of flea markets nationwide through the platform.

3.5 Recycling

In Taiwan, many valuable wastes, such as steel, paper, metals, plastics, etc., are collected by waste pickers and vendors. In 1988, the legislature amended the WDA to create an extended producer's responsibility law, which authorizes the TEPA to designate articles or packaging whose manufacturer, importer, and seller shall bear the responsibility to clear, treat, or dispose of such post-consumer wastes, if such wastes are difficult to clear, treat, or dispose of, contain materials that are difficult to decompose, or contain hazardous materials. From 1998 to 2014, the TEPA designated general containers, containers of agrochemicals, dry batteries, autos, motorbikes, tires, lead-acid batteries, lubricants, electrical and electronic appliances, information technology (IT) products, and light tubes as "regulated recyclable wastes" (RRW) whose responsible enterprises – namely, the manufacturers, importers, and sellers of the products or packaging – are obliged to collect, clear, and dispose of such wastes. The TEPA deregulated lubricants as RRW from 2012. Prior to 1997, the TEPA required the responsible enterprises to meet certain annual recycling rates by collecting and recycling the wastes by themselves or by an organization established jointly by several responsible enterprises. Lacking the mechanism to check the performance of the responsible enterprises, the legislature passed an amendment to the WDA in 1997. The new law mandated that the responsible enterprises pay recycling fees to eight item-specific recycling funds from 1997, which are managed by the eight fund management boards established by the TEPA to collect and recycle RRW. In June 1998, the TEPA set up the Recycling Fund Management Board (RFMB) to take over the businesses of the eight recycling fund management boards. The eight recycling funds then became one of the governmental funds of the TEPA subject to the budget review of the legislature.

Of the recycling fees paid by the responsible enterprises, 80 percent are distributed to trust funds and 20 percent to the special income fund. Trust funds are used to subsidize collectors and recyclers. The special income funds are used for the following purposes: (1) grants for recycling programs of enforcement authorities or non-profit organizations; (2) auditing and certification of collection and recycling volumes of collectors and recyclers; (3) auditing the sales or import volumes of responsible enterprises; (4) education and communication; (5) administration. In 2013, the trust fund expended NT$5,211,225,000 of subsidy, as shown in Figure 6.1. The special income fund expended NT$1,269,834,000, as shown in Figure 6.2 (on November 28, 2014, NT$31 = US$1).

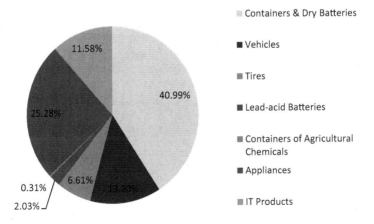

Figure 6.1 Trust fund expenditure of 2013

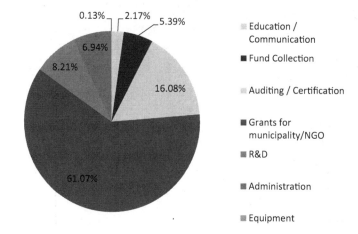

Figure 6.2 Special income fund expenditure of 2013

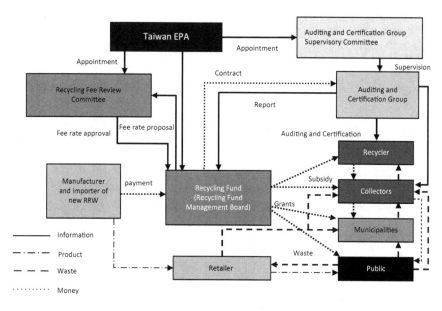

Figure 6.3 Framework of operation of the Resource Recycling Management Fund

The rates of recycling fee and subsidy is proposed by the RFMB, reviewed by the Recycling Fee Review Committee and then decided by the minister of the TEPA. Members of the Recycling Fee Review Commitee are appointed by the minister of the TEPA from members of business groups, consumer protection groups, the government, scholars, and experts.

Recyclers can apply with the TEPA for subsidy based on the volumes of the RRW certified by the audit and certification groups (ACGs) contracted by the TEPA.

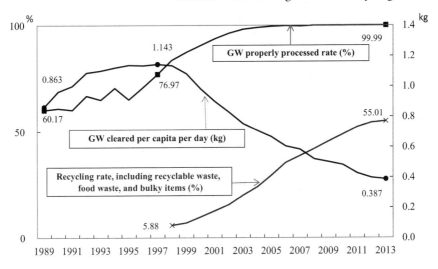

Figure 6.4 Trend of Taiwan's general waste clearance, treatment, and recycling

The ACGs check the volumes recycled by the recyclers and make sure that recyclers comply with the relevant standards set by the TEPA. The TEPA pays subsidies to recyclers based on the certificates issued by ACGs. The TEPA sets up a ACGs Supervisory Committee to monitor without prior notice ACG's on-site operations. The committee also evaluates ACGs' performance once a year. Figure 6.3 demonstrates the framework of the operation of Resource Recycling Management Fund.

3.6 Achievements of reduction and recycling of general wastes

Taiwan's properly processed rate of general waste rose from 60 percent in 1998 to 99.99 percent in 2013. General waste cleared per capita per day grew from 0.863 kg in 1989 to a peak of 1.143 kg in 1997, and then dropped year by year to 0.387 kg in 2013, a significant 66 percent reduction from 1997. The recycling rate of general waste increased from 5.88 percent in 1998 to 55.01 percent in 2013. Figure 6.4 shows the trend of Taiwan's general waste clearance, treatment, and recycling.

4 Management of industrial waste

4.1 Generation of industrial waste

In 2013, the industries reported 18.65 million metric tons of industrial wastes cleared and treated or recycled, 92 percent of which was general industrial waste and 8 percent of which was hazardous. Of all the industrial wastes, 87.1 percent was generated from factories or utilities, 10.1 percent from construction businesses, and less than 1 percent from agricultural or medical sources.

4.2 Clearance and disposal of industrial waste

Enterprises can clear and dispose of their industrial wastes by themselves, commission the work to a permitted company, or recycle the industrial wastes in accordance with the relevant rules. Enterprises above a certain scale announced by the TEPA shall submit an industrial waste clearance and disposal plan to the local EPB for approval before operation. Such enterprises shall also report online the quantities of feedstock used, products produced, and the circumstances of industrial wastes generated, cleared, or disposed of. Companies that clear, treat, dispose of, or recycle industrial waste shall report online the circumstances of their operations. As of October 2014, 3,699 companies were permitted for clearance, 175 companies were permitted for treatment or disposal, and 1,365 companies were permitted for recycling industrial wastes. To track industrial wastes, the TEPA has regulated in succession since 2002 that trucks shipping hazardous wastes, dead poultry or livestock, slaughterhouse scraps, non-hazardous waste liquids, construction wastes, coal ash or slags, shipping trucks of class A waste clearance companies, and tanker trucks of class B or C waste clearance companies should be equipped with global positioning system (GPS) certified by the TEPA. As of October 2014, there were 8,206 certified GPS-equipped waste shipping trucks.

The TEPA established the Industrial Waste Control Center in 2000 to ensure that industrial wastes are properly cleared and disposed of. Using information

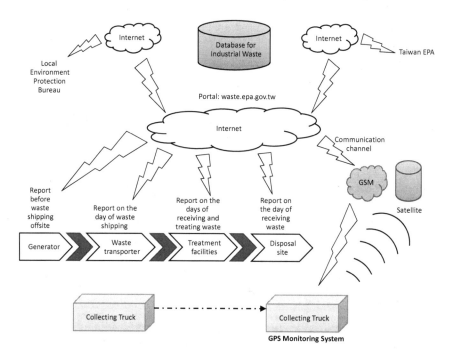

Figure 6.5 Framework of the reporting and tracking system of industrial wastes

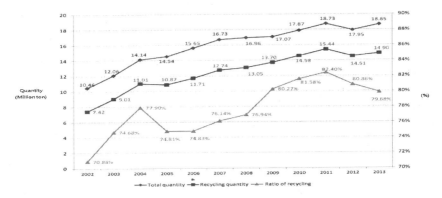

Figure 6.6 Quantities of industrial waste cleared and disposed of, quantities of industrial waste recycled, and the ratio of recycling from 2002 to 2013

systems and GPS, the center analyzed the data of industrial wastes reported online and the shipping routes of the waste to find possible violations. The TEPA then passed the case to the EPB or the TEPA's inspectorate for investigation. Figure 6.5 illustrates the framework of the reporting and tracking system of industrial wastes.

In 2013, the industrial waste recycled amounted to 14.9 million metric tons, of which 36 percent were coal ashes, 18 percent were slags from steelmaking blast furnaces, 11 percent were slags from steelmaking electric arc furnaces, and 10 percent were construction and demolition wastes. Figure 6.6 demonstrates the quantities of industrial waste cleared and disposed of, quantities of industrial waste recycled, and the ratio of recycling from 2002 to 2013.

5 Management of waste import and export

Taiwan regulates the import and export of wastes in accordance with the Basel Convention. The import, export, transit, or transshipment of wastes may commence only after receiving a permit from the EPB. For hazardous wastes, a permit from the EPB based on the approval from the TEPA is necessary. However, the requirement does not apply to 19 items of industrial feedstock announced by the TEPA, such as waste wood, thermoplastics, paper, steel, single metal, etc. Additionally, hazardous industrial wastes, except for degreased waste cables, waste leather scraps or powder, mixed waste metals, garbage, and ashes from incinerators, are banned from import.

From 2009 to 2013, excluding industrial feedstock, Taiwan exported 232,556 metric tons of wastes, nearly 94 percent of which were mixed waste metals, and mainland China was the major importer; imported wastes amounted to 31,686 metric tons, nearly 99.9 percent of which were mixed waste metals.

6 Conclusion

Taiwan's policy of waste management shifted gradually from end-of-pipe treatment to source reduction and recycling. Citing the concepts of sustainable materials management and a sound material-cycle society, the TEPA has integrated the WDA and the RRA and drafted a new law, the Waste Substance Recirculating and Reuse Act. The new draft sets a management framework from source reduction to proper final disposal in every stage of a product's lifecycle, starting from raw material extraction to manufacturing, recycling, and final disposal. To reduce consumption of natural resources and environmental loads, the TEPA is promoting the 6R policy – namely, Reduction, Reuse, Recycling, Energy Recovery, Land Reclamation, and Redesign of products with the cradle-to-cradle concept – in order to realize the national vison of zero waste and sustainable use of natural resources.

References

Records of 14 Years' of Recycling Fund Management Board. Retrieved from http://www.epa.gov.tw/cpDownloadCtl.asp?id=15525

Records of Waste Management. Retrieved from http://www.epa.gov.tw/cpDownloadCtl.asp?id=15508

Resource Recycling Act (2009) Retrieved from http://ivy5.epa.gov.tw/epalaw/search/LordiDispFull.aspx?ltype=17&lname=0010

Waste Disposal Act (2013) Retrieved from http://ivy5.epa.gov.tw/epalaw/search/LordiDispFull.aspx?ltype=07&lname=0010

Website of Taiwan Environmental Protection Administration. Retrieved from http://www.epa.gov.tw

Part III

Topics in recycling and regional waste trade

7 For "optimal resource circulation regimes" in East Asia

From a comparative study of the recycling policies of Japan, China, and Thailand

Takashi Sekiyama

1 Introduction

Venous industry recycles venous resources, such as used products, parts, and raw materials generated from arterial economic activities, back into raw materials for new production. Reusing used products, parts, and raw materials in the venous economy rather than discharging them into the environment would be ideal resource circulation. Otherwise, they can become pollutants instead of valuable resources. However, information asymmetry and price rigidity in the venous resource market make it difficult to achieve the desired resource circulation without government interventions (Hosoda, 2008). It is a costly effort to prevent such materials from becoming pollutants.

Economic agents engaged in recycling activities under a regime[1] that aims to realize the desired resource circulation are called formal actors. On the other hand, their counterparts are informal actors. The latter tends to generate more profits by extracting economically valuable materials from venous resources at a low cost with disregard for environmental destruction and health hazards.

A cross-border flow of venous resources will be established based on demand and supply. A legitimate but high-cost resource circulation flow is avoided, even when a regime to achieve ideal resource circulation has been successfully developed (Puchett and Smith, 2002). In trans-border venous resource trading, a large amount of resources are sold and transported to countries where informal actors are dominant. In Japan, for example, a favorable resource circulation system has been developed. Nevertheless, it has been pointed out that a fair amount of Japan's venous resources continue to be transported to neighboring East Asian countries, including China (Ministry of Economy, Trade and Industry, 2004; Kojima, 2005), and this flow contributes to the global spread of environmental pollution. Furthermore, the provider countries of products, parts, and raw materials often differ from the countries where they are recycled and offered as used items. The Basel Convention is intended to restrict the international transport of hazardous waste, but the burden of stopping all illegal traffic at country borders is simply too heavy.

In order to circulate venous resources properly, therefore, it is not enough that each country builds its own appropriate domestic regime. Moreover, international cooperation is required to help one another in this regard. Given that Japan has expanded its production and sales networks to East Asia, including China and ASEAN countries, the country must work with the entire region to properly handle venous resources produced in production and sales processes. Otherwise, ideal resource circulation cannot be achieved in this region.

Then, how do we define a regime for realizing the desired resource circulation called an "optimal resource circulation regime" in this study? And how should East Asian countries work together to achieve this regime? This chapter explores a possible form of international cooperation for establishing an optimal resource circulation regime. First, this chapter identifies a new concept of an optimal resource circulation regime and the effective policies to establish the regime with a game theoretic approach. Next, in light of this discussion, this chapter compares the recycling policies of some East Asian countries. The main subject of this comparative study is Japan, which lies at the center of the arterial and venous economies in the region. The study also selected China and Thailand, which have strong economic ties and large material flows with Japan. Finally, a suitable form of international cooperation for realizing the optimal resource circulation will be proposed with reference to the preceding discussions and study results.

2 Discussion

2.1 Social model for forming a recycling regime

Now, let us look at a hypothetical country consisting of two groups. Group 1 values the environment and endeavors to properly handle and recycle venous resources without turning them into pollutants. On the other side, Group 2 is unconcerned about potential pollutants, environmental pollution and health risks, and pursues economic gains by efficiently extracting recyclable materials from venous resources. Each group includes actors in the arterial and venous economies. Here, arterial actors include manufacturers of products, parts, and raw materials; vendors; and consumers. Actors in the venous economy include generators of used products, parts, and raw materials; collectors; and recyclers.

Apparently, Group 1, whose main concern is environmental conservation, wishes to develop a regime that suits their goals and is against the establishment of a regime that seeks only economic gain. In other words, Group 1 will be satisfied and gain positive utilities if Group 2 agrees to form a regime that encourages proper handling and recycling of venous resources. In contrast, Group 1 will be dissatisfied with the development of a profit-oriented regime and gain negative utilities.

On the other hand, profit-driven Group 2 is unconcerned about the lack of rules or regulations regarding recycling. They prefer building a regime that focuses on the efficient extraction of useful resources. Thus, this group is keen to avoid the establishment of a regime that forces its members to properly manage potential pollutants at a high cost. Group 2 will very much gain from agreeing

Table 7.1 Social situation surrounding the establishment of a recycling regime

	Group 1 (Focus on the environment)	Recycling with a focus on the environment	Recycling with a focus on economic benefits
Group 2 (Focus on the profit)			
Recycling with a focus on the environment	+, −		0, 0
Recycling with a focus on economic benefits		0, 0	−, +

with its counterpart to establish a regime that strives for economic benefits. But agreeing to develop an environmental regime dissatisfies Group 2.

The payoff matrix in Table 7.1 summarizes this logic. The columns represent the strategies of Group 1, and the rows are Group 2. The left symbol in each cell indicates the gain from the outcome for Group 1, and the right for Group 2.

In this situation, the left bottom cell is a Nash equilibrium. As this table shows, the best strategy for Group 1 would be the implementation of environment-friendly recycling, regardless of the intention of the other group. For Group 2, the best response would be economically beneficial recycling no matter what stance Group 1 takes. These two groups will not be able to reach an agreement on which regime to develop. This outcome confirms claims made by previous studies that a resource circulation regime cannot be established without the involvement of the public sector.

2.2 Optimal resource circulation regime

Under this circumstance, what way can make the society opt for an environmental recycling system that effectively utilizes used products, parts, and raw materials as resources in the arterial economy?

First of all, one possible answer is to change the payoff matrix to make green recycling the only equilibrium solution with some proper regulations and institutions (hard laws).[2] In the venous economy, the private costs individual actors face are usually lower than the favorable costs, which include social costs for environmental protection due to information asymmetry and the absence of relevant markets. Consequently, profits from recycling with a focus on economic benefits tend to be overestimated. In the same idea, profits of environmentally friendly recycling tend to be underestimated. To establish an environmentally friendly regime that can lead to optimal resource circulation, the incentive structure of society needs to be changed by adopting appropriate institutions to bring social costs into private costs.

Thus, for environmental recycling to become an equilibrium solution, society first needs to adopt hard laws to raise the costs for building and maintaining a profit-oriented regime (the right bottom cell of Table 7.1), thereby decreasing the resulting utilities. In setting or suggesting a price range for handling recyclable materials, necessary costs should be properly included, for instance, making a standard price publicly available. Reducing information asymmetry by adopting a waste manifest system is another effective approach. Similarly, hard laws to reduce the costs for establishing an environmental regime (the left bottom cell of Table 7.1) and to increase utilities may work. Utilities for the environmental regime can be increased by providing financial aid for the implementation of appropriate recycling, or by devising a standards system to ensure the safety of recyclable materials.

Secondly, the effectiveness of governance is also an important factor. The development of effective hard laws does not always guarantee that society will select an environment-oriented regime unless the hard laws are properly enforced. To control and punish illegal recycling practices, good governance is indispensable.

Thirdly, it is also crucial to raise environmental awareness (soft laws) among society members. Even if the conditions outlined earlier are met, the incentive structure may not always change as intended, and the implementation of environmental recycling may not be an equilibrium solution. This is usually because it is difficult to accurately estimate reasonable costs for establishing an environmental regime and its cost-effectiveness. If that is the case, what can be done? As Table 7.1 shows, there may not be a win-win scenario that leads to a unique compromise solution. Still, finding such a solution should be possible as long as each actor is able to receive benefits from a given regime. The key to reach a win-win scenario is appropriate norms and customs (Sekiyama, 2014). Educational and promotional activities to foster appropriate norms and customs and to raise environmental awareness among society members need to be conducted in such a way that favors an environment-oriented regime. The implementation of appropriate policies is essential.

In this chapter, a regime that has the appropriate hard laws, governance, and soft laws for realizing the desired resource circulation is called an "optimal resource circulation regime".[3] Hard laws needed to achieve the goal include (1.1) a system to raise the costs of profit-oriented recycling and (1.2) a system to expand the benefits of environmentally friendly recycling. Furthermore, (2) good governance to control and punish illegal recycling practices should be ensured. Otherwise, hard laws will not function effectively. In a regime with ineffective hard laws, (3) soft laws, such as norms and customs, that value the environment need to be fostered through educational and promotional activities.

Under the optimal resource circulation regime, each type of venous resources, including used home appliances, cars, and plastic items may form a sub-regime. The optimal resource circulation regime is a collection of such smaller regimes. Each national government should consider the characteristics of its own society and historical background in developing the optimal resource circulation regime.

2.3 Need for international cooperation

Even if one country successfully establishes such a regime, however, a considerable amount of its venous resources will flow out to other countries where dominant informal actors dodge the legitimate but costly resource circulation flow. Therefore, a true optimal resource circulation regime must be established beyond national borders through international cooperation. In principle, waste materials should be disposed of where they are generated. It surely makes sense to do so, given the high costs of long-distance transportation and the hazards of handling waste. In reality, however, production and sales networks extend globally, and thus we need to be aware that the place of origin of a given product, where its parts and raw materials have been consumed, is often different from where the product is used and becomes waste.

This expansion of the arterial economy calls for a broad, global perspective on the venous economy flow – namely, collecting, transporting, treating, and recycling parts and materials extracted from venous resources – in order to properly utilize these materials to produce new products. Japan, in particular, must work with other East Asian countries in treating and recycling venous resources generated from its economic activities because its production and sales networks have expanded across the entire region, including China and Southeast Asia.

As stated above, the optimal resource circulation regime consists of the appropriate hard laws, governance, and soft laws for realizing the desired resource circulation. A comparison of these aspects should make it easier for East Asian countries to identify and overcome their own weaknesses by learning from other countries and sharing their strengths with others. Each country should be able to improve its weaknesses and reinforce its strengths through working with its neighboring countries.

3 Results of the comparative study

Based on previous discussions and their implications, this section examines recycling policies in East Asian countries and their impact on the establishment of the optimal resource circulation regime. This study compared Japan, as the center of the East Asian arterial and venous economies, and its major economic partners China and Thailand. Recycling policies and their effectiveness in the three countries were compared in terms of hard laws, governance, and soft laws to assess their progress towards the establishment of the optimal resource circulation regime. Table 7.2 briefly summarizes the results of the comparison.

Table 7.2 Implementation status of recycling policies in Japan, China, and Thailand

Policies		Japan	China	Thailand
Hard laws	(1) Raising the costs of economy-oriented recycling	Good	Poor	Poor
	(2) Increasing the benefits of environmental recycling	Poor	Good	Poor
Governance	Monitoring and penalties	Good	Poor	Poor
Soft laws	Education and promotion	Fair	Poor	Fair

3.1 Japan[4]

Since the 1960s, Japanese society has faced the diversification and rapid increase of waste materials due to the concentration of population in urban areas and the development of industrial activities. In this context, the Waste Management and Public Cleaning Act came into effect in 1970 to preserve healthy living conditions and improve public hygiene by controlling the generation of waste and by treating such materials properly. The law defined the responsibilities of citizens, business entities, and the national and local governments and specified the handling of waste. During the 1970s and 1980s, the amount and types of waste materials continued to increase with the further development of economic activities and changes in lifestyles. These increases resulted in a shortage in waste treatment facilities and posed a risk to the environment. Moreover, inappropriate treatment of waste, such as illegal dumping, became a serious social problem.

With the aim to solve these issues, Japan began adopting policies in the 1990s to promote the collection and recycling of recyclable waste and reduce the negative impact on the environment. For example, in 1991 the Waste Management and Public Cleaning Act was amended to reduce waste, promote recycling, and ensure proper treatment of waste materials. This law has been revised many times over the years in response to the diversification of waste and related issues. In the same year, the Law for the Promotion of Effective Utilization of Resources was enforced for the purpose of encouraging the effective use of resources, reducing the generation of waste, and protecting the environment. The law urged business entities to recycle their products after use and required them to develop products in view of recycling and to use recycled resources for manufacturing. Moreover, sorted waste collection by material type, such as steel and aluminum, became an important component of the promotion of recycling. Thus, the law stipulated that manufacturers indicate the raw materials used for their products. In the 1990s, the Container and Packaging Recycling Law and the Home Appliance Recycling Law came into force, and the development of a legal framework for recycling progressed significantly. The former was enacted in 1995 to reduce the amount of waste and make more effective use of resources by reusing waste materials obtained from used containers and packaging, such as glass and PET bottles, to produce new products. The latter was implemented in 1998 to achieve the same objective by collecting used appliances such as air conditioners, televisions, refrigerators, and washing machines from households and offices and recycling usable parts and raw materials.

These ad hoc recycling laws, however, failed to reduce the amount of waste, and it became increasingly difficult to secure the required number of waste treatment facilities each year. In addition, issues such as increasing illegal dumping made it more complex and difficult to reduce the burden on the environment.

To solve such waste issues, the Japanese government enhanced its measures for recycling goods and resources and adopted more drastic measures for reducing waste generation and promoting recycling in the early 2000s. It embarked on the promotion of the 3Rs, namely "reduce," "reuse," and "recycle". "Reduce" indicates a reduction in waste generation by saving resources for manufacturing and extending product lifetime. "Reuse" represents efforts to reuse old parts obtained from used products. "Recycle" refers to collecting used products and making use of recyclable resources.

In 2000 the Basic Law for Establishing the Recycling-Based Society was enacted as a legal framework for waste recycling measures. This law is positioned as a basic law in recycling policies and sets out (1) the implementation of the 3R initiative, (2) the responsibilities of manufacturers and (3) the basic plans to create and promote a recycling-based society. The implementation of this basic law pushed forward revisions to the related individual waste recycling laws. In the same year, the Law for the Promotion of Utilization of Recycled Resources was significantly amended and renamed the Law for Effective Utilization of Resources. To reduce the generation of waste, the law obliges business entities to (1) save resources for manufacturing products such as cars, home appliances, personal computers, and gas and oil appliances; (2) improve product durability; (3) standardize product parts; and (4) produce repairable products to extend product life. Furthermore, for the purpose of promoting recycling, manufacturers are required to reuse by-products, including slag and sludge, generated during production processes. As for the recycling of used goods other than containers, packaging waste, and home appliances, the Construction Material Recycling Act, the Food Recycling Law, and the Law for the Recycling of End-of-Life Vehicles took effect in succession from 2000. More recently, the Act on Promotion of Recycling of Small Waste Electrical and Electronic Equipment, covering mobile phones, digital cameras, portable music players, and game consoles was passed in August 2012 and enacted in April 2013.

As all these laws indicate, Japan has been successfully developing hard laws for recycling venous resources that include containers, packaging waste, home electronic products, construction materials, food waste, and automobiles. These hard laws stipulate that manufacturers and distributors must recycle used products based on the principle of extended producer responsibility (EPR). These laws based on EPR raise the costs of economic activities that will likely harm the environment and public health so as to return recyclable products, parts and raw materials to the arterial economy instead of turning them into pollutants. On the whole, it can be said that hard laws, as well as the system for monitoring and penalizing illegal waste treatment, are working fairly well in Japan.

Of course, it would be an exaggeration to claim that Japanese hard laws for recycling are flawless. In particular, the current recycling laws still need to be further refined to increase the benefits of environmentally friendly recycling. For example, the country has not offered economic support or grants for recycling waste or ensured the safety of recyclable resources by means of standardization. That is, the existing hard laws have not increased the benefits of the environmental approach.

As for soft laws, public awareness of recycling is relatively high in Japan. According to the Public Opinion Survey on Environmental Problems conducted by the Cabinet Office in 2012, 86.8 percent of respondents said they make daily efforts to recycle waste; yet only 31.2 percent are willing to purchase recycled products, although the percentage has increased from the 16 percent level of the last few surveys (Cabinet Office of Japan, 2012). Still, we should note that consumers have not stimulated manufacturers strongly enough to develop environment-friendly products.

3.2 China[5]

The Law on the Prevention and Control of Environmental Pollution by Solid Waste was introduced in China in 1995. This basic and general law concerning waste covers the treatment of industrial, household, and hazardous waste. It was amended in 2004 to clarify the mandatory responsibility of manufacturers to prevent pollution caused by waste materials. The Cleaner Production Promotion Law enacted in 2002 requires business entities to adopt production processes that generate fewer pollutants and to produce goods that are easy to collect, recycle, and reuse during their life cycle. The Circular Economy Promotion Law of the People's Republic of China came into force in 2008 to define extended producer responsibility (EPR) with regard to waste recycling and to provide for the utilization of industrial waste and the reuse and recycling of recyclable resources.

Under these basic laws, the Chinese government has been endeavoring to manage and promote the recycling of automotive industrial waste and electrical and electronic waste, which are expected to increase in amount and produce high economic gains through recycling. In 2001, the government passed a law to regulate the collection and recycle of end-of-life vehicles.[6] In China, illegal trading of end-of-life vehicles and reuse of worn parts are posing a threat to road safety. To improve the situation, the law stipulates that automobiles and motorcycles be collected and recycled under the supervision of the government, and prohibits the reuse of major parts, including engines, direction indicators, transmissions, suspensions, and frames. Automotive dismantlers must recycle them as iron scrap. For electrical and electronic waste, a bill was introduced and posted for public comment in 2004. After some twists and turns, the Management Regulations for Recycling and Disposing of Consumer Electronics and Electronic Waste was finally promulgated in 2009. This is the Chinese equivalent to Japan's Home Appliance Recycling Law. The five items covered in this law include washing machines, refrigerators, televisions, air conditioners, and personal computers. The law requires that (1) consumer electronics retailers collect these items, (2) manufacturers collect and provide dismantlers with funds for disassembling waste equipment, and (3) dismantlers be certified. Besides, similar to RoHS in the European Union (EU), the 2007 Administrative Measure on the Control of Pollution Caused by Electronic Information Products covers a wide range of electrical and electronic products and urges manufacturers to reduce the amount of hazardous substances, such as lead and mercury, in their products to a standard level.

As examined above, China has developed hard laws comparable to those in Japan and the EU to some extent. In particular, the unique characteristic of China's recycling policies is that economic aid, like subsidies, is provided to expand the benefits of environmental recycling, as in the case of home appliance recycling. The Chinese government encourages the recycling of automotive industrial waste and electrical and electronic waste. This may be because these wastes are expected to increase in amount and produce high economic gains as venous resources.

On the other hand, hard laws regarding many other types of venous resources, including containers, packaging, construction, and food waste, have yet to be established. Also, the Chinese government has not adequately adopted measures to incorporate extended producer responsibility that requires manufacturers and distributors to recycle used products. In other words, the country has not yet developed the means to raise the costs of economic activities that cause environmental destruction and health risks.

In regard to soft laws, awareness of the effective use of recyclable resources has been growing in China also. As the Cleaner Production Promotion Law and the Circular Economy Promotion Law indicate, the country has made progress in formulating rules for reusing and recycling waste. However, it has not managed to reduce the burden on the environment by controlling the generation of waste. Comprehensive measures like Japan's 3Rs have not been adopted. Furthermore, China is faced with governance issues. It lacks an effective system for monitoring and penalizing the illegal handling of waste. As many observers have noted, hard laws are not enforced properly despite their adequate preparation.

These points suggest that waste recycling in China is not designed to reduce the environmental burden by preventing the generation of waste. Rather, the main objective is to make more effective use of venous resources for the sake of economic development. The government appears to be playing an active role in promoting proper waste treatment, but as a developing country whose national income per capita is below USD$10,000, economic development is the first priority in China. Increasing amounts of waste resulting from the concentration of population in urban areas and the development of industrial activities have made China the world's largest producer of municipal solid waste. With its increasing population, Beijing generates around 18,000 tons of waste per day, and the volume is growing by 8 percent annually (MOE 1969–2014). Since most waste materials end up in landfills, the shortage of such sites is now a growing concern.

3.3 Thailand[7]

China is not the only country that emphasizes economic development when formulating recycling policies to expand its underdeveloped economy. The recycling policies of Thailand, which is on the same economic level as China, will be discussed in this section.

Having experienced industrial development earlier than other East Asian countries, Thailand now faces urgent environmental issues resulting from rapid economic development. For instance, air pollution near industrial parks and large cities has been worsening due to discharge from those industrial facilities and vehicle emissions. Moreover, contamination of urban rivers and water channels, including the Chao Phraya River, is increasingly serious. The management of a massive amount of waste is also a major environmental issue.

In Thailand, the Department of Industrial Works (DIW) oversees industrial waste management, and the Pollution Control Department (PCD) oversees domestic waste. Of 26 million tons of industrial waste generated in the country per year, non-hazardous waste accounts for 90 percent, of which 87 percent are reused or recycled and 9 percent ends up in landfills. Another 3 percent is exported overseas. In particular, used batteries are sent to the Netherlands. For hazardous waste, 15 percent is incinerated, and only 16 percent of the total amount generated is properly disposed of at landfill sites. Waste management companies need permission from DIW to handle waste materials. The General Environmental Conservation (GENCO) is a leading company in waste treatment and disposal services. Even though it is not government-owned, it pursues Thailand's national interests.[8] According to Japanese companies in Thailand, the company has a high level of technology but charges high handling fees (Sasaki, 2008, 197). Twenty percent of 16 million tons of household waste generated per year is sent to waste-to-energy facilities. Each year, 400 thousand tons of used home appliances are collected as electrical and electronic waste. The weight of household hazardous electrical and electronic waste, including fluorescent lights, collected annually is estimated at 150 thousand tons.

In domestic waste collection, private recycling companies – or so-called junk shops – play a key role. The country adopted a registration system for those companies and 5,000 are now officially registered; however, unregistered, illegitimate ones engage in the business, treating waste materials inappropriately with no regard for environmental and health consequences. One third of used electrical and electronic products are collected by private recycling companies. Given that virtually no company can dispose of such waste materials properly, they are likely being disposed of inappropriately. Some companies charge handling fees for collecting such waste or collect it for hidden illegal purposes. There are numerous unregistered recycling businesses near a temple 30 kilometers from Bangkok where a market for selling used electrical and electronic products is held.

People who do not trust private recycling businesses have no means of disposing of used electrical and electronic products and thus keep them at their homes. The amount of such electrical and electronic waste is estimated to account for one third of the total amount. An official of PCD interviewed for this paper confessed to having kept an old cathode ray tube at home because there is nowhere to take it. The last third seems to be dumped illegally or exported. One notable issue is that hazardous and non-hazardous electrical and electronic waste is disposed of together through open dumping and burned to reduce the volume.

To address this situation, soft laws for environmental protection have been growing lately in Thailand. The recent urbanization and industrialization have caused various environmental problems, including water, air, and waste pollution. This has given rise to growing public awareness of the environment. Some private recycling companies strive to provide environmental education to local residents and promote environmental awareness in cooperation with local governments (Sang-Arun et al., 2013). In parallel, the national government has been

Table 7.3 Major waste regulations in Thailand

The Enhancement and Conservation of National Environmental Quality Act	This is a basic law on the development of environmental standards and plans, and the management of environment monitoring. It also covers waste management.
Public Health Act	This act facilitates the management of general, infectious and bodily waste. Hazardous domestic waste must be handled under this law.
Factory Act	This act regulates the operation of factories, and the handling of hazardous and non-hazardous industrial waste is specified in detail in the secondary law. Waste materials generated by offices, residential houses, and canteens are excluded from this act.
Hazardous Substances Act	This act specifies the management of hazardous substances. A list of such substances includes hazardous waste that must be handled as a hazardous substance in compliance with this act. A waste manifest system is defined in the secondary law.

Source: Umeyama (2011), p. 28.

enhancing its 3Rs policies by implementing a promotion pilot project in each region, offering training programs for local government officials and residents, developing guidelines for 3Rs promotion, and encouraging the collection of used mobile phones.

In terms of hard laws, on the other hand, Thailand lacks a comprehensive legal framework for waste management and recycling. In Thailand, the basic environment law was enforced as early as 1975. Then it was amended and renamed the Enhancement and Conservation of National Environmental Quality Act in 1992. The further revision of this act has been discussed for long time but not carried out yet. As a result, individual laws and their secondary regulations separately touch on waste management and recycling as shown in Table 7.3. Even though the country regulates the management of hazardous waste to a certain extent, measures to achieve ideal resource circulation have not been proposed or adopted. The government must work hard to improve the management of general waste.[9]

4 Conclusion

What is a suitable regime for achieving ideal resource circulation? How should East Asian countries work together to establish such a regime? This chapter proposed the concept of an "optimal resource circulation regime" and compared the recycling policies of Japan, China, and Thailand in light of this concept.

The Japanese regime of recycling is closer to the optimal resource circulation regime when compared with China and Thailand, which are Japan's major economic partners in the region. Therefore, the country should share its experience and know-how with surrounding countries to facilitate the development of such a regime. On the other hand, this comparative study also revealed that Japan should also learn from neighboring East Asian countries, even though it leads in building a resource circulation regime. Japan does not have a system to provide economic support, like subsidies for recycling, or a standards system to ensure the safety of recyclable resources. In short, the country has not created sufficient hard laws to expand the benefits of the environmental approach. In contrast, China has adopted such means, including the implementation of an electrical and electronic waste recycling system. Japan should learn from Chinese recycling policies.

China has made good progress in establishing recycling hard laws. It is noteworthy that it took measures like subsidies and a recycling company designation system to enhance the benefits of environmental recycling. However, the country has not succeeded in introducing hard laws to raise the costs of economic activities that will likely harm the environment and public health, or to incorporate extended producer responsibility into its recycling policies. In addition, for hard laws to work effectively, governance and soft laws need to be significantly improved in China. Japan should assist China in strengthening its governance and soft laws to build a resource circulation regime through human resource development and educational activities.

In Thailand, all of hard laws, governance, and soft laws remain to be developed. This is where Japan comes in to support Thailand in the construction of a legal framework, the development of human resources, and the implementation of educational and awareness-raising activities. In particular, Thailand has not enforced its hard laws regarding waste management and recycling. It has yet to raise the costs of the economic-oriented approach based on extended producer responsibility and develop hard laws to maximize the benefits of the environmental approach by providing subsidies. For Thailand to promote proper treatment of waste and recycling, educating its citizens on proper waste management practices and sorting of recyclable materials is essential. The most significant hurdle in East Asian countries in this regard is that the people are not used to sorting recyclables. What makes recycling difficult in Thailand, for example, is that many homes have only one garbage bin. To fix the problem, local governments have been frequently conducting educational activities in local communities and schools. Some private recycling companies work with local governments to actively provide environmental education to residents and promote recycling. Even though recycling laws have not been enforced yet, hazardous waste materials such as fluorescent lights, mobile phones, and batteries have begun to be collected voluntarily. This type of undertaking proves a growing awareness of environment and health issues and is expected to lead to improvement in Thailand's waste management. The country should also seek assistance from Japan, China, and other countries with which it has strong ties in the venous economy. Since the country emphasizes economic development over environment protection, much like China, Japan should play an active role in supporting Thailand to improve its governance and soft laws through developing human resources and conducting educational and awareness-raising activities.

Needless to say, specific individual policies in one country cannot be introduced to another without taking their social characteristics and historical backgrounds into consideration. Moreover, the rough comparison of the recycling policies of Japan, China, and Thailand presented in this chapter does not necessarily provide an accurate understanding of the situations in these countries. Nonetheless, the analytic framework presented here for establishing the optimal resource circulation regime should make it easier to compare recycling policies in general and each type of venous resource in a number of countries. The framework will be useful in identifying the strengths and weaknesses of the recycling policies in each country and in achieving optimal resource circulation across national boundaries.

Notes

1 *Regime* is a concept developed in the field of international politics. According to Krasner, *regime* refers to "institutions possessing norms, decision rules, and procedures which facilitate a convergence of expectations" that govern the behavior of doers (Krasner 1983, p. 2).
2 Hard laws are defined as binding laws such as a set of rules and ministerial and local ordinances. Soft laws refer to non-binding norms and customs that influence the behavior of doers.
3 Hosoda (2014) points out that countries need to develop a system in which hard and soft laws are consistent with each other by sharing knowledge and information with neighboring countries.
4 The history of Japanese waste recycling regulations in this section is drawn from MOE (1969–2014) and from Sekiyama (2013).
5 The waste regulations in China described here were written according to Yoshida (2006), Du et al. (2011), Gao and Gao (2011), Sekiyama (2013), Hosoda (2014), Hosoda and Someno (2014), and field work by the author.
6 In China, "laws" mean legislative laws enacted by the National People's Congress as well as ordinances and regulations, administrative and ministerial regulations.
7 The description about waste regulations in Thailand was in accordance with SANG-ARUN et al. (2013), Umeyama (2011), and field work by the author. In particular, the data on waste materials presented in this section are based on information obtained from the Pollution Control Department in October 2014.
8 According to the Pollution Control Department, GENCO pays 30 percent of its profits to DIW even though such payment is not required by law as of October 2014.
9 According to the Department of Industrial Works, the Thai government has been preparing to implement three recycling laws: the Basic Recycling Law, the Solid Waste Management Law and the WEEE Management Law. The Basic Law has already been drafted and is expected to be enforced soon under the military regime. The law is designed to build a legal structure based on the principle of extended producer responsibility and promote proper treatment of waste materials by means of economic measures such as provision of subsidies.

References

Cabinet Office of Japan (2012) *Public Opinion Poll on Environmental Issues.* Retrieved from http://www8.cao.go.jp/survey/h24/h24-kankyou/index.html (accessed on 28 August 2014).

Du, H., F. Yoshida, and Z. Fu (2011) "Electrical and electronic waste recycling and related legal policies in China," *Environmental Technology,* Japan Association of Engineering Management for Waste Treatment Facility, Tokyo, No. 143, pp. 109–113, in Japanese.

Gao, Weijun, and Yongzhi Gao (2011) "A study on the current situation of home appliance recycling and a projection of future engine displacement in urban areas in China," *A Viewpoint to East Asia,* September, pp. 12–22.

Hosoda, Eiji (2008) *Resource Circulation Society: System Design and Policy Perspective,* Keio University Press, Tokyo, in Japanese.

Hosoda, Eiji (2014) "Problems and prospects of international resource circulation in the East Asian region," *Safety Engineering,* Vol. 53, No. 1, pp. 27–34.

Hosoda, Eiji and Kenji Hosono (2014) "New development of the venous business in China," *The Economic Studies (Hokkaido University),* Vol. 63, No. 2, pp. 13–27.

Kojima, Michikazu, ed. (2005) *Trading of Recyclable Resources in Asia,* Institute of Developing Economies, Makuhari, Japan.

Krasner, Stephen D., ed. (1983) *International Regimes,* Cornell University Press, Ithaca, NY.

METI (Ministry of Economy, Trade and Industry) (2004) *A Guide to the Home Appliance Recycling Law,* The Research Institute of Economy, Trade and Industry, Tokyo.

MOE (Ministry of the Environment, Japan) (1969–2014) *White Paper.* Rerieved from http://www.env.go.jp/en/wpaper/ (accessed on 30 January 2016).

Puchett, J. and T. Smith (2002) *Exporting Harm: The High-Tech Trashing of Asia. The Basel Action Network (BAN) and Silicon Valley Toxics Coalition (SVTC).* Retrieved from http://archive.ban.org/E-waste/technotrashfinalcomp.pdf (accessed on 30 January 2016).

Sang-Arun, J., M. Bengtsson, T.L. Chong, L. Jinhui, P. Wanpen, P. Modak, S. Gilby, Z. Nana, S. Batia and S. Buachum (2013) *Promoting Recycling in Municipal Solid Waste Management Through Suitable Business Models: Improving the Supply Chain for Recyclables,* Commissioned Report, Institute for Global Environmental Strategies, Hayama, Japan.

Sasaki, So (2008) "The Current Situation of Industrial Waste Management and Recycling in Thailand: The Deregulation Policy," in Michikazu Kojima, ed. *Recycling in Asia,* London: Routledge, pp. 193–224.

Sekiyama, Takashi (2013) "A paradox in China's environmental management: An argument from a comparative study on waste recycling policies between China and Japan," *Chinese Business Review,* Vol. 12, No. 6, pp. 425–434.

Sekiyama, Takashi (2014) "Coordination, compromise, and change: An implication of the repeated games of the 'Battle of the Sexes'," *Journal of Mathematics and System Science,* Vol. 2, No. 8, pp. 557–568.

Umeyama, Kenichi, ed. (2011) *A Guide to the System of Environmental Laws in Thailand,* Envix.

Yoshida, Aya (2006) "Recycling in China," in Michikazu Kojima, ed. *Recycling in Asia,* IDE-JETRO, Chapter 5, pp. 99–120, in Japanese.

8 Extended official responsibility and the red card rule in China

Eiji Sawada and Yirui Xu

1 Introduction

Recently, the extended producer responsibility (EPR) strategy was introduced to the production of home appliances as part of the waste and recycling policy in China. From 2009 to 2011, a national old-for-new home appliances replacement scheme (HARS) was implemented. Since 2012, regulations on the management of the recovery and treatment of waste from electrical and electronic equipment (WEEE) have been in effect (Saito et al., 2015). Under both policies, home appliance producers are obliged to pay a recycling fee. In addition, these waste and recycling policies include schemes for paying subsidies to recycling firms. These types of reward and punishment schemes are expected to promote a sound material-cycle society in China.

However, the development and passage of hard laws and the enforcement of these laws are two separate matters. In fact, in our field studies in China from 2012 to 2015, we observed cases in which policy was undermined in various regions. For example, subsidy payments to recycling firms are often delayed or require a long time for approval, which encourages the implementation of informal recycling activities. If recycling and waste policies are not implemented well, they become useless no matter how sound they are. Therefore, we need to promote not only good policies but also good governance to implement these policies; as Sekiyama notes in Chapter 7 of this volume, an optimal resource circulation regime requires a good mix of soft law, hard law, and governance.

Usually, good governance means that officials are able to enforce policies with firms. This idea implicitly supposes that officials have incentives to implement policies but that firms do not have incentives to follow these policies. However, this is not always true in the case of China. Because of the specific way in which policy decisions are made, officials often do not have enough incentives to implement policies. In this chapter, we examine the reason why current waste and recycling policies are sometimes badly implemented as a result of policy decisions in China. We use the term "bad governance" to denote those situations in which insufficient funds are budgeted for environmental improvements as a result of a lack of policy implementation incentives. Because EPR gives the producers of home appliances incentives to proceed under the Design for the Environment

(DfE) policy, officials also require a system that will give them appropriate incentives to implement these policies.

In Section 2, we present an overview of the earlier research by Sawada and Xu (2014), which examined the hierarchical structure of competitive promotion among officials as well as that of the policy decisions in China. Uniquely, in China, officials do not develop policies to maximize the social welfare in their governing areas but rather to increase their chances of being promoted to the upper levels of government. This system is now well known as the political selection tournament system (PSTS). Under this system, officials sometimes underfund policies that will not bring significant results in the short run; this is an important contribution to bad governance. The way in which policies will be viewed when an official is evaluated for promotion is often considered by the official to be more important than how the policies work.

In Section 3, we re-examine the ways to avoid bad governance under PSTS in a simple economic model. The so-called "red card rule" (RCR), which is based on the right to specifically appoint personnel who have chosen to proceed with environmental improvement, is essential to the argument against the PSTS. Some important roles of the RCR have already been shown by Sawada and Xu (2014). However, we now show some additional roles of the RCR. The RCR can be a reliable threat to officials. The central government does not always set a standard that is equal to its environmental goals because officials work to achieve targets for fear of being demoted. Finally, in Section 4, we summarize our conclusions.

2 Policy decisions and the promotion race among officials in China – an overview of Sawada and Xu (2014)

2.1 Political selection tournament system

A growing number of economic studies have examined the performance of personnel control in China, including a study by Li and Zhou (2005), which is a leading study in the literature. The study analyzed the relationship between the promotion of local officials and the growth rate of regional economies between 1979 and 2002 by using provincial-level data. According to this examination, there is a clear correlation between the probability of promotion and provincial GDP growth. Thus, the higher the provincial GDP growth rate is, the higher the probability that officials in the provincial-level government will be promoted. We cannot ignore this key relationship when analyzing policy decisions in China.

Moreover, Zhou claimed in another paper that upper-level governments control lower-level governments by exercising a "political selection tournament system". Central governments often promote regional economic growth by exercising their personnel rights and by giving strong incentives to local officials, selecting them on the basis of the economic growth in their governing areas. Thus, local officials invest more funds and resources in projects that result in greater economic growth and increased tax revenue in order to be promoted to the upper levels of government.

Evaluation for promotion is not only based on economic growth but also on a wide variety of political functions. However, some functions are difficult to include in the auditing standards of PSTS. Two factors prevent political functions from being evaluated for PSTS:

- Measurability of the administrative roles
- Length of the planning period

Some administrative roles have indexes that are easy to measure (e.g., GDP for economic growth), while others do not. Environmental improvement, however, is an example that is difficult to measure quantitatively. How can we evaluate the state of the environment when it has such a wide variety of components? Each environmental component must be measured individually because components such as air quality, water quality, and the efficient use of resources, among others, mostly have their own indexes. We need to be careful when including such administrative roles into an evaluation.

Even if some outcomes of policies are easily measurable, other problems remain. Local officials are unwilling to invest funds and resources in projects with delayed effects. In other words, they prefer policies that bring about substantial results in a short period, thereby underfunding policies that can potentially influence long-term economic growth in their regions but have insignificant effects during the period these officials are in office. Therefore, environmental improvement is difficult to achieve under the PSTS system of promotion. The process for promotion and evaluation should be designed to require environmental improvement so that officials cannot underfund environmental improvement projects.

2.2 Policy decisions in a hierarchical structure

Sawada and Xu (2014) examined the multiple policy decisions under PSTS with an economic model that captures the hierarchical structure of officials' promotions. In our analysis, we make several assumptions. First, we use the "elimination tournament model" with four homogeneous officials and two selections. The general framework of the elimination tournament was initially proposed by Rosen (1986). Second, selection is based on the relative performance of the officials. Performance is evaluated by the weighted sum of GDP and the level of environmental improvement achieved within a governing area. Third, officials can obtain a private financial benefit depending on the extent of economic growth in their governing areas. This private benefit is sometimes formal and sometimes informal. In our framework, both interpretations are possible. Fourth, officials distribute funds budgeted by the government for economic growth and environmental improvement so that their expected profit, with and without considering a promotion, is maximized. Fifth, the upper-level government controls the local officials' incentives for environmental improvement by adjusting the "promotion weight" on the GDP level and on the environmental level, which explains how these levels are emphasized more when offering a promotion.

Based on the above framework, we show two major properties of policy decisions under PSTS. First, the rights of personnel to be promoted do not always provide enough incentives to officials to achieve certain environmental improvements. If the profit after the promotion is not sufficiently large or if the profit when they fail to be promoted is not sufficiently small, economic agents abandon the promotion and distribute no funds for environmental improvement. That is, officials are willing to hold their existing positions and maximize their private benefit by only considering economic growth in the areas they govern.

Second, we show that there exists a trade-off relationship between the achievement targets of upper-level governments and those of lower-level governments. Suppose that the promotion weight on the environmental level of the upper government is adjusted to aim for a higher environmental target in the areas under the upper government's purview. Then, officials decrease the expenditure on economic growth, which results in less profit for the officials in the upper government. This makes officials in the lower governments unwilling to be promoted. Finally, environmental targets cannot be achieved in the lower governments no matter how great the environmental accomplishments are weighted in promotion decisions. Conversely, if a local government prioritizes achieving environmental targets, then it has to reduce its emphasis on the environment to increase the profit of the officials in the upper government. These results were uniquely obtained from an analysis of a framework in which the participants in the tournament decide the policies. This framework makes it difficult to give appropriate incentives to officials in every selection period.

2.3 Two possible approaches to restore efficiency to the PSTS

In the previous section, we explained some scenarios in which policy decisions under the PSTS fail to achieve policy targets. Considering this, how can we avoid failure? In our analysis, we examined the following two possible approaches:

- Budget control while sustaining the original incentive structure
- Additional rules for the promotion process that will change the incentive structure

The profit gap between being promoted and not being promoted becomes important in the PSTS. The wider the profit gap is, the more officials become willing to be promoted. There are three options to enlarge the profit gap. One way is to simply adjust the salary level, setting the salary level for upper-level government above that of the lower-level government. Another way is to adjust private benefits directly and indirectly. The direct way is possible only when the private benefit is formal. In fact, as far as attracting investments, local officials can sometimes gain certain commission fees privately if they succeed in attracting firms to their area. Private benefits can also be adjusted indirectly through policy budgets. The amount of the policy budget influences the scale of the economic policy and the resulting economic growth. Thus, a larger policy budget will result in greater private benefit. In the sense that all these options are categorized as budget control, our results support the opinion of Xu (2014) that a dual-control system of personnel control and budget control can create a desirable state of economic targets as well as other targets, such as environmental issues and social security.

Another approach is to add more rules to the promotion process. In contrast to the previous approach, rewards to officials and government budgets need to be fixed. However, we can achieve similar results by changing the incentive structure in the PSTS. The design and development of promotion rules are important to appropriate decision making under the PSTS.

2.4 Red card rule

The RCR is a specific example of such an additional rule. Under the RCR, the central government has inserted a strict standard for evaluating social stability into the PSTS. That is, if any incident occurred that could have a negative impact on social stability, any local official involved in the incident would not be promoted, no matter how high that official's evaluation in other respects. The RCR was initially introduced as an environmental protection measure in Changxing prefecture, Zhejiang province in 2004. Since then, the rule has been applied to various environmental protections, including pollutant treatment plant construction, energy savings, emissions abatement, etc.

One example of the RCR is the censure system established in the 11th five-year plan. This system introduced targets of energy saving to reduce the GDP-specific energy consumption to 20 percent below the 2005 levels. These targets are an important index for the evaluation of officials, and an RCR was applied to the targets. Under this censure system, local officials and executives of firms are called to account for the evaluation results when their energy savings are reviewed. In the case of a failure to achieve the targets, orders for improvement are issued to provinces and firms. If they are unable to show improvements within the given periods, the evaluation of the officials will be substantially lower.

The RCR often serves as a safety net to ensure that the worst possible outcome of an environmental issue (when control has failed) does not surpass a certain low level. In the following chapter, we re-examine the role of the RCR. As we show later, the RCR has some other roles, in particular, the use of personnel control to facilitate the achievement of certain targets. Several properties of the RCR have been demonstrated by Sawada and Xu (2014), but herein, we will show additional properties of the RCR.

3 A simple economic analysis

3.3 Model

In this section, we analytically examine the reason why bad governance often arises. In addition, we examine the role of the RCR and show that the RCR can be applied to waste and recycling policies as a possible solution to bad governance.

Sawada and Xu (2014) developed a mathematical model for policy decisions in China that is an application of Rosen's framework (1986). Here, we adopt a simpler framework than Sawada and Xu (2014) did. To preliminarily explain our framework, we consider a tournament with two officials (i = 1, 2) and only one selection.[1] Figure 8.1 shows a representation of our economic model. The winner is selected based on the relative performances of the officials. This promotion race can be sometimes interpreted as the promotion from the township level to the county level and sometimes from the county level to a higher level of government (e.g., a province-level government).

The official i distributes the policy budget B (in most of the following analysis, this is assumed to be 1) for economic growth b_i^f and environmental improvement b_i^g ($1 = b_i^f + b_i^g$). Depending on the amount of expenditures, the GDP level $F\left(b_i^f\right)$ and the environmental level $G\left(b_i^g\right)$ are determined (both are assumed to be C^2, increasing and concave functions). If more funds are to be distributed for environmental improvement, the undermining of the policy by the delay of subsidy payments to recycling firms must decrease. Therefore, in our framework, too little government spending on environmental improvement indicates bad governance.

Moreover, we assume that salary levels are common among the officials and are constant through a tournament. Furthermore, we assume that the more officials win in a tournament, the more private benefits they can receive as their governing areas become larger and richer. Thus, officials can receive private benefits according to the extent of economic growth in their governing areas. We simply assume that private benefits are expressed as an increasing function of the budget distribution to economic growth, and this allows the private benefit of official i to be $R\left(b_i^f\right)$. If the official succeeds in being promoted to the upper government, then he or she can receive even greater private benefits $\bar{R}$, which is greater than the private benefit fully budgeted to the economic growth (Figure 8.2). This becomes the incentive for officials to seek promotion to the upper government.

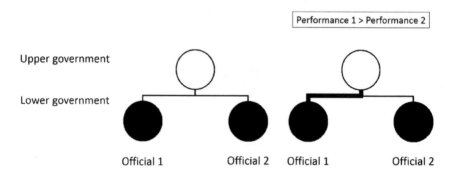

Figure 8.1 Political selection tournament system with two officials

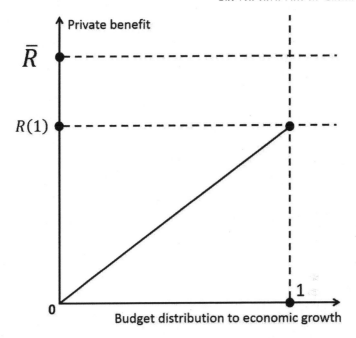

Figure 8.2 Increasing private benefits according to the budget distribution for economic growth

The probability of the promotion of official i is defined by

$$P_{ij}\left(h_i^g, h_j^g\right) = \frac{Performance\, i}{Performance\, i + Performance\, j},$$

where the numerator is the performance of official i and the denominator is the sum of the performances of both officials. Thus, this promotion probability expresses the relative performances of officials. The performance of official i is expressed by the weighted sum of the GDP level and the environmental level $F\left(b_i^f\right) + \alpha G\left(b_i^g\right)$, where α is the promotion weight on the environmental level. Here, we can interpret this promotion weight as a level of official responsibility for the results of their policy implementation. If the environmental level worsens as a result of bad governance, then their promotion probability becomes lower. Upper government can control the level of official responsibility by adjusting the promotion weight so that given environmental targets can be achieved.

Officials decide the budget distribution to maximize their expected profit. As we mentioned, what is special and important in this model is that officials do not develop policies to maximize the social welfare in their governing areas but rather to increase their relative performances to achieve promotion to the upper government:

$$\Pi\left(b_i^g;b_j^g\right) = \max_{b_i^g \in [0,1]}\left[P_{ij}\left(b_i^g;b_j^g\right)\left(W+\bar{R}\right)\right.$$
$$\left.\left(1-P_{ij}\left(b_i^g;b_j^g\right)\right)\left(W+R\left(1-b_i^g\right)\right)\right].$$

With a probability $P_{ij}\left(b_i^g;b_j^g\right)$, officials promoted to the upper government can receive W plus the largest private benefit $\bar{R}$. With a probability $1-P_{ij}\left(b_i^g;b_j^g\right)$, they fail to be promoted and obtain W plus a private benefit, depending on the budget distribution $R\left(1-b_i^g\right)$. By solving these problems, we obtain Nash equilibrium budget distributions and corresponding GDP levels, environmental levels, and profit levels denoted by $b_i^{fN}, b_i^{gN}, f\left(b_i^{fN}\right), g\left(b_i^{gN}\right)$, and $\Pi^N := \Pi\left(b_1^{gN};b_2^{gN}\right) = \Pi\left(b_2^{gN};b_1^{gN}\right)$, respectively. Using comparative statistics, we can obtain the following two important properties:[2]

- The environmental level at Nash equilibrium increases as the official's responsibility increases.
- The official's profit at Nash equilibrium decreases as the official's responsibility increases.

If the officials become responsible for the results of their implementation of environmental policy, does the environment improve? The first result is very intuitive. Greater official responsibility drives an official to implement environment policy effectively. However, why does the official's profit decrease? The answer is closely related to the private benefit received according to the GDP level. With greater responsibility, officials are forced to distribute more funds to environmental improvement to succeed in being promoted. At the same time, a lower distribution of funds for economic growth decreases private benefits, and profits at the Nash equilibrium also decrease.

The second result causes another problem. As the officials' profits decrease and as their official responsibility increases, do they continue to increase the distribution of funding for environmental improvement? The answer is negative. We can easily show that officials have incentives to deviate from the Nash equilibrium and to consider no environmental improvement if the profit after promotion is small enough. At the time the profits in the Nash equilibrium become lower than the profit with no environmental improvement, it becomes more beneficial for them to abandon their promotion and choose to distribute all funds to economic growth so that their profits without promotion are maximized. Let the profit of official i with no budget distribution for environmental improvement be $\Pi^D := \Pi\left(0;b_j^g\right)$. Then, the maximum profit of official i is formally expressed by

$$\Pi\left(b_i^g;b_j^g\right) = \begin{cases} \Pi^N, & \Pi^N \geq \Pi^D \\ \Pi^D, & \Pi^N < \Pi^D \end{cases}.$$

The maximum profit in Nash is 1 as far as it does not decline less than the profit with no environmental improvement. However, once the profit exceeds the threshold, officials do not distribute any funds for environmental improvement no matter how high their official responsibilities are.

Figure 8.3 shows the relationship between the level of official responsibility and the environmental level. The left figure shows the case when the profit after promotion is large enough. In this case, any environmental level from $G(0)$ to $G(1)$ can be achieved by adjusting the extent of official responsibility. The right figure shows the case when the profit after promotion is small enough. Here, officials increase the distribution to environmental improvement up to a certain level as their official responsibility increases. However, once the profit becomes lower than the profit with no environmental improvement, they cease improving the environment at all. In the right figure, the environmental level sticks to the horizontal axis after an official's responsibility increases and the environment is improved to point A.

The effects of uncertainty are not well examined by Sawada and Xu (2014). However, it is quite natural for the results of policies to be uncertain sometimes. How does the uncertainty of the results impact the analysis? Here, we will briefly examine the impact of uncertainty. The effect of uncertain policies is somehow straightforward. If officials do not prefer risk, then they underestimate the results with uncertainty. Thus, if the environmental policy is uncertain, then environmental improvements have to be evaluated as greater to give similar incentives to those without uncertainty. On the other hand, uncertain policies do not affect promotion abandonment at all because promotion probability is always 50 percent as long as officials are considered homogenous.

The effect of uncertain private benefits is more significant. Generally, it is not obvious that uncertain private benefits make abandonments of promotion less frequent because the uncertainty of private benefits not only makes the benefit with abandonment smaller but also makes the expected benefit after the promotion

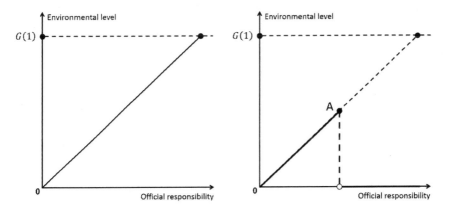

Figure 8.3 Environmental level and the extent of official responsibility

smaller. The results depend on the relative magnitude of benefits, which is also a specific property that obtained only in the hierarchical structure.

3.4 Two failures with low and high responsibility for officials

Based on our understanding of the previous section, we would like to examine what causes the scarce distribution of funding for environmental improvement in more detail. Here, the following two key ideas become important:

- The level of the environmental target
- The failure to set an appropriate level of official responsibility

We will first consider the first idea listed above. Upper-level governments set the official responsibility of lower-level governments so that officials in the lower governments have incentives to distribute enough funding to environmental improvement and to achieve certain environmental targets. Here, we only consider high and low environmental targets and corresponding official responsibility α_L and α_H ($\alpha_L < \alpha_H$). By setting the official responsibility to α_L if the environmental target is low or by setting the official responsibility to α_H if environmental target is high, then environmental targets can be achieved as long as officials do not abandon their promotions (Figure 8.4).

In Figure 8.4, the left figure shows the case when the profit after promotion is large, and the right figure shows the case when the profit after promotion is small, as shown in Figure 8.3. In the left figure, both target points B and C are achieved by setting official responsibility appropriately. In contrast, in the right figure, if the environmental target is high and the upper government sets the official responsibility at α_H, then officials choose to make no distribution of funds for environmental improvement. Point C cannot be achieved, no matter how high

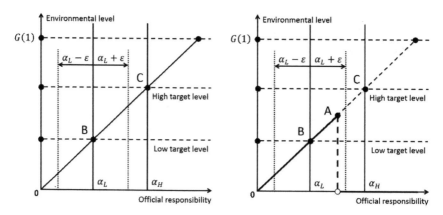

Figure 8.4 Environmental target and the result of setting a false extent of responsibility

Table 8.1 Likelihood of bad governance with small and large profit after promotion

Environmental target	Official responsibility				Environmental target	Official responsibility		
	Small	Appropriate	Big			Small	Appropriate	Big
High	Bad governance				High	Bad governance	Bad governance	Bad governance
Low	Bad governance				Low	Bad governance		Bad governance

the official responsibility is. Even worse, reaching point C could result in a worse state, with no environmental improvement and with greater responsibility. This is the case of bad governance because of the high environmental target.

Even if environmental target is low and seems relatively easier to achieve by adjusting the official responsibility, it is still problematic because there is no guarantee that the upper government correctly sets the extent of responsibility. It is natural that if the government fails to set the correct level, the responsibility level sometimes becomes lower and sometimes becomes higher. In the figure, ε expresses the margin of error in the appropriate responsibility level to be set. In the left case, depending on whether the error is negative or positive, the resulting environmental improvements can become lower and higher. On the other hand, in the right figure, the level of environmental improvement can become lower not only with a negative error but also with a positive error. In the figure, official responsibility with a positive error $\alpha_L + \varepsilon$ exceeds point A, where officials cease any environmental improvement.

Table 8.1 provides a summary of the likelihood of bad governance. The table on the left is a case in which an official receives a large profit after promotion, and the table on the right is a case in which an official receives a small profit after promotion. If the profit after promotion is large, then bad governance occurs only when official responsibility is set too low. On the other hand, if the profit after promotion is small, then bad governance always occurs except when the target level is low and official responsibility is set to the appropriate level. We have to be cautious because bad governance is not necessarily brought about by low environmental targets and less official responsibility. In other words, policies are not necessarily implemented well, even if environmental targets are higher or if officials are more responsible for their policy implementation.

3.5 Effects of the introduction of the RCR

In this section, we incorporate an additional promotion rule, the red card rule, into our framework. We add the following conditions:

- Let the environment standard be $\bar{G}$. If the environmental level becomes lower than the standard, then officials will be demoted in rank no matter how high the GDP level is.

- After demotion, officials have the lowest private benefit $\hat{R}$. Then, the profit after demotion becomes $\hat{\Pi} := W + \hat{R}$.

"Environmental target" and "environmental standard" are two distinct terms, defined as follows:

- An environmental target is the environmental level that is socially expected to be achieved.
- An environmental standard is the threshold of the environmental level at which officials are demoted in rank.

Formally, the expected profit of officials after the introduction of the RCR is expressed as follows:

$$\Pi\left(b_i^g; b_j^g\right) = \begin{cases} \Pi^N, & \Pi^N \geq \Pi^D \wedge G\left(b_i^g\right) \geq \overline{G} \\ \Pi^D, & \Pi^N < \Pi^D \wedge G\left(b_i^g\right) \geq \overline{G}. \\ \Pi, & G\left(b_i^g\right) < \overline{G} \end{cases}$$

As long as the environmental level satisfies the standard, the maximized profit is still decided at the Nash equilibrium or at the profit level with promotion abandonment. Figure 8.5 shows the effect of the introduction of RCR. For any level of responsibility, the environmental level never becomes lower than $\overline{G}$ because as soon as it becomes lower than the standard, the official will be demoted in rank and receive the lowest profit. This is an important function of the RCR, which guarantees the lowest environmental level determined as a standard.

The RCR has another important role. In the previous section, we said that the profit gap becomes important because it allows officials to have enough incentives to promote environmental improvement. Introducing the RCR enlarges the profit gap. By our definition, the magnitude of the relationship among profits with promotion, without promotion and with demotion is

$$W + \overline{R} > W + R\left(b_i^f\right) > W + \hat{R}.$$

The gap further increases as the lowest private benefit $\hat{R}$ decreases.

In Figure 8.5, a higher environmental target can also be achieved by adjusting official responsibility (point C is now on the solid line). This target achievement was impossible before introducing the RCR. The RCR enlarges the possible environmental-level area of control by adjusting official responsibility to point D. This additional role gives two further benefits when the upper government fails to set the responsibility correctly. Before introduction, if the error is nega-tive, then the environmental level becomes too low. However, in this case, the

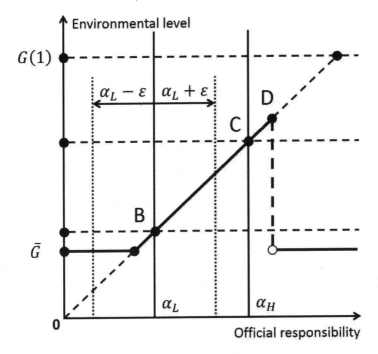

Figure 8.5 Effects of the red card rule

Table 8.2 Likelihood of bad governance with small and large profit following promotion after the introduction of the RCR

	Official responsibility				Official responsibility		
Environmental target	Small	Appropriate	Big	Environmental target	Small	Appropriate	Big
High — At least standard level				**High** — At least standard level			Bad governance
Low — At least standard level				**Low** — At least standard level			Bad governance

environmental level never becomes lower than the target level; therefore, the impacts of government failures are mitigated. Furthermore, because of the larger controllable area, it becomes unlikely that the positive error will exceed the threshold that causes officials to abandon environmental improvement. Bad governance happens only when the false extent of responsibility $\alpha_L + \varepsilon$ exceeds point D, whereas before introduction, the threshold is point A.

Table 8.2 summarizes the likelihood of bad governance after introducing the RCR. Three changes become evident. In both tables, even if bad governance arises because responsibility is too low, the resulting environmental level is at least at the standard level. Second, the environmental target can be achieved with appropriate levels of responsibility even if the profit after promotion is small. Third, although it does not appear in the table, the environmental target becomes more unlikely to exceed the threshold and result in bad governance as a result of inappropriate official responsibility in the case of small profit after promotion.

3.6 Use of the RCR as a reliable threat

We show that the RCR can reduce bad governance. However, bad governance still exists. In this section, we examine ways to completely reduce bad governance with two approaches. One way is by changing the level of the standard, and the other is by changing the level of $\hat{R}$.

The first approach is very simple and requires setting the standard to be equal to the target level. Then, the environmental level must be greater than the standard level, as far as the standard is within the controllable area. However, this does not enlarge the controllable area itself. After the environmental standard exceeds the controllable maximum, officials cannot choose a level without a standard. They have no incentives to achieve more than the standard or less than the standard. The left figure in Figure 8.6 expresses this situation. When setting the standard to $\bar{\bar{G}}$, official responsibility has little effect. This is similar to direct control. As such, an adjustment of the standard level can allow the achievement of any environmental target.

A second approach is to enlarge the controllable area. As we repeatedly noted, the profit gap critically affects the incentives in this tournament system. Thus, we can easily show that by maximally setting demotion (e.g., demoted to the lowest position), the profit gap is further enlarged. As a result, the area that is controllable by adjusting the official responsibility will also be enlarged and any environmental level can be achieved by controlling responsibility. Figure 8.6 shows this situation. All environmental levels greater than the standard are covered by the solid line. This

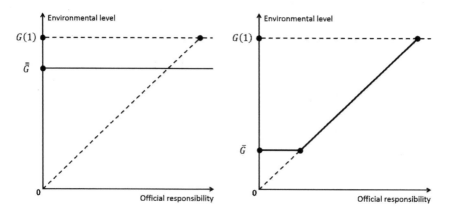

Figure 8.6 Red card rule with a sufficiently high standard

Table 8.3 Likelihood of bad governance with small and large profits after a promotion that follows the introduction of the RCR

		Official responsibility					Official responsibility		
		Small	Appropriate	Big			Small	Appropriate	Big
Environmental target	High	At least standard level				Environmental target	High	At least standard level		
	Low	At least standard level					Low	At least standard level		

is the third role of the RCR. The severity of the rule functions as a reliable threat to officials and gives them sufficient incentives to improve the environmental level.

Table 8.3 summarizes the results found in this section. Even when omitting the case with direct control, the RCR has the potential to further reduce bad governance. Appropriately setting the official responsibility can result in the achievement of any environmental target. False responsibility with a positive error no longer causes bad governance. False responsibly with a negative error is also avoidable by setting the standard as low as possible.

4 Concluding remarks

In this chapter, we examined the reasons why bad governance is often observed in the implementation of waste and recycling policies in China. The introduction of EPR will make producers shift their activities toward the production of more environmentally friendly processes and products. However, not only producers but also officials should be required to be somehow responsible for the results of their policy operations. In this sense, multiple extensions of responsibility are required in China.

Officials with less responsibility occasionally do not distribute sufficient funds to implement waste and recycling. However, it is more obvious that greater official responsibility also brings about bad governance. We showed that bad governance can be caused by variations in the mix of the level of environmental targets, the profit gap between the upper and lower governments, and a false setting for responsibility. We also showed that the RCR is a possible solution to such a situation. It is expected that introducing this rule to waste and recycling policies will result in less bad governance.

In 2011, the national council reported two important developments. First, as a reform proposal to achieve green growth, the council approved the expansion of fiscal expenditures for use in achieving appropriate personnel appointments and for the appropriate allocation of financial resources. Second, it introduced the RCR for environmental protection as an important basis for the selection of officials. If officials cannot achieve the given environmental targets, then the central government may temporarily stop the examination of the budget except for civilian projects, energy saving, environmental protection, and infrastructure construction. Moreover, the council now holds the officials responsible for leadership. This social atmosphere will encourage the introduction of the RCR to waste and recycling policies.

Finally, our analysis still has some problems, and various expansions are left for future studies. We shall mention two especially important expansions. First, our analytical framework only considers general environmental policy and does not much specify waste and recycling polices. Therefore, by incorporating a specific feature of waste and recycling policies in China, our study will provide further insights into the discussion of bad governance in the implementation of waste and recycling policies. Secondly, our analysis is limited within an analytical approach and does not contain any quantitative analysis with actual data. Available data are now increasing. A quantitative examination of our results will also provide more detailed insights.

Notes

1 Because it does not have a hierarchical structure, our economic model is closer to a rank-order tournament model than it is to an elimination tournament model. See Sawada and Xu (2014) for an explanation of the political selection tournament system with a hierarchical structure.
2 See Sawada and Xu (2014) for details on this derivation.

References

Li, H. and L. Zhou (2005) "Political turnover and economic performance: the incentive role of personnel control in China," *Journal of Public Economics*, Vol. 89, pp. 1743–1762.

Rosen, S. (1986) "Prizes and incentives in elimination tournaments," *The American Economic Review*, Vol. 76, No. 4, pp. 701–715.

Saito, T., E. Sawada, and K. Sato (2015) "Home appliance recycling system to promote resource circulation," *Review of Environmental Economic Studies*, Vol. 8, No. 1, pp. 103–106.

Sawada, E. and Y. Xu (2014) "Environmental policy decisions incentives and the possibility of environmental improvements," *Public Governance Review*, No. 2, pp. 24–36.

Xu, Y. (2014) *Economic Growth and Land-Debt Problem of China: Between the Public Finance System, the Government with Competition and Adjustment*, Keio University Press, Tokyo.

9 Evaluating future end-of-life household appliances

Time-series material flow analysis and impact assessment

Jun Nakatani

Background

Significance of estimation of future waste quantities and impact assessment of waste

To establish a household appliance disposal and recycling strategy, it is required to accurately estimate changes in the types and quantities of end-of-life appliances that will be disposed from homes and offices in the present through the future. Note that periods of time from their procurement (demand occurrence) to disposal are not constant, and future demands for every product cannot be predetermined. In countries that have a high population and have shown significant improvement in living standard levels corresponding with economic development, quantities of disposed products are expected to increase significantly in the future as demands for products continue to increase. However, the aforementioned conditions prevent us from accurately predicting future quantities of disposed products by only observing the statistical data obtained thus far. Therefore, we need an effective tool that numerically estimates the future waste quantities (i.e., quantities of end-of-life products) by modeling the product lifetime, including the occurrence of demand, a period of use, and product disposal.

While studying the proper disposal and recycling of consumer durables such as household appliances, note that their characteristics differ from those of food waste, containers, and packaging waste. Since consumables such as foods, containers, and packaging have short periods of time from their procurement to disposal (i.e., they have a short product lifespan), production, procurement, consumption, and disposal of these products will occur at nearly the same time. Owing to these characteristics, the changes in waste quantities of consumables are predictable as long as the changes in demand and ratio of disposal can be estimated. Conversely, consumer durables have a longer product lifespan, with time lags of several years or a few decades between their production/procurement and disposal. Another difficulty estimating waste quantities is that the product lifetime varies among consumers even if the same type of consumer durables is used. To estimate the quantities of disposed consumer durables, a more sophisticated analysis method is required that is based on the product demand from the past to the future on a multidecadal scale and product lifespan distribution.

Some consumer durables can be utilized as secondary resources if they are recycled at the end of their lifetimes. However, note that improper processing of components containing toxic substances such as metals can have adverse impacts on human health and the ecosystem if these substances are released into air, water, or soil. Therefore, a simple prediction of waste quantities is insufficient for planning a proper control and recycling. Such evaluation should consider the content of materials or substances contained in products that will be eventually disposed, although these materials can differ among products depending on their production year. Every material or substance needs to be assessed to determine its potential value as a resource as well as to determine its toxicity. Then, more realistic measures would be proposed for the development and introduction of disposal and recycling technologies to control and/or recover those materials. In particular, to enhance recovery of secondary resources as well as lower the environmental impacts of waste from the medium- to long-term perspective, a strategic recycling system must be established. As the basis for planning such a system, it is necessary to estimate the quantities of disposed end-of-life products on a multidecadal scale, and to assess and analyze quantities of secondary resources that could be recovered from waste and the potential impacts of toxic substances on human health and the ecosystem in the medium- to long-term future.

Objectives of this chapter

As stated above, it is important to numerically evaluate the maximum effect of resource recovery and recycling in the future with quantitative indicators so that the recycling will not become an end in itself. In this chapter, household appliances among various consumer durables are selected as objects to investigate the method and framework for assessing and analyzing the potential impacts of waste from both viewpoints of resource availability and toxicity. Results of the assessment and analysis presented herein can serve as fundamental data to establish a strategic recycling system. To help further understanding the analysis method, a case study of a television (TV) set disposal in China is described by referring to the study by Habuer et al. (2014).

This chapter is composed as follows. We describe analytical tools applicable to the estimation of waste quantities in the future and impact assessment, and introduces existing studies that applied these tools in the next section. The method and procedure used in the estimation and assessment are further described in the later part of this chapter using the study of TV set disposal in China. We describe the estimation of quantities of end-of-life products in the medium- to long-term perspective. Then we discuss the impact assessment of recovered secondary resources on the resource availability, and the potential toxicity of the substances contained in household appliances. Finally, issues remaining in the estimation/assessment method are discussed.

Analytical tools

Analytical tools to estimate future waste quantities

Material flow analysis (MFA) is applicable for estimating the quantities of waste. MFA either physically or calorimetrically analyzes the input of resources from the ecosphere into the economic sphere, the flow of materials and products in the economic sphere, and the emission of substances from the economic sphere into the ecosphere. The analysis method can be called product flow analysis (PFA) when it is used to analyze the flow at the product level, substance flow analysis (SFA) when it is used to analyze the flow at the element level, and material stock analysis (MSA) or material flow and stock analysis (MFSA) when the estimation of stock in the economic sphere is part of the analysis. All these analytical tools have a fundamental concept in common. In the case of consumer durables with long product lifespans and time lags between their production/procurement and disposal, the analysis covers periods of several years to a few decades. This type of MFA in which the elapse of time is included is sometimes called time-series MFA (Habuer et al., 2014).

Numerous MFA studies have selected electrical and electronic equipment, including household appliances from consumer durables, as targets of analysis. In Japan, survey and analysis of substance flow in waste treatment processes (such as disassembly, crushing, and separation processes) have been reported regarding 55 types of metals contained in electrical and electronic equipment (Oguchi et al., 2012). In the United States, MFA has been conducted for personal computers (PCs) and TV sets, focusing on the technology transition in the market until 2030 (Lam et al., 2013). Some studies have estimated the quantities of end-of-life household appliances in China in the medium- to long-term future (Liu et al., 2006; Zhang et al., 2011, 2012; Habuer et al., 2014).

Analytical tools to assess the resource and toxicity impacts of waste

The impact assessment or characterization methods developed for life cycle assessment (LCA) are applicable for assessing the resource impacts of recovery and recycling of secondary resources and the toxicity impacts of substances emitted into the environment. The international standards for LCA (i.e., ISO 14040: 2006 and ISO 14044: 2006) mandate that the phases of goal and scope definition and life cycle inventory (LCI) analysis are followed by the life cycle impact assessment (LCIA) phase, which is "aimed at understanding and evaluating the magnitude and significance of the potential environmental impacts for a product system throughout the life cycle of the product".

This LCI analysis, as with MFA described above, is the phase in which the material flow is analyzed. LCI analysis differs from MFA in that the entire flow in the product life cycle of interest, including the input of energy and auxiliary materials, is analyzed retroactively, taking into account the input of natural resources from the ecosphere to the economic sphere and the emission of pollutants from the economic sphere to the ecosphere (i.e., elementary flow). On the other hand, the objectives of LCIA are to assess the impacts on the ecosphere imposed by the extraction of natural resources from the ecosphere and the emission of pollutants into the ecosphere. Given these characteristics of the analytical tools, it is reasonable to apply LCIA to the quantities of accumulated and recovered resources as well as emitted substances estimated using MFA. Therefore, this approach can be used for assessing the potential resource and toxicity impacts of waste by focusing on substances contained in the product.

Since the early 1990s, various LCIA methods have been developed, mainly in Europe, the United States, and Japan. Almost all impact assessment methods consider resource depletion or resource consumption as an impact category. Several methods distinguish mineral resources and fossil resources (or fossil fuels) as different impact categories. Characterization models differ among methods. A typical midpoint approach is the CML, 2002 (Guinée 2002), in which the reserves of every resource are used in the characterization, whereas a typical endpoint approach is the Eco-indicator 99 (Goedkoop and Spriensma, 2001), in which surplus energy that would be required for the future extraction of every resource is used in the characterization. ReCiPe, 2008 (Goedkoop et al., 2013; ReCiPe HP) is the most recently published method among dominant LCIA methods in Europe. In this method, the endpoint impact category of resources is considered as resource availability and its indicator is the surplus cost (in USD). Damages caused by resource extraction are assessed as the future increase in social costs. It is conceivable that an assessment method with such an economic indicator has certain significance in the study of a strategic recycling system in that the introduction of such an indicator enables the comparison of social costs with recovery/recycling costs.

In the same framework of the LCIA methods as the resource depletion is analyzed, it is also possible to assess the impacts that emissions of various substances (e.g., metals) into the air, water, and soil has on human toxicity and ecotoxicity. In ReCiPe, 2008, human toxicity and ecotoxicity are characterized based on the damage respective to human health and ecosystem diversity as the endpoints (Goedkoop et al., 2013; ReCiPe, HP).

Previous studies have used the LCIA methods to examine the resource and toxicity impacts of metals contained in end-of-life household appliances. Lim and Schoenung (2010) used the characterization factors in the TRACI (Bare et al., 2002; U.S. EPA, HP), which was developed by the United States Environmental Protection Agency (U.S. EPA), for estimating the potential adverse effects of heavy metals used in liquid crystal display (LCD) TV sets, monitors, laptop computers, and plasma TV sets on human health in terms of carcinogenic and noncarcinogenic impacts and on ecotoxicity. Lam et al. (2013) used the characterization factor in the USEtox model (Rosenbaum et al., 2008; Hauschild et al., 2011) to estimate the potential adverse impacts of heavy metals on human health in terms of carcinogenic and noncarcinogenic impacts and on ecotoxicity. The effects of waste treatment processes (such as disassembly, crushing, and separation processes) of household appliances in China have also been studied on multiple impact categories, including resource depletion, human toxicity, and ecotoxicity, using the LCIA methods (CML, 2002 and Eco-indicator 99) developed in the Netherlands (Song et al., 2013).

Time-series material flow analysis

Parameter projection to estimate future waste quantities

The first step in the analysis is to project changes in parameters that are used to estimate the number of domestic sales and disposals of household appliances in the medium- to long-term future. The parameters include changes in the number of households, household appliance possessions, lifespan distribution, and penetration rates for the types of products or technologies in the region or nation of interest. The estimation of parameters described in this chapter is relative to cathode ray tube (CRT) and flat panel display (FPD) TV sets in China for the period 1995–2030. The parameter projection process consists of the following four steps.

Projection of the number of households in urban and rural areas

Obviously, the number of household appliance possessions in an area of interest largely depends on the number of households in the area. Although it is difficult to accurately estimate the number of households in the future, it is possible to easily make a reasonable estimation on the basis of the publicly available population projection if the average number of people in a household can be calculated. Note that the possession rate of household appliances differs between urban and rural areas owing to differences in household economic levels; this is especially true in emerging countries. Therefore, separate estimations must be conducted in urban and rural areas.

For calculating the number of households in urban and rural areas in China until 2010, the data were obtained from the China Statistical Yearbook (NMBC, 1995–2010) in terms of population in urban and rural areas every year, household size (i.e., average number of people in a family household) excluding single-person households, and the number of single-person and family households every 10 years. It was assumed that 75 percent of households are families in urban areas. In addition, urban and rural population projections (IIASA HP) in 2020 and 2030, shown in Scenario B2 of the Greenhouse Gas Initiative (GGI), were used to project the number of households in urban and rural areas until 2030 (Figure 9.1). In this projection, it was assumed that the average number in a family would not change from that reported in 2010. The number of households in rural areas is estimated to decrease owing to urbanization of the rural areas and outflow of rural population into urban areas, although the total number of households in China is expected to increase until 2030.

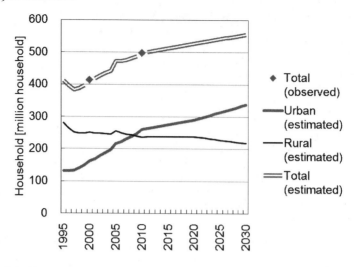

Figure 9.1 Changes in the number of households projected in urban and rural areas in China.

Note: Observed data adapted from NMBC (1995–2010)

Estimation of the number of TV set possessions in urban and rural areas

In the second step, the household appliance ownership rate is estimated. Note that the ownership rate in this chapter is defined as the ratio of the total number of appliances in the area of interest to the total number of households in the area, rather than the ratio of households possessing appliances to the total number of households. Nonetheless, Equation (1) proposed by Tasaki et al. (2001) and Liu et al. (2006) can be used to estimate future possessions.

$$p(t) = p_{max} / \left(1 - b_0 \cdot e^{-b_1 \cdot (t - t_0)} \right) \tag{1}$$

$p(t)$: Ownership rate at the end of year t [unit/household]
p_{max}: Maximum ownership rate [unit/household]
b_0, b_1: Estimated parameters

Using this equation, the parameters are estimated on the basis of observed data of the ownership rate in urban and rural areas until 2010 obtained from NMBC (1995–2010); the ownership rate in China until 2030 is then calculated (Figure 9.2). The least-squares method is used for the parameter estimation, and the maximum ownership rate is given as an a priori condition. In this estimation, the saturation level of the ownership rate in Nanjing (Zhang et al., 2011), 1.496 unit/household, is used as the maximum ownership rate both in urban and rural areas.

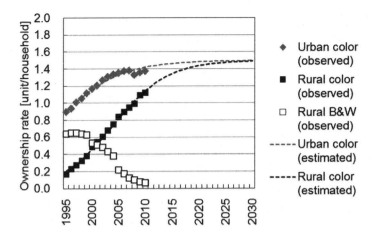

Figure 9.2 Changes in ownership rates of TV sets in urban and rural areas in China.
Note: Observed data adapted from NMBC (1995–2010)

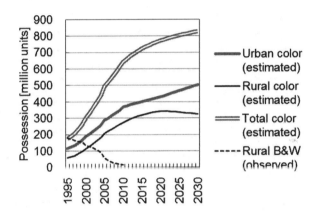

Figure 9.3 Changes in the number of TV set possessions in urban and rural areas in China

The total number of TV set possessions in urban and rural areas (Figure 9.3) was obtained by multiplying the estimated ownership rates by the number of households in the areas (see Figure 9.1). The ratio of the number of black-and-white TV sets in 2010 is small, approximately 6 percent in rural areas, when compared with the number of color TV sets. Therefore, only color TV sets are analyzed in the remainder of this chapter.

Lifespan distribution of TV sets

In the third step, the distribution of the lifespans of household appliances of interest is estimated. The Weibull distribution expressed by Equation (2), which has been discussed in papers reported by Tasaki et al. (2001, 2004) and Oguchi et al. (2006, 2008, 2010), is applicable to the distribution estimation. The average lifespan and the parameter are estimated using the least-squares method such that the difference between the number of TV set possessions estimated from the number of domestic sales, using Equation (4), and that estimated above can be minimized.

$$W(y) = 1 - \exp\left[-\left(\frac{y}{\bar{y}}\right)^b \left\{\Gamma\left(1 + \frac{1}{b}\right)\right\}^b\right] \tag{2}$$

$W(y)$: Cumulative distribution function of Weibull distribution
$\bar{y}$: Average lifespan [year]
b: Estimated parameter

Using this estimation method, the lifespan distribution of TV sets in China was determined. The survival probability of TV sets (i.e., the ratio of the number of appliances not yet disposed to the number of appliances that have been procured) as well as that of other household appliances is estimated and shown in Figure 9.4. It is assumed that the lifespan distribution is unchanged through 2030. Note that in the analysis in this chapter, it is assumed that the lifespan distribution of CRT TV sets is identical to that of FPD TV sets.

Ratio of CRT and FPD TV set production

In recent years, TV technology has progressed from old type (i.e., CRT) to new type (i.e., FPD). Therefore, the impact of recovered secondary resources on the resource availability and the potential toxicity of the substances contained in the disposed products are assessed by taking into consideration the changes in

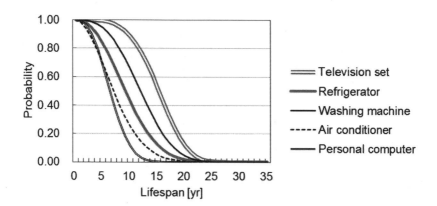

Figure 9.4 Survival probability of household appliances in China

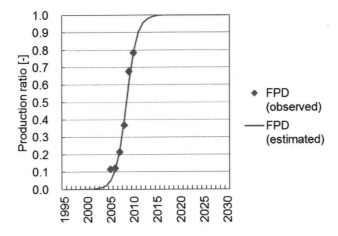

Figure 9.5 Changes in ratio of FPD TV set production to the total TV set production in China

penetration for each type of TV sets. In this estimation, the penetration rate in terms of production and sales is considered.

The ratio of FPD TV set production to the total TV set production in China was estimated for the period 1995–2030 (Figure 9.5). This ratio was based on the observed data of CRT and FPD TV set production between 2005 and 2010 (Yearbook of China Information Industry, 1995–2010). The logistic regression expressed by Equation (3) is applied to the ratio of FPD TV set production.

$$r(t) = \exp(b_0 + b_0 \cdot t) / \{1 + \exp(b_0 + b_0 \cdot t)\} \tag{3}$$

$r(t)$: Ratio of new type production in the year t (number of FPD TV sets/total number of TV sets in production)
t: Year ($t = 0$: 2000)
b_0, b_1: Estimated parameters

Assuming that the ratio of CRT TV sets and FPD TV sets in production is identical for domestic sales, the ratio of the number of domestic sales of CRT TV sets to that of FPD TV sets (Figure 9.6) can be estimated. Furthermore, the penetration rate of CRT and FPD TV sets (i.e., the number of CRT and FPD TV sets/total number of TV set possession) can be estimated using the lifespan distribution expressed by Equation (2).

Estimation of quantities of end-of-life household appliances

In this step, the flow of materials in the medium- to long-term future is analyzed at the product and element levels using the parameters estimated above. That is,

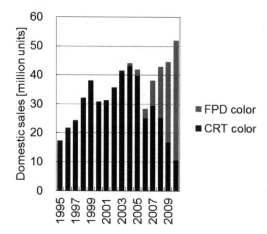

Figure 9.6 Changes in the number of domestic sales of CRT and FPD TV sets in China

the number of household appliance sales and that of disposed end-of-life household appliances in the future are estimated, and the quantities of accumulated and recoverable materials are then calculated on the basis of the content of various materials contained in the appliances. The number of domestic sales and disposals of CRT and FPD TV sets as well as accumulated and recoverable quantities for 15 types of metals were analyzed in China until 2030.

Number of domestic sales and disposals of CRT and FPD TV sets

Thus far, the number of end-of-life TV sets can be estimated as the flow of materials at the product level on the basis of the number of domestic sales from the past to the present; the ratio of CRT and FPD TV set production and lifespan distribution. The number of domestic sales and disposals of TV sets in the future can be calculated by successively applying Equation (4) to the number of TV set possessions for each year estimated above.

$$P(t) = P(t-1) + S(t) - D(t) \tag{4}$$

$P(t)$: Number of possessions at the end of year t [million units]
$S(t)$: Number of domestic sales in the year t [million units]
$D(t)$: Number of disposals in the year t [million units]

The number of domestic sales of color TV sets in China until 2010 was calculated from the number of production and the number of imported/exported TV sets (NMBC, 1995–2010; GAC, 2005–2010). On the basis of this observed data of the number of domestic sales, the ratio of CRT and FPD TV set production,

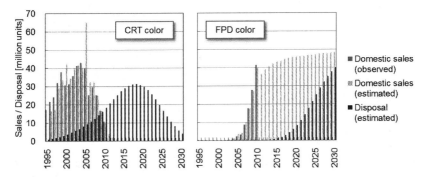

Figure 9.7 Changes in the number of domestic sales and disposals of TV sets in China

and lifespan distribution of TV sets, the number of domestic sales and disposals of TV sets every year until 2030 were estimated (Figure 9.7).

Quantities of accumulated and recoverable metals contained in CRT and FPD TV sets

Quantities of the accumulated and potentially recoverable materials (i.e., the total weights of every materials contained in end-of-life household appliances) can be estimated as the flow of materials at the element level. To this end, the content of various materials and the number of domestic sales and disposals of appliances estimated from Equation (4) are used. As reported by Habuer et al. (2014), it is effective to use the weight of each component of household appliances and the content of materials in each component for the estimation. Tables 9.1 and 9.2 show examples of the weights of components of various appliances and those of materials, including 15 types of metals (Al, Fe, Co, Ni, Cu, Zn, Sr, Pd, Ag, Sn, Sb, Ba, Au, Pb, and Bi), respectively.

The accumulated and potentially recoverable quantities of the above 15 types of metals contained in TV sets sold domestically in China were estimated using their content in CRT and FPD TV sets shown in Tables 9.1 and 9.2. The content of these metals in FPD TV sets was estimated on the basis of every component of LCD TV sets. Changes in accumulated and recoverable metallic element weights of the six heaviest metals are shown in Figure 9.8.

Resource Impact Assessment

Characterization of resource availability in ReCiPe, 2008

Using the resource characterization method developed in LCIA studies, it is possible to assess the potential reduction in social costs by recovering and recycling the secondary resources estimated in the previous section, assuming that the total weights of every materials contained in the disposed end-of-life products

Table 9.1 Weights of various components of household appliances

	CRT TV	PDP TV	LCD TV	Desktop PC	Laptop PC
Ferrous material	127	295	461	474	96
Aluminum material	1	133	41	0	12
Copper cable and material	39	10	9	9	5
Other non-ferrous material	10	8	2	0	0
Unidentified metallic material	60	0	0	0	65
Plastic casing and other plastic parts	179	99	259	28	270
CRT printed circuit board	71	0	0	0	0
LCD printed circuit board	0	65	97	90	143
CRT panel glass	244	0	0	0	0
CRT funnel glass	131	0	0	0	0
LCD outer glass	0	112	55	56	134
LCD inner glass	0	235	42	0	0
Drives	0	0	0	164	0
Battery	0	0	0	0	135
Cold Cathode Fluorescent Lamps	0	0	9	0	1
Others	139	43	26	179	141

PDP: plasma display panel; LCD: liquid crystal display
Units: [g/kg]

Table 9.2 Weights of materials contained in various components of household appliances

	Al	Fe	Co	Ni	Cu	Zn	Sr	Pd	Ag	Sn	Sb	Ba	Au	Pb	Bi	Plastic
Ferrous material	0	1,000	0	0	0	0	0	0	0	0	0	0	0	0	0	0
Aluminum material	1,000	0	0	0	0	0	0	0	0	0	0	0	0	0	0	0
Copper cable and material	0	0	0	0	1,000	0	0	0	0	0	0	0	0	0	0	0
Other non-ferrous material	0	0	0	0	0	0	0	0	0	0	0	0	0	0	0	0
Unidentified metallic material	0	0	0	0	0	0	0	0	0	0	0	0	0	0	0	0
Plastic casing and other plastic parts	0	0	0	0	0	0	0	0	0	0	0	0	0	0	0	1,000
CRT printed circuit board	62	34	0	3	72	5	1	0	0	18	3	2	0	14	0	0
LCD printed circuit board	63	49	0	0	10	20	0	0	0	29	0	0	0	1	0	0
CRT panel glass	11	1	0	0	0	3	74	0	0	0	3	79	0	0	0	0
CRT funnel glass	18	1	0	0	0	1	5	0	0	0	2	3	0	215	0	0
LCD outer glass	0	0	0	0	0	0	0	0	0	0	0	0	0	0	0	0
LCD inner glass	0	0	0	0	0	0	0	0	0	0	0	0	0	0	0	1,000
Drives	0	0	0	0	0	0	0	0	0	0	0	0	0	0	0	0
Battery	0	0	0	0	0	0	0	0	0	0	0	0	0	0	0	0
Cold Cathode Fluorescent Lamps	0	0	0	0	0	0	0	0	0	0	0	0	0	0	0	0
Others	0	0	0	0	0	0	0	0	0	0	0	0	0	0	0	0

Units: [g/kg]

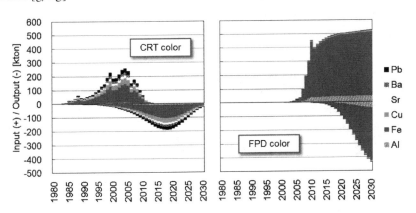

Figure 9.8 Changes in weights of accumulated (input) and recoverable (output) metallic elements contained in TV sets in China

have been recovered. As described above, various models are used to characterize resource depletion or consumption. This chapter describes the characterization factors of resource availability, which is proposed in ReCiPe, (2008; Goedkoop et al., 2013), the most recently published LCIA method in Europe.

In this model, the damage to resource availability (i.e., surplus cost) is defined as "the additional net present costs that society has to pay as a result of an extraction" or "the increased cost for future extractions" (Goedkoop et al., 2013). The practical interpretation is that the consequence of extracting 1 kg of a commodity will cause a cost to society equivalent to its characterization factor. The impact category at the midpoint level associated with the resource availability (endpoint) consists of mineral resource depletion and fossil fuel depletion in indicator units of [kg Fe eq] and [kg oil eq], respectively. Both midpoint indicators are presented as the ratio of the endpoint characterization factor to that of iron (Fe) or oil for every resource type, and the characterization models of the midpoints are identical to those of the endpoint. Therefore, the characterization at only the endpoint level is described in this chapter.

The characterization model of mineral resources follows these steps (Goedkoop et al., 2013): (i) A marginal increase in yield [$] caused by an extraction of a deposit results in a marginal lower grade [$/kg] of the deposit. (ii) A marginal decrease in grade [$/kg] results in extra mining cost [$/kg]. (iii) The marginal cost increase on deposit level [($/$)/$] is calculated by combining the step (i) and (ii). (iv) The average weighted yield of the cost increase of all deposits that contribute to the production of the commodity is calculated. (v) The marginal cost increase on commodity level [($/$)/$] is converted using the value of the commodity and expressed for a mass extraction. Thus, the characterization factor is obtained as expressed by Equation (5).

$$CF_c = \sum_t \left(MCI_c \cdot P_c \cdot \frac{1}{(1+r)^t} \right) \tag{5}$$

CF_c: Characterization factor of commodity c for mineral resource depletion [$/kg]
MCI_c: Marginal cost increase due to extracting commodity c
P_c: Annually produced amount of commodity c [kg/year]
r: Discount rate (3 percent/year)

Among the 15 types of metals shown in Table 9.2, the characterization factors of 11 metal types for resource availability are calculated in ReCiPe, (2008). The characterization factors of those 11 types of metals are listed in Table 9.3. For

Table 9.3 Endpoint characterization factors of metals for resource availability

	MDP [$/kg]		MDP [$/kg]		MDP [$/kg]
Al	$6.44 \cdot 10^{-3}$	Cu	$3.05 \cdot 10^0$	Sn	$9.09 \cdot 10^1$
Fe	$7.15 \cdot 10^{-2}$	Zn	$1.61 \cdot 10^{-1}$	Au	$5.00 \cdot 10^3$
Co	$7.22 \cdot 10^{-2}$	Pd	$2.73 \cdot 10^2$	Pb	$1.26 \cdot 10^{-1}$
Ni	$8.96 \cdot 10^{-1}$	Ag	$2.05 \cdot 10^1$		

MDP: mineral depletion potential
Note: Adapted from ReCiPe (HP).

example, the characterization factor of Fe (0.07 \$/kg) indicates that the future increase in social costs caused by extraction of 1 kg of Fe is equivalent to \$0.07 of the present value when a discount rate of 3 percent is used.

Assessment of potential reduction in social costs by recovery of secondary resources

In this estimation, the characterization factors [\$/kg] of metals for extraction in each year from the past to the future was calculated by discounting the factors listed in Table 9.3 using the discount rate of 3 percent. For every metal type, the characterization factor is multiplied by the accumulated quantity in each year. Then, the product of each metal is summed to estimate the social cost increase due to the extraction of primary resources needed to produce and sell the household appliances every year. The potential reduction in social costs due to recovery of secondary resources from end-of-life household appliances can also be estimated by summing the products of the characterization factors and the quantities of recoverable metals. Figure 9.9 shows the increase in social costs (bars in the positive direction) due to the primary resource extraction for domestic sales of CRT and FPD TV sets in China as well as the potential reduction in social costs (bars in negative direction) due to the resource recovery from the end-of-life TV sets.

The increase and reduction in social costs shown in Figure 9.9 are allocated to the year when the factor contributing to the increase or reduction (i.e., domestic sales or resource recovery) occurs. Thus, note that the timing of this increase or reduction calculation is different from the timing at which the extraction cost actually increases.

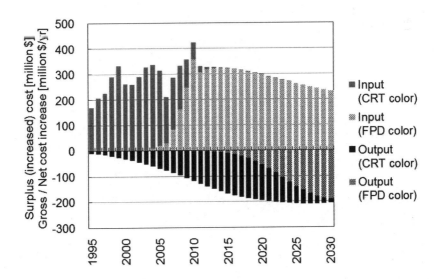

Figure 9.9 Increase and reduction in social costs due to domestic sales of TV sets and secondary resources recovered from end-of-life TV sets in China

As shown in the figure, CRT TV sets contributed to the social cost increase until around 2005. Beginning at around 2010, FPD TV sets had a higher contribution to the social cost increase, whereas CRT TV sets largely contributed to the reduction in social costs through recovery of secondary resources until around 2015. The impact of primary resource extraction due to TV set production and sales gradually diminished in around 2010 and thereafter because the discount rate is applied to the future resource extraction. On the other hand, as the number of end-of-life TV sets increases (see Figure 9.7), the potential reduction in social costs will reach its peak in 2027. Thus, it can be estimated that the reduction in social costs (maximum effects) by recovery of secondary resources from TV sets disposed in China will reach the same level as that of the increase in social costs due to TV set production and sales around 2030.

Toxicity impact assessment

Characterization of human toxicity and ecotoxicity in ReCiPe (2008)

The impact categories associated with metals emitted into the environment include human toxicity and ecotoxicity. ReCiPe (2008) classifies ecotoxicity as terrestrial, freshwater, and marine impacts. Human toxicity and ecotoxicity are related to the endpoints as damage to human health and ecosystem diversity, respectively. Damage to human health includes mortality and morbidity, whereas damage to ecosystem diversity is represented by the loss of species. Because the magnitude of the toxicity impact varies among initial emission compartments (air, water, and soil), the characterization factors are calculated for each compartment. Among the 15 types of metals shown in Table 9.2, the characterization factors of 9 metal types for human toxicity and ecotoxicity are calculated in ReCiPe (2008). The characterization factors of those 9 types of metals emitted into soil are listed in Table 9.4.

Table 9.4 Endpoint characterization factors of metals emitted into soil for human toxicity and ecotoxicity

	HTP 100 [DALY/kg]	TETP 100 [species.yr/kg]	FETP 100 [species.yr/kg]	METP 100 [species.yr/kg]
Co	0	$2.59 \cdot 10^{-6}$	$1.09 \cdot 10^{-8}$	$5.81 \cdot 10^{-10}$
Ni	$6.12 \cdot 10^{-7}$	$1.61 \cdot 10^{-6}$	$4.58 \cdot 10^{-9}$	$5.39 \cdot 10^{-10}$
Cu	$6.19 \cdot 10^{-8}$	$2.57 \cdot 10^{-6}$	$1.77 \cdot 10^{-9}$	$9.86 \cdot 10^{-11}$
Zn	$1.89 \cdot 10^{-6}$	$7.80 \cdot 10^{-7}$	$2.33 \cdot 10^{-10}$	$1.33 \cdot 10^{-11}$
Ag	$5.53 \cdot 10^{-4}$	$1.55 \cdot 10^{-4}$	$4.78 \cdot 10^{-8}$	$4.47 \cdot 10^{-9}$
Sn	$1.27 \cdot 10^{-8}$	$4.24 \cdot 10^{-8}$	$5.72 \cdot 10^{-12}$	$4.61 \cdot 10^{-13}$

(*Continued*)

Table 9.4 (Continued)

	HTP 100 [DALY/kg]	TETP 100 [species.yr/kg]	FETP 100 [species.yr/kg]	METP 100 [species.yr/kg]
Sb	$1.42 \cdot 10^{-4}$	$6.37 \cdot 10^{-7}$	$2.76 \cdot 10^{-9}$	$3.44 \cdot 10^{-10}$
Ba	$4.03 \cdot 10^{-5}$	$1.03 \cdot 10^{-7}$	$6.57 \cdot 10^{-10}$	$8.52 \cdot 10^{-11}$
Pb	$1.62 \cdot 10^{-6}$	$3.01 \cdot 10^{-9}$	$1.11 \cdot 10^{-12}$	$8.70 \cdot 10^{-14}$

HTP 100: Human Toxicity Potential (100-yr time horizon)
TETP 100: Terrestrial Ecotoxicity Potential (100-yr time horizon)
FETP 100: Freshwater Ecotoxicity Potential (100-yr time horizon)
METP 100: Marine Ecotoxicity Potential (100-yr time horizon)
Characterization factors are not available for Pd, Au and Bi.

Note: Adapted from ReCiPe (HP).

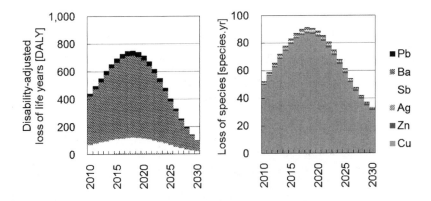

Figure 9.10 Changes in potential magnitudes of human toxicity and ecotoxicity of TV sets disposed in China

Assessment of potential human toxicity and ecotoxicity caused by metals contained in end-of-life household appliances

This section assesses potential human toxicity and ecotoxicity due to disposal of household appliances using the endpoint characterization factors in ReCiPe (2008), assuming that all the metals contained in end-of-life household appliances are emitted into the environment. In this assessment, the characterization factors for soil emission (Table 9.4) are used because most of the metals contained in electrical and electronic equipment will eventually be landfilled during the waste treatment process (Lim and Schoenung, 2010; Oguchi et al., 2012). Moreover, the metal content in end-of-life TV sets is same as the recoverable quantities estimated above. The potential magnitudes of the impacts on human toxicity and ecotoxicity of disposals of TV sets in China are assessed every year (Figure 9.10) by multiplying the characterization factors by the content of various metals contained in TV sets followed by summing the products of all the metals.

This assessment revealed that barium (Ba) causes the most damage to human health and copper (Cu) causes the most damage to ecosystem diversity. The magnitudes of human toxicity and ecotoxicity will reach their peaks in 2018, matching the peak of disposals of CRT TV sets (see Figure 9.7). The contents of Ba and Cu contained in FPD TV sets are less than those in CRT TV sets (see Figure 9.8). Thus, changes in potential human toxicity and ecotoxicity depend on the quantities of end-of-life CRT TV sets.

Discussion

One issue that remains in the estimation method described in this chapter is that improvement, or at least sensitivity analysis, is needed in the reliability of the average lifespans used to estimate the lifespan distribution and the saturation levels used to estimate the ownership rates of household appliances. In addition, various characterization models and factors have been proposed to assess the resource impacts in LCIA studies. Therefore, it is necessary to investigate the degree to which the assessment will be affected by the choice of characterization methods.

Note that the quantities of recoverable materials and the reduction in social costs were calculated under the assumption that all metals contained in end-of-life household appliances are recovered as secondary resources. In other words, the recoverable quantities and the social cost reduction estimated in this chapter are the maximum expected values. Similarly, the potential magnitudes of human toxicity and ecotoxicity were calculated under the assumption that all metals are emitted into the environment, including soil; these magnitudes are also the maximum expected values. Thus, the potential magnitudes of toxicity impacts and the quantities of recoverable materials are mutually exclusive events because the metals recovered as secondary resources will not be emitted into the environment. To resolve or mitigate this contradicting situation, it is necessary to establish scenarios of the material flows in the recovery, fixation, and emission of metals contained in end-of-life household appliances, including the ratio of metals disposed through landfilling or fixation under proper controls. Such scenarios should be technically feasible in present and future waste treatment and recycling processes for end-of-life household appliances.

Acknowledgements

This research was supported by the Environment Research and Technology Development Fund from Ministry of the Environment, Japan (3K123002), and a Grant-in-Aid for Young Scientists (B) from the Japan Society for the Promotion of Science (No. 26820220).

References

Bare, J.C., G.A. Norris, D.W. Pennington, and T. McKone (2002) "TRACI: The tool for the reduction and assessment of chemical and other environmental impacts," *Journal of Industrial Ecology*, Vol. 6, No. 3, pp. 49–78.

GAC: General Administration of Customs (2005–2010) *China Custom Statistical Yearbook 2005–2010*. China Customs Press, Beijing.

Goedkoop, M., R. Heijungs, M. Huijbregts, A. De Schryver, J. Struijs, and R. Van Zelm (2013) *ReCiPe 2008. A Life Cycle Impact Assessment Method Which Comprises Harmonised Category Indicators at the Midpoint and the Endpoint Level, First edition, revised*, Report I: Characterisation. Ministry of Housing, Spatial Planning and Environment (VROM), Den Haag.

Goedkoop, M. and R. Spriensma (2001) *The Eco-Indicator 99. A Damage Oriented Method for Life Cycle Impact Assessment. Methodology Report*, Third edition. PRé Consultants, Amersfoort.

Guinée, J.B., ed. (2002) *Handbook on Life Cycle Assessment. Operational Guide to the ISO Standards*, Kluwer Academic Publishers, Dordrecht.

Habuer, J. Nakatani, and Y. Moriguchi (2014) "Time-series product and substance flow analyses of end-of-life electrical and electronic equipment in China," *Waste Management*, Vol. 34, No. 2, pp. 489–497.

Hauschild, M.Z., O. Jolliet, and M.A.J. Huijbregts (2011) "A bright future for addressing chemical emissions in life cycle assessment," *International Journal of Life Cycle Assessment*, Vol. 16, No. 8, pp. 697–700.

IIASA: International Institute for Applied Systems Analysis (HP) GGI scenario database version 2.0.1. Retrieved from http://webarchive.iiasa.ac.at/Research/GGI/DB/index.html/?sb=5

Lam, C.W., S.R. Lim, and J.M. Schoenung (2013) "Linking material flow analysis with environmental impact potential: Dynamic technology transition effects on projected E-waste in the United States," *Journal of Industrial Ecology*, Vol. 17, No. 2, pp. 299–309.

Lim, S.R. and J.M. Schoenung (2010) "Human health and ecological toxicity potentials due to heavy metal content in waste electronic devices with flat panel displays," *Journal of Hazardous Materials*, Vol. 177, No. 1–3, pp. 251–259.

Liu, X., M. Tanaka, and Y. Matsui (2006) "Generation amount prediction and material flow analysis of electronic waste: A case study in Beijing, China," *Waste Management Research*, Vol. 24, No. 5, pp. 434–445.

NMBC: National Bureau of Statistics of China (1995–2010) *China Statistical Yearbook 1995–2010*, China Statistics Press, Beijing.

Oguchi, M., T. Kameya, T. Tasaki, N. Tamai, and N. Tanikawa (2006) "Estimation of lifetime distributions and waste numbers of 23 types of electrical and electronic equipment," *Journal of the Japan Society of Waste Management Experts*, Vol. 17, No. 1, pp. 50–60, in Japanese.

Oguchi, M., T. Kameya, S. Yagi, and K. Urano (2008) "Product flow analysis of various consumer durables in Japan," *Resources, Conservation and Recycling*, Vol. 52, pp. 463–480.

Oguchi, M., S. Murakami, T. Tasaki, I. Daigo, and S. Hashimoto (2010) "Lifespan of commodities, part II: Methodologies for estimating lifespan distribution of commodities," *Journal of Industrial Ecology*, Vo.14, No. 4, pp. 613–626.

Oguchi, M., H. Sakanakura, A. Terazono, N. Tamai, and H. Takigami (2012) "Fate of metals contained in waste electrical and electronic equipment in a municipal waste treatment process," *Waste Management*, Vol. 32, No. 1, pp. 96–103.

ReCiPe (HP) "ReCiPe." Retrieved from http://www.lcia-recipe.net/

Rosenbaum, R.K., T.M. Bachmann, L.S. Gold, M.A.J. Huijbregts, O. Jolliet, R. Juraske, A. Koehler, H.F. Larsen, M. MacLeod, M. Margni, T.E. McKone, J. Payet, M. Schuhmacher, D. Van de Meent, and M.Z. Hauschild (2008) "USEtox – The UNEP-SETAC toxicity model: Recommended characterisation factors for human toxicity and freshwater ecotoxicity in life cycle impact assessment," *International Journal of Life Cycle Assessment*, Vol. 13, No. 7, pp. 532–546.

Song, Q., Z. Wang, J. Li, and X. Zeng (2013) "The life cycle assessment of an E-waste treatment enterprise in China," *Journal of Material Cycles and Waste Management*, Vol. 15, No. 4, pp. 469–475.

Tasaki, T., M. Oguchi, T. Kameya, and K. Urano (2001) "A prediction method for the number of waste durable goods," *Journal of the Japan Society of Waste Management Experts*, Vol. 12, No. 2, pp. 49–58, in Japanese.

Tasaki, T., T. Takasuga, M. Osako, and S. Sakai (2004) "Substance flow analysis of brominated flame retardants and related compounds in waste TV sets in Japan," *Waste Management*, Vol. 24, No. 6, pp. 571–580.

U.S. EPA (HP) Tool for the Reduction and Assessment of Chemical and Other Environmental Impacts (TRACI). Retrieved from http://www.epa.gov/nrmrl/std/traci/traci.html

Yearbook of China Information Industry, ed. (1995–2010) *Yearbook of China Information Industry 1995–2010*.

Zhang, L., Z. Yuan, and J. Bi (2011) "Predicting future quantities of obsolete household appliances in Nanjing by a stock-based model," *Resources, Conservation and Recycling*, Vol. 55, No. 11, pp. 1087–1094.

Zhang, L., Z. Yuan, J. Bi, and L. Huang (2012) "Estimating future generation of obsolete household appliances in China," *Waste Management Research*, Vol. 30, No. 11, pp. 1160–1168.

10 Input-output analysis on Chinese urban mines

Kazuaki Sato

1 Introduction

China has made striking progress on its way to become the world's largest economy. Along with the sudden economic growth, living standards of China's citizens have also improved, and many manufactured goods have become commonplace. China's entry into a mass consumption society is one of the largest factor behind the dramatic rise in costs for global resources. The issues of China's economy are, from the perspective of quantity, issues of the global economy. From a quality perspective, they also provide a touchstone for many newly developing countries. In analyzing China's economy, we are focusing on an economic analysis of the venous industry that is important aspect of circular economy and includes disposal of waste, recycling and urban mines. It is an important milestone not only for analyzing the Chinese economy, but also for discerning the flow of global resources both now and in the future.

Economic development brings with it the development of a venous industry, with such areas as waste disposal and recycling. Moreover, increased wage levels means more ownership of physical goods, and the goods made from many resources accumulate in an economic circulation as worthy resources. Wealth as shown by national accounts tell us how many products were sold rather than the extent to which people are stockpiling resources in their homes. In other words, national accounts show us added value not as economical stocks but as economic flows. However, from a material perspective, stocks are as important as these flows. Circular economy is composed of arterial economic flows where goods are produced and consumed, and of venous economic flows where consumed goods are disposed and recycled. However, stocked goods between arterial economy and venous economy, or under consumption are released for venous economic flows. Therefore, the urban mine as stocked goods accumulation has great impact on venous industry. To develop urban mines becomes all the more important of a political issue in the situation where the price of virgin mineral resources from mines rises.

Among these physical stocks, we have a particular interest in the widespread adoption of home appliances. First of all, the speed with which home appliances have been adopted is astounding. Second, voluntary recycling has proceeded apace even without government policies for the appropriate recycling of home appliances. However, inappropriate disposal methods harm the environment; the recycling of home appliances brings with it a strong potential for pollution. Especially, improper treatment of informal sector more damaged the environment (Chia et al., 2011). Third, many government policies have attempted to tackle home appliance recycling (Hosoda, 2007). We cannot avoid an assessment of these government policies when we consider the future of resource recycling policies in China.

This paper analyzes home appliance recycling policies that cause the recirculation of previously disposed of physical stocks, both from the perspective of a circulation economy, and as urban mines. Urban mines are a way of thinking of home appliances in households as a certain type of resource. Wang et al. (2013) have treated the ownership of home appliances in China, and their disposal, in detail. Tong et al. (2013) estimated WEEE output from Chinese policy by estimation. We shall afterward discuss these details, though suffice it to say that the ownership rate of home appliances in China is rising rapidly, and that of urban areas is in a state of saturation. In the future, these home appliances will be disposed of, and this requires an analysis from the perspective of resource policies and the circulation economy, and not just simply from waste policies. In particular, estimates have been made of WEEE levels discharged, though there have been few analyses made of their economic value. This paper analyzes the economic induced effect of home appliance disposal in the venous industry using input-output tables, in order to calculate the economic value of disposed home appliances as resources.

This paper is comprised as follows. Section 2 is a brief explanation of Chinese home appliance recycling policies. Section 3 is an explanation of an analytical model and data used in an analysis. Section 4 is an explanation of the results of our analysis.

2 Policy on WEEE and urban mines in China

2.1 Subsidy of home appliances going to countryside policy

Prior to examining China's home appliance recycling policies, it would be appropriate for us to first explain that country's policies for home appliance proliferation. This is because, from the long-term perspective, the proliferation of home appliances and policies to promote that proliferation have an enormous impact on resource circulation. Economic development and wage increases, technological development that accompanies the proliferation of new home appliances, and the adoption of information technologies and lifestyle changes all alter the quality and quantity of home appliances that people buy, own, and use. In particular, a country experiencing startling economic growth like China will see a rapid adoption of home appliances, in conjunction with increased wages, in order to reduce housework and make lifestyles more convenient. Further, many countries have put in place policies to accelerate home appliance adoption or to promote replacing older home appliances with newer appliances having more functions, better designs, or perhaps more efficient energy consumption. Economic, political, or financial resources are often invested in these policies. Home Appliances going to Countryside (HAGC) policies in China are one such example we should consider.

Since China began its reform and opening-up policy, ever-expanding social gaps have become a huge issue. Policies were the driving force not to aid all regions of the country equally in economic growth, but to first focus investment along the coastal regions, and then to realize dramatic economic growth nationwide. In other words, the country employed economic policies based on "xian fu lun", or "getting rich first". These policies were very successful, and in addition to bringing about rapid economic growth in China, they firmed up the country's position in the global economy. However, once China embarked on a path of economic growth based on capitalism, domestic inequality only increased. The economic gaps among regions has made the country more like multiple states within one country, and the earning gap among individuals even within a single region is extraordinarily large. China's Communist party emphasizes socialistic values, and while the expanding gaps can to a certain extent be overlooked, or perhaps eyes may be temporarily closed to the gaps, in essence it is an issue that strikes at the *raison d'etre* of the party and the state. The gaps between urban regions and agricultural areas, and between city dwellers and farmers, is particularly acute.

Chinese citizens in principle do not have the freedom of mobility. Those that are born in farming villages are required to live there, and likewise those born in cities are required to live in cities. Of course, there are many migrant workers, called "nongmin'gong", that receive extremely low wages, enabling China to become the world's factory. Even today, workers from farming villages may work in cities, but they receive lower wages than their counterparts from urban areas. Without a doubt, this phenomenon has become the basis for the development of labor-intensive industry. However, the policy that citizens from farming villages and those from urban areas are differentiated in their civil registries and are not allowed to move has the social policy benefit to control excessive domestic population movements, while it has also had the side effect of firming up interregional and civil gaps. This has led to the adoption of "san nong", or "the three rural issues", a policy based on the theory of a "harmonious society".

The "three rural issues" refer to farming villages, farmers, and farming, and San Nong is a policy that aims for the removal of decisive unfairness between urban and rural areas by invigorating farming as an industrial unit, improving earning standards for farmers, and promoting the development of farming villages. Within the San Nong policy is another set of policies called "xia xiang". These policies were sparked by the slogans of Mao Zedong, and mean to bring wealth into the countryside. Xia xiang includes a number of policies, such as increased use of cars and motorcycles in rural areas; one such policy is HAGC.

HAGC began on a trial basis in 2008 in the three provinces of Shandong, Henan, and Sichuan, as well as the city of Qingdao, as a way to increase the adoption of home appliances in farming villages; the subsidies were rolled out

nationwide over a four-year period beginning in 2009. According to this policy, part of the purchase price of home appliances was subsidized for those whose registered domicile was in a rural village, in order to positively impact the heretofore-feeble amount of home appliances in rural villages. Xia Xiang meant sending more than twenty million youth to rural villages during the Cultural Revolution, though the 11th 5-year plan defined Xia Xiang as spreading the use of home appliances and cars to rural villages as part of the Ministry of Commerce budget.

Products falling under this program are televisions, refrigerators, washers, and mobile phones. Each household in a rural village can receive a subsidy of 13 percent of the purchase price per appliance. There is a list of subsidized products, with upper limits of USD$309[1] for televisions and USD$154 for mobile phones. That said, earnings for farmers are low, and many farmers cannot bear the cost of a television, for example, even when receiving the maximum subsidy.

However, rural villages stopped being a pressing social issue due to achieving the striking economic growth that was part of the 11th 5-year plan. In their place, social gaps within urban areas became the number one problem, followed by the realization that a change was required from economic growth based on external demand and investment to economic growth based on internal demand and consumption. A third factor was the increasing importance of energy conservation and resource conservation along with the arrival of the mass consumption society. It was then that the national old-for-new Home Appliances Replacement Scheme (HARS) policies for home appliances appeared, their aim being to promote the replacement of older home appliances in urban areas, and the recycling of those older appliances.

2.2 The national old-for-new Home Appliances Replacement Scheme

HARS started as an experiment in nine cities and provinces including Beijing in 2009, the same year HAGC began. As a policy, HARS' intent was promoting sales of home appliances and improving the circulation of resources, and the scope expanded to add twenty cities and provinces from June 2010 to the end of 2011.

Subsidies beginning in 2009 in model businesses were for purchases of home appliances and the collection of older appliances. The scope of subsidized products included televisions, refrigerators, washers, air conditioners, and personal computers. Among model businesses, maximum subsidy amounts were set by providing old appliances when purchasing new home appliances, with up to 10 percent of the purchase price subsidized. The maximum subsidy was set at USD$62 for televisions, USD$46 for refrigerators (including freezers), USD$39 for washing machines, USD$54 for air conditioners, and USD$62 for personal computers. Moreover, a freight subsidy was implemented based on the number of old appliances collection companies sold. The source of the subsidies was, like HAGC, 80 percent from the central government and 20 percent from the provincial government.

When HARS was rolled out nationwide, changes were made to transportation subsidies. The biggest change was the setting of subsidies for recycling firms when dismantling appliances. Further, transportation subsidies went from being based on the quantity of appliances collected to being distributed based on appliance type, standards, and transportation distances. Subsidies for dismantling were disbursed when a specific appliance dismantling company collected and dismantled a used appliance within a specified period. In regards to HARS, the subsidies to consumers for the purchase of new appliances were budgeted by the Ministry of Commerce. It is thought that the Ministry of Commerce allowed old appliances to stay in circulation in order to create an economy based on resource circulation.

At the same time, subsidies for transportation and dismantling came from the budget of the Ministry of Environmental Protection. Even if many waste appliances were allowed to circulate into the waste appliance market, if products were to be disposed using improper methods such as open burning of plastic parts or leakage of contaminated water, pollution would become even more of a problem even though a circulation-based economy was created. Thus, the intent of the Ministry of Environmental Protection was the proper disposal of old appliances at each stage: collection, disposal, and recycling.

Because of this, the government authorized small numbers of appliance disposal companies and handed out subsidies, causing a consolidation among what were previously dispersed recycling companies, and improving control and guidance. Companies receiving subsidies for dismantling were large, with both technological capabilities and capital. Sometimes they were state-owned or affiliated with major appliance manufacturers. However, in regards to the means of appliance collection, there were many bit players already in operation, and they were not consolidated due to the impact on employment. It was in these circumstances that the structure of a venous industry, with diverse ways of collection and consolidated disposal, was created.

However, the intent of the Ministry of Environmental Protection did not come to full fruition. Waste appliances in the interior of provinces were basically managed by one or two companies that handled recycling, but sometimes waste was transported between provinces. In addition, China already had an informal waste disposal industry, and it was sometimes not necessarily logical for collection companies to sell old appliances to disposal companies. The proper disposal of old appliances incurs costs, and not even transportation subsidies always provided an advantage in a price war. In other words, the setting of subsidy levels perhaps could not sufficiently reflect external diseconomies. Moreover, an interview survey of multiple recycling companies revealed that, for disposal companies that did not have their own means of collection, the existence of many companies that disposed of waste improperly raised purchase prices in negotiations between collection companies and disposal companies, and disposal companies that did not have their own collection route had difficulties making profits.

That said, HARS enabled the rapid increase in the number of waste appliances circulating through the appliance recycling market, and it certainly accelerated the development of a venous economy with resource circulation. However, the transition in policies from HAGC to HARS resulted in an awareness of these economic policies as stimuli for individual consumption. From a macro-economic policy perspective, they can well be said to have brought on a mass consumption society.

According to an announcement by China's Ministry of Commerce, the number of home appliances sold via the HAGC as of April 2012 was 241 million, or USD$88 billion in sales. USD$10 billion in subsidies was disbursed through the program. The average prices of these appliances was approximately USD$365, and about 12 percent of that, or USD$43, was subsidized through HAGC. The number of HARS-related home appliances sold up to 2011, including the pilot period of 2009, was 92.48 million, or USD$53 billion in sales, USD$4.6 billion of which was subsidized. The average selling price was 1.57 times that of HAGC, at USD$573, and the average subsidy per appliance was about 1.2 times that of HAGC, or USD$50, no more than 9 percent of the sales price.

2.3 Regulations on the management of the recovery and treatment of WEEE

The HARS policy without a doubt nurtured the venous industry in China, and served to promote the circulation of resources. However, as was noted above, it was an economic policy designed to stimulate consumer appetites, as well as a policy for subsidizing home appliances purchases in urban areas, which was balanced with the HAGC in rural areas. In addition, it was a macro-economic policy to correct China's GDP, which relied on equipment investments and had low individual consumption. Regulations on the Management of the Recovery and Treatment of WEEE (WEEER) were series of policies to promote resource circulation that was discussed long before HARS.

An Ordinance for the Control of Waste Electronics Disposal, used for appliance recycling subsidies, was enacted by the 23rd executive meeting of the State Council on August 20, 2008, and was issued on February 25, 2009, taking effect January 1, 2011. HAGC and HARS were both in place prior to that, and were used both as economic policies to stimulate consumption and as social policies for San Nong and those with low incomes. However, just as these policies were beginning, another legal basis for full-scale recycling had come into being after long consideration. This ordinance governed collection activities for waste electronics, and was enacted for the comprehensive usage of resources and the development of a circulation economy, as well as for health and environmental protection.

WEER, like HARS, had many means of collection and assumed consolidated disposal. Thus, it established a system to authorize disposal companies and subsidies for those companies. Authorized companies alone were allowed to dispose of waste appliances, and only those companies could receive subsidies. Subsidies amounted to USD$14 for televisions, USD$13 for refrigerators, USD$6 for washing machines, USD$6 for coolers, and USD$14 for personal computers; based on the information obtained from the HARS system, these subsidies were set at a level that ensured proper disposal.

In addition, the fiscal system adopted a completely different method than HARS, focusing on extended producer responsibility and expenditures for the disposal of old appliances by the appliance manufacturers. This is a different design than the extended producer responsibility of Japan's appliance recycling system. In Japan, where old appliances have no value as resources, consumers (i.e., disposers) bear the cost of recycling, though appliance manufacturers do the actual recycling. In that regard, Japan's structure fulfills the producer responsibility.

The methods used to collect disposal costs when disposing of waste can lead to illegal dumping. Thus, some in Japan feel that disposal costs should be collected when an appliance is sold, though this has not yet been implemented. On this point, China's appliance recycling system is structured to have an amount set by the appliance manufacturers for each product remitted to a fund established by the above ordinance. From there, this fund is used to pay for the disposal of appliances on a per product basis. This structure makes illegal dumping less likely to occur. However, in China waste appliances still have value, and the appliances themselves are typically not dumped illegally. Rather, the issues are different, with open burning and other methods of improper disposal creating environmental problems.

Monies for subsidies are collected from appliance manufacturers and importers based on the principle of extended producer responsibility. However, those monies are managed through a Waste Electronics Disposal Fund. The fund was set up by electronics manufacturers, recipients of imported electronics, or their representatives, but opinions of manufacturers and disposal companies, as well as associations of related industries and professionals regarding collection standards and subsidy standards were to be heard. However, negotiations between the government and industry regarding the cost burden ran aground, and enactment of the Ordinance for the Control of Waste Electronics Disposal was delayed until July 2012. The targets of fee collection and recycling subsidies were televisions, refrigerators, washers, air conditioners, and personal computers, with one amount being set for each of these five categories based on the principle of "one tax, one subsidy". Three billion yuan is expected to be collected in the first year.

Under this system, meeting strict environmental standards is required to receive subsidies for appliance recycling. These standards are the same as for HARS, and in order to stop externalities such as corruption caused by entrusting the venous industry to a free market economy, the government recognized monopolistic recycling by a small number of companies with technological capability and capital. In addition, the government applied strict environmental standards, and set up a structure for monitoring and control. However, by subsidizing the additional costs incurred by proper disposal methods, the government showed concern that recycling companies not be unprofitable, and that these companies stay competitive with smaller companies that used illegal and improper disposal methods.

Another characteristic of this ordinance was that, unlike HARS for appliances, the system disbursed subsidies only to companies that disposed of waste appliances. As will be discussed in the next section, within the venous industry market, whether an appliance has worth or incurs a fee (for disposal), it is the consumer that supplies the goods and the producer (or, in this case, the disposer) that accepts it. The market is affected depending on to whom a subsidy is given, just as normal taxation and subsidies impact the market. It should also be noted that the subsidy per appliance given under this ordinance was less than one third that under HARS. Subsidy setting under this system was done after surveying and researching cost structures of the recycling industry under HARS, and subsidies were set such that recycling companies made a slim profit.

Further, an important point is the fact that this system is based on a special accounting system for forming funds. As was noted above, HAGC and HARS were highly affected by the economy and market fluctuations, and this made it difficult to implement these policies according to budget. Sometimes expenditures were required that went several times over budget. This was a limiting factor for local governments and the central government that wanted to have stable fiscal situations. Moreover, putting the burden of appliance recycling costs on manufacturers based on extended producer responsibility seems proper, just as with appliance recycling in Japan.

3 Model and data

3.1 Procedure and definitions

The concept of urban mines does not originate in policy; as with many advanced nations, the targets of policies are often closely statistically surveyed for the first time after implementation of the policies, making it possible to become aware of economic realities. Urban mines in China are much like this. Prior to being regulated by WEEER, no one grasped just how many old appliances were going to waste in real, and not just estimated, terms. Of course, HARS created data, though it was deficient, as to the amount of appliances being disposed of. For this paper, available HARS waste appliance data for 2011 and likewise available WEEER data from 2013 was used to calculate economic induced effects.

The following procedure was used to combine appliance waste data with the above input-output table. This paper does not attempt an analysis of fluctuations in environmental standards, and it does not use data as quantities, but rather converts data into costs. The amount of major and useful resources included in each old appliance are calculated, though the disposal data used here are subsidy disbursements, thus this data was prepared as accurate statistical data. It should be kept in mind that voluntary recycling with no subsidies is not part of this calculation.

Resource volumes are next multiplied by the sales price of resources, which provides the economic value of a resource produced in the venous industry. The resource value in this case is used as data from "ScrapMonster". In actuality, the value of a resource can fluctuate over the course of a year, and there may be regional differences in cost, but a simple average value for the year was used in this analysis. While there may be some amount of variation, there are no non-linear cost changes, and likely no major differences in estimated values. More important are the differences in price due to the varying levels of quality in the recycled resources produced. Waste appliances may be of high quality, and if a company has a high technological level and investment level, it is likely they will produce high quality goods with a high value add. However, one cannot assume that products in the same industry sector but of varying quality and varying price will be manufactured. Accordingly, the lowest prices were used to ensure estimates of economic effects were not exaggerated, and there is a strong possibility that this paper underestimates values, and that at a minimum there was the level of impact seen here.

Compositional data of emissions amounts was used to calculate resource volumes, and these resource volumes were then multiplied by resource prices to arrive at total production value. This figure was then multiplied by the annual average yuan/dollar prices to get the same units as the input-output table. It was assumed that iron, copper, aluminum, and gold were assumed to be produced in the metals industry, even though they were actually manufactured by the recycling industry. If an input-output table for specific categories of ferrous and non-ferrous metals were used, it would be possible to separate out these metals, but if there are no major differences in economic induced effect in these sectors, then it can be assumed that it is not possible to get any more information than the estimated results of this paper. Waste plastics were treated as products of the plastics industry, and waste glass was categorized as a product of the "other" industry.

In regards to metals production in particular, intermediate products are necessary to calculate units of metal produced based on the mining industry to a certain extent. In the venous industry, this is not typical mining; because consumers are in possession of urban mines, the economic induced effect of urban mines as analyzed in this paper is called the urban mine effect. Two points must be kept in mind regarding the urban mine effect. In considering material flow, certainly traditional mines are vastly different than urban mines, and there are major differences in the use of intermediate goods necessary for production, as well as the value add. Modern mining industries use large-scale equipment, and production is capital-intensive. The urban mining industry has many waste collectors, and is very labor-intensive. Moreover, intermediate inputs differ between the two industries. Intermediate inputs in the capital-intensive mining industry are taken from nature, where value added rate per capita is higher. On the other hand, intermediate inputs in the labor-intensive urban mining industry come from consumer stocks with less added value per capita.[0]

While there are these sorts of defects, there are also many benefits in this analysis, rather than examining the appliance recycling sector alone and simply summarizing the intermediate inputs, value add, final consumption, and import and export in a consistent fashion. First, it is possible to correctly analyze the impact of urban mining and resource circulation policies on the national economy by actually treating urban mining as metals, plastics, and glass production. Second, the analysis is highly objective, since it does not depend on unique surveys and estimates. Third, for the above reasons, it is possible to use this data to do a

simple comparison and confirm the results of estimates. In particular, an input-
output analysis is different than a complex general equilibrium model, in that
reproducibility of results simply and by anyone is a strength. This is another
reason why this analysis is significant.

However, care must be taken so that the data is not limited to a confirmation of
the effect of policies. In the background are the combined effects of two policies
used to leverage urban mining and old appliances that are automatically disposed
of in the market economy based on economic growth, income improvements,
product development, resource cost fluctuations, and other factors. Because the
disposal of old appliances prior to these policies is unknown, it is difficult to separate out the policy effects from the baseline.

3.2 Data of WEEE and policies

Tables 10.1 and 10.2 show the "possession of home appliances and electronic
equipment per urban household in China. In urban areas, each household has
about one of each appliance. While rural areas may have more than one color
television per household, the proliferation of other types of appliances is much
lower. Disposal of old appliances is advancing year by year, as household ownership of appliances is still not at a point of full saturation, and it can thus be
predicted that the disposal of old appliances in the future will continue to grow
substantially.

Table 10.2 shows the composition of resources in each home appliance, as
well as the recycled resource price for each in China. Most televisions disposed of

Table 10.1 Possession of home appliances and electronic equipment per urban household

	1990	1995	2000	2005	2009	2010	2011
Color TV	0.59	0.9	1.17	1.35	1.36	1.37	1.35
Refrigerator	0.42	0.66	0.8	0.91	0.95	0.97	0.97
Washing machine	0.78	0.89	0.91	0.96	0.96	0.97	0.97
Air conditioner	0	0.08	0.31	0.81	1.07	1.12	1.22
Computer	–	–	0.1	0.42	0.66	0.71	0.82

Source: Wang et al. (2013), Table 3.

Table 10.2 Possession of home appliances and electronic equipment per rural household

	1990	1995	2000	2005	2009	2010	2011
Color TV	0.05	0.17	0.49	0.84	1.09	1.12	1.15
Black-and-white TV	0.4	0.64	0.53	0.22	0.08	0.06	0.02
Washing machine	0.09	0.17	0.29	0.4	0.53	0.57	0.63
Refrigerator	0.01	0.05	0.12	0.2	0.37	0.45	0.63
Air conditioner	–	–	0.01	0.06	0.12	0.16	0.23
Computer	–	–	–	0.02	0.07	0.1	0.18

Source: Wang et al. (2013), Table 3.

today have CRTs, which explains the use of CRT composition data and the high amount of glass. In regards to gold, all home appliances contain some amount of gold, though only data for televisions and personal computers was available and used herein. Because only the annual average prices of scrap of the lowest purity in China are used for each metal resource prices herein, these prices should be considered as minimums. The average prices of scrap glass and plastics in China are not available, thus prices for these items exported from Japan to China are used in this analysis. In addition, the prices of gold in London were used.

Table 10.3 shows the amount of resources included in WEEE, and the resource prices that are not virgin resource prices but scraped or recycled resource prices. Table 10.4 shows the number of waste appliances disposed in 2011, when HARS was implemented, and 2013, when WEEER actually began. These

Table 10.3 Resource content of WEEE and resource price

Kg/unit	TVs	Refrigerators	Washing machines	Air conditioners	Computers	Resource price (US$/ Mil. tons) 2011	2013
Iron and steel	3.6	52.0	19.6	27.0	7.2	1,470	1,394
Copper	0.9	2.0	1.6	9.0	0.3	2,102	1,992
Aluminum	0.3	4.0	0.4	4.5	0.4	2,067	1,959
Plastic	7.8	33.0	17.2	8.0	2.8	602	571
Glass	15.9	–	–	–	–	15	15
Gold (mg, US$/kg)	4.5	–	–	–	1.4	50	45
Others	1.5	9.0	1.2	1.5	0.4	–	–

Source: Estimated by author

Table 10.4 Total output and estimating value as resource of WEEE, and subsidy from central government

	WEEE output (thousand units) 2011	2013	Estimating value (US$/ UNIT) 2011	2013	Subsidy (1,000US$) 2011	2013
TVs	51,485	37,654	13	12		16,811
Refrigerators	2,452	601	54	52		201
Washing machines	4,290	1,612	43	41		50
Air conditioners	306	5	73	69		4
Computers	2,268	–	14	13	Total (Million US$) 52,940	17

Source: Estimated by author

amounts are the formal subsidized quantities from disposal companies, and thus do not include appliances disposed of with no subsidies. In addition, the data shows resource prices for each appliance, and reflect that year's exchange rate. Moreover, the table also shows the amount of subsidies for each appliance. For HARS subsidies, only the total amount of subsidies is shown; a comparison of monetary amounts cannot be done since the total amount includes subsidies for the purchase of new home appliances. However, disposals of waste appliances of all types are declining, and lower resource prices means that the price per unit is also declining. In particular, the disposal of non-television waste appliances is declining steeply.

The following three points can be derived from this data. First is the decline in disposals of waste appliances. Considering the continued proliferation of appliances, this can be understood as being caused by policy changes. HARS is a policy for replacement purchases of appliances, making simple comparisons impossible. However, from the standpoint of urban mine use, an assessment would conclude that policies caused a retreat. Second, it would appear that subsidy amounts are set in inverse proportion to resource values of waste appliances. Recycling costs for waste appliances are not considered in this paper, making an assessment of subsidy setting difficult, but the overtones of waste policies serving to reimburse the costs of proper disposal are stronger than their promotion of resource circulation. Third, we know that subsidies are falling steeply. A simple comparison is impossible because policy objectives are different, but WEEER, which is based on fiscal EPR, keeps total subsidies to a bare minimum, and this slows down disposal of old appliances. However, in evaluating circulation economy policies, there is a possibility that HARS subsidies were set too high, making it difficult to assess which policy was the best.

3.3 Input-output table and models

Using the above data, it is possible to better understand what resource amounts and at what prices reintroduce resource values back into the Chinese economy. An input-output analysis using prices for resources reintroduced into the Chinese economy through WEEE disposal was done, and the economic induced effect was calculated. This paper uses input-output table from World Input Output Database(WIOD), national IO table(NIOT) of China.[2]

The input-output analysis showed that one unit of production led to one unit of final demand. For example, one unit of final demand of iron led to an increase in iron production, which necessitated various intermediate production inputs. The total increase in direct and indirect production is the economic induced effect. Total output vector X expresses the Leontief inversed matrix $(I-A)^{-1}$ with matrix of coefficients A and final demand F^d,

$$X = (I - A)^{-1} F^d$$

and political effect is represented by added final demand.

The fact that there is an economic induced effect means that there is that amount of value added in that industry. If it is assumed that, in conjunction with an increase in production, the ratio of inter-sector total production volumes to total value add does not change, then the induced effect of value added can be derived with gross value added inducement coefficients; in other words, this shows the level of increases in wages and distributions caused by an increase in production.

In addition, this model uses a non-competitive import model with domestic direct input coefficients A^d.

$$X = \left(I - A^d \right)^{-1} F^d$$

The urban mine model of resource circulation policies does not feature the promotion of resource imports, but rather aims to restrain them. Thus, this paper operates under the hypothesis that imports are not generated through appliance recycling. In actuality, the possibility of increased exports due to policies to promote home appliance recycling cannot be excluded, and it must be assumed that the maximum induced effect is estimated herein.

4 Analysis results

This section provides an explanation of the estimated results. Tables 10.5 and 10.6 are the resource volumes recycled from waste appliances that were subsidized and disposed of properly for each year. The impact on overall resource volumes depends on televisions, where much of the waste was created. Based on the characteristics of components of televisions, glass and plastic volumes are high. Among metal resources, iron waste is the highest, while copper and aluminum were not very high.

Tables 10.7 and 10.8 show an assessment of recycled resource volumes by price for each year. Iron has the highest value among resources produced via recycling, followed by plastics, and while the price is low, volume is high. Glass volumes are high, though prices are low, and gold volumes are low, but prices are high. These two categories create about the same level of economic values.

Table 10.5 Total output of resources from WEEE in 2011

Billion tons	TVs	Refrigerators	Washing machines	Air conditioners	Computers	Total
Iron and steel	185	127	84	8	16	421
Copper	46	5	7	3	1	62
Aluminum	15	10	2	1	1	29
Plastic	402	81	74	2	6	565
Glass	819	–	–	–	–	819
Gold (tons)	232	–	–	–	3	235
Others	77	22	5	0	1	106

Source: Estimated by author

Table 10.6 Total output of resources from WEEE in 2013

Billion tons	TVs	Refrigerators	Washing machines	Air conditioners	Computers	Total
Iron and steel	136	31	32	0	–	199
Copper	34	1	3	0	–	38
Aluminum	11	2	1	0	–	14
Plastic	294	20	28	0	–	341
Glass	599	–	–	–	–	599
Gold (tons)	169	–	–	–	–	169
Others	56	5	2	0	–	64

Source: Estimated by author

Table 10.7 Total value as resources from WEEE in 2011

Million US$	TVs	Refrigerators	Washing machines	Air conditioners	Computers	Total
Iron and steel	272	187	124	12	24	620
Copper	97	10	14	6	2	129
Aluminum	32	20	4	3	2	61
Plastic	242	49	44	1	4	341
Glass	12	–	–	–	–	12
Gold	12	–	–	–	0	12
Total	668	267	186	22	31	1,174

Source: Estimated by author

Table 10.8 Total value as resources from WEEE in 2013

Million US$	TVs	Refrigerators	Washing machines	Air conditioners	Computers	Total
Iron and steel	199	46	47	0	–	292
Copper	71	3	5	0	–	79
Aluminum	23	5	1	0	–	30
Plastic	177	12	17	0	–	206
Glass	9	–	–	–	–	9
Gold	9	–	–	–	–	9
Total	488	65	70	0	–	625

Source: Estimated by author

Table 10.9 shows the economic induced effect for each year by WEEE industry type. From the same table the following two facts can be ascertained. First, production induced effects and added value induced effects dropped by about half. The reduction in appliance waste is a major factor, though the large bias towards the category of televisions in appliance disposals is also important. Second, the relationship between production induced effects and added value induced effects shows a variance of around 26 percent, depending on the appliance type and year.

Table 10.9 Production induced effects and added value induced effects by WEEE

Million US$		TVs	Refrigerators	Washing machines	Air conditioners	Computers	Total
Production	2011	1,898	747	524	62	87	3,318
induced effects	2013	1,291	170	183	1	–	1,645
Added value	2011	497	197	137	16	23	870
induced effect	2013	337	44	48	0	–	429

Source: Estimated by author

Table 10.10 Direct and indirect induced effect on directly affected industries, "urban mining sector", and top 5 indirectly affected industries

Million US$	Production induced effects		Added value induced effect	
	2011	2013	2011	2013
Urban mining sectors				
Rubber and plastics	476	269	89	50
Other non-metallic mineral	44	24	12	7
Basic metals and fabricated metal	1334	625	263	123
Chemicals and chemical products	253	137	52	28
Mining and quarrying	201	97	94	45
Top 5 indirectly affected industries				
Electricity, gas, and water supply	163	79	46	23
Machinery, nec	89	39	21	9
Coke, refined petroleum, and nuclear fuel	76	37	14	7
Wholesale trade and commission trade, except of motor vehicles and motorcycles	67	33	40	20
Financial intermediation	58	28	40	19

Source: Estimated by author

Table 10.10 shows the economic induced effect per year for each industry sector. Metal resources have a direct impact on "basic metals and fabricated metal". Plastics have a direct impact on "rubber and plastics". Glass has a direct impact on "other non-metallic minerals". The monetary amount of the industry sectors shown is the total production volume and value added indirectly increased by the induced effect and directly increased by appliance recycling.

The sector most indirectly impacted by the economic induced effect due to metal resource production is "mining and quarrying". This sector can be thought as an urban mine generated directly from recycling. Likewise, urban mines can be thought as economic stimuli for households, and in essence must be processed as household income improvements, though they are calculated in this paper as inducing an effect similar to that of the mining sector. The sector most impacted by plastics recycling is "chemicals and chemical products". This sector can also be thought of as an urban mine. In waste plastics production, the induced amount is growing in comparison to metal resources.

In addition to the industry sectors above directly impacted, five industries actually receive an indirect economic effect outside of the urban mining sector, which has an effect equivalent to that of the household sector. They are: electricity, gas, and water supply; machinery, nec; coke, refined petroleum, and nuclear fuel; wholesale trade and commission trade, except of motor vehicles and motorcycles; financial intermediation. The first three sectors show greatly impacted by urban mining sectors indirectly in production-induced effect. The latter two are greatly impacted by recycling policy indirectly in added-value-induced effect. They can be seen as having a growing induced amount of value added due to the low amount of intermediate products.

5 Concluding remarks

It is clear that, when natural resources are understood to be limited, the importance of a circulation economy will increase. In particular, recycling policies in China, which has a high population and high economic growth, will have a huge impact on not just China, but the direction of the world's resource prices. This paper analyzed HARS and WEEER, two recent policies that exerted a major impact on the venous industry in recent years. Conducting an economic assessment of home appliance recycling in 2011 and 2013 using input-output table analysis is significant in that it shows new findings gleaned in relation to prior research that focused only on the volume of resource circulation. That said, there are two major issues with this paper. One is that it does not consider the costs of appliance recycling. It is hoped that a major macro-level survey estimating home appliance recycling costs in China will be done. The second problem is that of how to deal with urban mines. The industry sector called urban mining is in actuality indicating the household sector. The induced effect of the mining sector takes a different route than that of income increase effects in the household sector, but in this paper that difference was not sufficiently taken into account.

Three important facts were identified through this paper's analysis. The first is in regards to the direction of the venous industry that disposes of waste appliances. It was noted in the beginning of this paper that China's venous industry is just getting started, but when one examines only the volumes of disposed appliances, one notes that it is shrinking. Two factors may be behind that. One is the possibility that HARS created excess disposals of old appliances. The primary purpose of HARS was to promote sales of appliances, and in light of the ballooning of subsidies, the possibility that policies had an outsize impact on the urban mine situation cannot be discounted. On the other hand, there is the possibility that the WEEER subsidies were not set at appropriate levels. In examining the adoption of home appliances, one notes that televisions were the first to be adopted, through when comparing HARS and WEEER, non-television appliance disposals have dropped dramatically. Even taking the relatively high cost incurred for proper disposal of a CRT television into consideration, there is a possibility that subsidies for other waste appliances are set too low. In addition, fiscal EPRs are providing funding, and it is even possible that the total amount of subsidies may be insufficient. Seeking out a better circulation economy will require the setting of subsidies in ways that consider the value of resources obtained through recycling, and not merely proper disposal costs.

The second fact regards the value of resources in waste appliances. The amount of resources included depends on the type of appliance, though even so, iron and plastics account for most resources by far. This is one reason for the bias of waste appliances towards televisions, though refrigerators and washing machines also have large amounts of iron and plastics. One cannot choose resources by the recycled appliance. In this paper's analysis, resource prices are a given. Pushing policies for appliance recycling will lead to an oversupply of iron scrap and waste plastics, and they may serve to reduce the price of resources.

Third, this paper identifies an economic induced effect. In addition to recycled resources produced through appliance recycling, a broad economic induced effect was confirmed in improvement of household income by utilizing urban mines, as well as energy, machinery, trade, and financing due to the properly recycled resources. The resource circulation policies have a large impact, depending on the sector, though the economic induced effects of home appliance recycling were no more than 3.318 billion US dollars in 2011, and 1.645 billion US dollars in 2013, the percentage of intermediate goods production for each year being no more than 0.023 percent and 0.009 percent, respectively. The value added induced effect was no more than 870 million US dollars and 429 US million dollars respectively, and the percentage of GDP was no more than 0.015 percent and 0.006 percent respectively. While the impact on the overall economy is small, from the perspective of proper recycling and final disposal that does not create environmental issues and damage to health, as well as policies for resource circulation, the direction of home appliance recycling policies in China are an area of concern.

Notes

1 Based on 2011 average exchange rate, CNY\1 = USD$0.1548.
2 National Input-Output Tables, Released November 2013 (http://www.wiod.org/new_site/database/niots.htm).

References

Chia, Xinwen, Martin Streicher-Porteb, Mark Y.L. Wanga, and Markus A. Reuterc (2011) "Informal electronic waste recycling: A sector review with special focus on China," *Waste Management*, Vol. 31, pp. 731–742.
Hosoda, Eiji (2007) "International aspects of recycling of electrical and electronic equipment: Material circulation in the East Asian region," *Journal of Material Cycles and Waste Management*, Vol. 9, No. 2, pp. 140–150.

Timmer, M. P., E. Dietzenbacher, B. Los, R. Stehrer, and G. J. de Vries (2015), "An illustrated user guide to the world input–output database: The case of global automotive production," *Review of International Economics*, 23, pp. 575–605.

Tong, Xin, Yifan Cai, and Lin Yan (2013) "Generation and collection of WEEE in pilot areas of HARS: An empirical study," *Ecological Economy*, Vol. 7, No. 269, pp. 38–42.

Wang, Feng, Ruediger Kuehr, Daniel Ahlquist, and Jinhui Li (2013) *E-waste in China: A Country Report*, United Nations University, Bonn, Germany.

11 The effect of cost fluctuation on waste trade and recycling in East Asia

Masashi Yamamoto

1 Introduction

There is no doubt that the trade between two or more countries increases the welfare among them. This advantage of the trade has been shown by many literatures in economics for a long time, from both theoretical and empirical points of view. It seems, however, that the analysis has been rather limited within the trade of "goods", and the literature has not discussed welfare improvement through trading "bads", or wastes.

Indeed, the amount of waste in the world trade was trivial until very recently. Two things make the volume of the waste traded larger and larger. First, the per capita consumption level has been getting higher and higher in the last several decades. The increase has been remarkable, especially in the emerging countries in the last decades, and this leads to not only more generation of waste but also more demand for natural resources, which could be substituted with the recyclables from the waste. The second is the ever-stronger regulation against environmental pollution, mainly in the developed countries. More wastes have been losing their final destinations because increasingly strict regulation restrains wastes from being dumped nearby.

With the increase in the generation of wastes, the surge in demand for recyclables in developing countries, and the disappearance of dumping options in the developed countries, the potential demand for waste trade is now exceptionally high – historically so. In fact, the total waste trade in the world has been rapidly growing and has reached about 200 million tons (Kellenberg, 2013). It is easier to understand how much waste that is when we compare it with the total debris created by the massive tsunami attack in Japan on March 11, 2011, which is 26.7 million tons,[1] and the 1.6 million tons resulting from the September 11, 2001, attacks in New York (Kellenberg, 2013).

Despite waste's strong presence in the international trade, economists have not been paying enough attention to this issue. There is plenty of previous research in the field of natural resources and their trade (e.g., Li et al., 2012; Agostini, 2006). There is not so much in the area of the waste trade and recycling except the seminal works by Slade (1980) or Gomez et al. (2007). Only recently, Baggs (2009) and Kellenberg (2013) consider the waste trade from the perspective of international trade. They are based on a so-called *gravity model*. This chapter, however, tries to understand the basic features of the waste trade from a different perspective by concentrating the focus on its transportation cost.

In the next section, we develop a simple economic model to describe why the transportation cost is important when we analyze waste trade. Section 3 provides a brief overview of the waste trade between China and Japan. In Section 4, the result of the time-series analysis is presented; the final section summarizes the discussion.

2 The role of transportation cost

One of the biggest problems when waste is exported to developing countries is that there are substantial numbers of informal sectors dedicated to the waste treatment and recycling business in developing countries. As far as the author understands, the inappropriate treatment of (toxic) wastes was first revealed by the Basel Action Network (BAN). The report published by BAN (2002) introduced a small town called Guiyu in Guangdong Province located in Southern China, close to the border of Hong Kong. In Guiyu, more than 100,000 workers dedicated themselves to breaking apart and processing old computers imported from developed countries such as Japan and the US. The working environment was horrible; proper equipment to prevent workers from inhaling toxic substances was not provided. The residuals from the recycling process for high tech appliances have been abandoned without appropriate precautions against environmental damage.

As we show later in this chapter, China has swallowed a lot of so-called e-waste (PC, mobile phone, and other small electric appliances) since the late 1990s. Not a small amount of the e-waste shipped from the developed countries is recycled by these informal sectors. We would like to examine how important the transportation cost is given the existence of informal sectors. For an efficient recycling framework, waste trade is inevitable. The cheap labor cost supports a labor-intensive breakup process, but advanced technology in developed countries can play an important role when it comes to dealing with recyclables that are difficult to process. It is very important to understand the role of transportation cost when we exchange waste between two countries.

Suppose there are two countries. One country has a formal firm to recycle and the other one has an informal sector. Here we define an informal sector as a firm that does not consider environmental damage properly. We assume that, because of its definition, an informal sector has smaller marginal cost of recycling compared to the formal one.

In order to understand the feature of the transportation cost in our setting, we develop the famous Hotelling model of the linear city. Suppose there is a linear city in $[0,1]$ with uniformly distributed residents. There are also two recycling firms: one is formal and located at a in $[0,1]$ and the other one is informal and located at b with lower marginal cost. The resident has one unit of recyclables that he/she never wants any more. The utility function of the resident is as follows:

$$U = r - ty - p_i, \quad \text{where} \quad i = \{a, b\} \tag{1}$$

where r is the reservation price for a resident. We assume that r is big enough so that every resident has an incentive to give up the recyclable. Furthermore, y denotes the distance between where a resident lives and recycling firm i, t denotes transportation cost, and p_i means the price charged by firm i. Then there exists a resident $\hat{x}$ who is indifferent about buying from firm a or firm b. This resident can be defined as follows:

$$r - t\hat{x} - p_a = r - t(1 - \hat{x}) - p_2 \rightarrow \hat{x} = \frac{1}{2} + \frac{p_b - p_a}{2t} \tag{2}$$

It is natural to assume that a formal recycling firm has higher marginal cost. If firm a is a formal one, then a profit-maximizing problem for each firm could be:

$$\Pi_a = (p_a - c_a)\left(\frac{1}{2} + \frac{p_b - p_a}{2t}\right) \tag{3}$$

$$\Pi_b = (p_b - c_b)(1 - \hat{x}) = (p_b - c_b)\left(\frac{1}{2} - \frac{p_b - p_a}{2t}\right). \tag{4}$$

Solving (3) and (4), we get:

$$\begin{cases} p_a = \dfrac{t + c_a + p_b}{2} \\ p_b = \dfrac{t + c_b + p_a}{2} \end{cases} \tag{5}$$

Using (5), we can derive the equilibrium price for each firm, and then substituting it in (2), we have:

$$\hat{x} = \frac{1}{2} + \frac{1}{2t}\left(\frac{c_b - c_a}{3}\right). \tag{6}$$

In this model, the market area for firm a is from 0 to $\hat{x}$. If firm a is in the formal sector, we can say $c_b < c_a$. Then the sign of the second term in (6) is negative, which means that the market share for two firms is different and in fact the informal sector firm (firm b) has larger market area at the equilibrium. This difference does not happen if there is no informal sector; in other words, if $c_b = c_a$. In that case, two firms share the market area equally regardless of the unit transportation cost, although the competitive price would be different according to the level of the unit transportation cost.

Turning back to the transportation cost, the share difference between informal sector and formal sector becomes smaller as the transportation cost becomes larger. When the transportation cost is small, the difference of marginal costs between two firms has been relatively more meaningful than is the case with higher transportation cost. All these results suggest that the transportation cost is more important when there exists an informal sector.

3 Waste trade among East Asian countries

Among waste trades in the world, we concentrate here on the trade between East Asian countries. This is because the region covers the most trade in terms of the volume. Figure 11.1 is the percentage of the waste trades by countries, which is

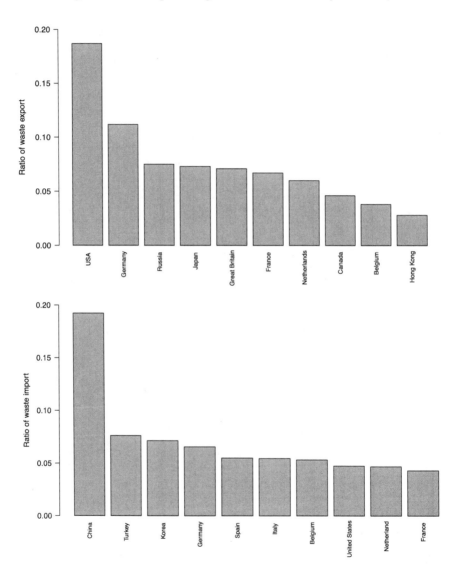

Figure 11.1 Shares of waste trade (upper panel: export, lower panel: import)

Source: Yamamoto (2013)

summarized by Kellenberg (2013) using the UN's Comtrade data set. It includes 62 six-digit HS codes for commodities. The typical commodity examples are, for example, municipal waste (HS382510), copper waste and scrap (HS740400), and aluminum waste and scrap (HS760200).[2]

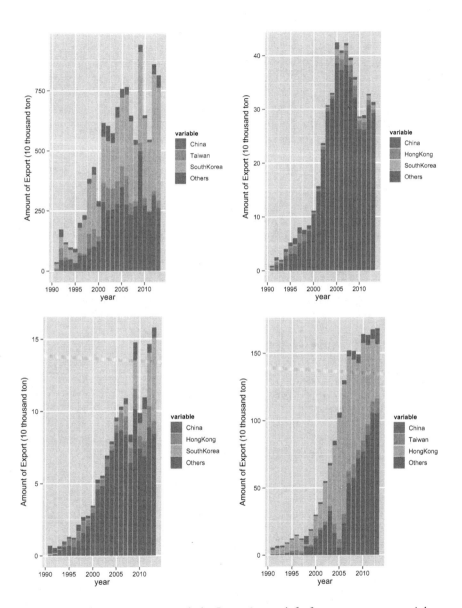

Figure 11.2 Changes in waste trade by Japan (upper left: ferrous scrap, upper right: copper scrap, lower left: aluminum scrap, lower right: plastic scrap)

Source: Trade Statistics of Japan (each year)

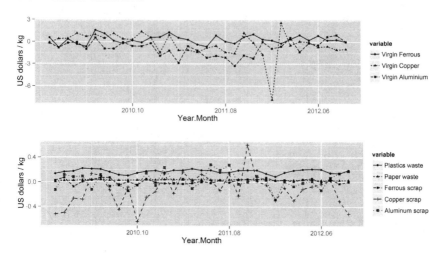

Figure 11.3 Change in transportation cost (upper: final good, lower: scrap)

Source: Author's calculation based on UN Comtrade data

The US has the largest share of exports at about 20 percent; Germany, Russia, and Japan follow it, each with around 10 percent. All the countries in the top 10 rankings are the developed countries. When it comes to the import of waste, China has the largest share at 20 percent. Reflecting its rapid economic growth, Turkey is ranked as the second, but the share is less than half of China's. In a sense, China deals with one fifth of the world's waste. This simply indicates China's importance when we consider the waste trade in the world.

Figure 11.2 shows the changes in waste export by Japan. All four graphs indicate that China has been the biggest importer of its waste since the late 1990s.

South Korea in ferrous scrap and Hong Kong in plastic scrap are similar to China in import rates, but China is a dominant importer from them, as well. In fact, it is said that most of the plastic scrap imported by Hong Kong is shipped again to China. In what follows, we limit our research only to the waste trade between China and Japan.

It is usually very hard to obtain transportation costs, but in trade data sets, it is feasible to derive a kind of transportation cost. The point is that there are two different records for the same trade. When a good is exported, the value of the transaction is recorded by the exporting country in the manner of FOB (Free on Board), which includes only the good's own value as a commodity and excludes all fees for ocean transportation, tariff, and insurance. On the other hand, the importing country records the same transaction in the manner of CIF (Cost, Insurance, Freight), which includes all the tariff and transportation costs. Given no changes to tariff and other fees during shipment, import value minus export value is considered a generalized transportation cost of the trade. Figure 11.3 depicts the change in the (generalized) transportation cost between China and Japan.

Figure 11.3 is based on the data set provided by the UN (UN Comtrade). Since Chinese data is limited in the UN Comtrade, our data set is from January 2010 to October 2012. Carefully looking at Figure 11.3, we see that the transportation cost per kg is higher for the final good compared to the scrap. Another point that should be mentioned is that some of the transportation costs are negative during the sample period, which does not make sense economically. There might be several reasons for this. One of the reasons might the time lag between the day the contract was actually made and the real transaction of the cargo. We must be careful if we try to compare the average transportation costs, but our main interest is what affects the transportation cost. In the next section, we analyze the waste trade between Japan and China by using the time-series analysis tools.

4 Time-series analysis of waste trade

The first step for our time-series analysis is to check how the data behaved during the sample period. Figure 11.4 shows the changes in the oil price index and in iron ore, copper, and aluminum prices. All data is taken from the IMF database

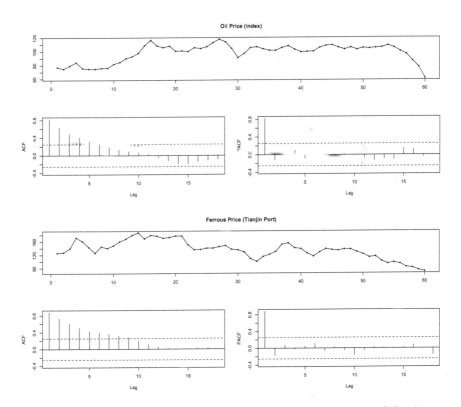

Figure 11.4 Time-series plot, ACF, and PCF, for oil, iron ore, copper, and aluminum

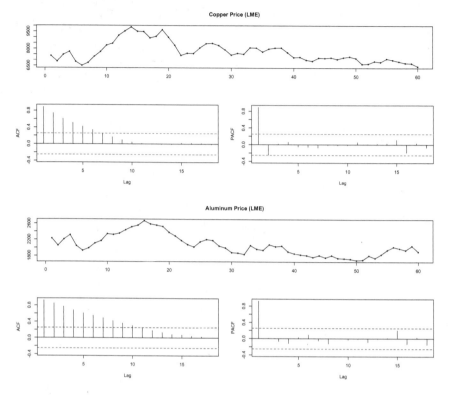

Figure 11.4 continued

(*IMF Primary Commodity Prices*).[3] The oil price index here means "Crude Oil (petroleum), Price index, 2005 = 100, simple average of three spot prices; Dated Brent, West Texas Intermediate, and the Dubai Fateh" while the iron ore price is from China's import price at Tianjin port. The copper and aluminum prices are the grade A LME spot price and 99.5 percent minimum purity spot price at LME, respectively. Each commodity has three graphs; original series of the data at the top, the autocorrelation function (ACF) at the lower left, and partial autocorrelation function (PCF) at the lower right. Contrary to the transportation cost that we show in the previous section, this data contains 60 months, from January 2010 to December 2014. Note that all the prices are in US dollar. In the time-series plots, the oil price marks a remarkable sharp decline during the last six months. The other three time series are also showing a decreasing trend.

Let y_t be time-series data where $t = \{1, \cdots, T\}$. Then autocorrelation between time t and k is defined as follows:

$$\rho_{kt} = Corr\left(y_t, y_{t-k}\right) = \frac{Cov\left(y_t, y_{t-k}\right)}{\sqrt{Var\left(y_t\right) \cdot VAR\left(y_{t-k}\right)}} = \frac{\gamma_{kt}}{\sqrt{\gamma_{0t} \cdot \gamma_{0,t-k}}} \tag{7}$$

Looking at each ρ_{kt} as the function of k, we call it an autocorrelation function. In the ACF panel in each commodity, dotted lines are drawn to show the significance level to reject the null hypothesis that $\rho_{kt} = 0$. All ACF graphs are in favor of positive autocorrelation for at least 6 months and the clear downward trend of the autocorrelation is the major difference from other variables considered below.

Next we compare scrap price and transportation cost. Here we pick up three major resources.

- **Ferrous**: HS7202 ferroalloys for final commodity and HS7204 ferrous waste and scrap, remelt scrap iron/steel ingot for scrap material
- **Copper**: HS7402 unrefined copper, copper anodes for electrolytic refining for a final commodity and HS7404 copper waste and scrap
- **Aluminum**: HS7604 aluminum bars, rods, and profiles and HS7602 aluminum waste and scrap

Figures 11.5–11.7 are the time-series plot, ACF, and PCF for scrap price (upper) and its transportation cost (lower) for ferrous, copper, and aluminum

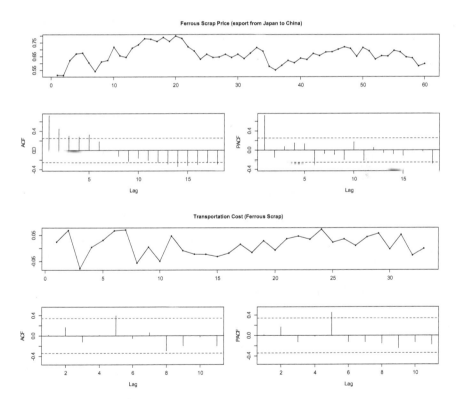

Figure 11.5 Time-series plot, ACF, and PCF, for ferrous scrap price and transportation cost

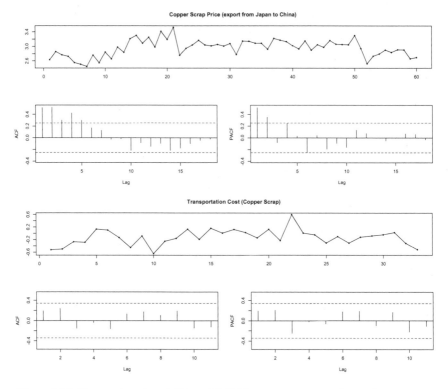

Figure 11.6 Time-series plot, ACF, and PCF for copper scrap price and transportation cost

traded between Japan and China. For the scrap price, the sample length is again 60 months while the transportation cost has only 20 months because of data limitations on the Chinese side. As for the time-series plot, scrap prices are rather consistent compared to previous LME prices for the same commodity. Especially for copper scrap, the price seems to be higher than that of 60 months ago. Table 11.1 summarizes the result of the unit test (Augmented Dickey – Fuller test: ADF test) for each variable. The null hypothesis of the ADF test is that the data has a unit root. The fact that only transportation cost for scrap materials can reject the null hypothesis is the strong evidence for its stationarity.

We now understand that the transportation cost, especially for scrap transaction, is relatively stable. Our next step is to detect what causes the transportation changes. The most popular tool is the Granger causality test. It is common practice to say that variable x Granger-causes y if x is useful to predict y. Suppose there are two time-series data $\{x_t\}$ and $\{y_t\}$. Let

$$\sigma^2(x_t \mid x_{t-1}, x_{t-2}, \cdots) \qquad (8)$$

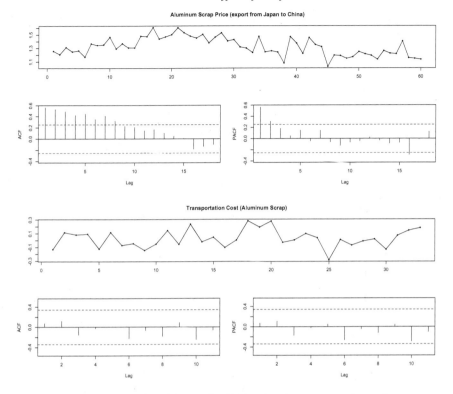

Figure 11.7 Time-series plot, ACF, and PCF for aluminum scrap price and transportation cost

Table 11.1 Results of ADF test

	Ferrous	*Copper*	*Aluminum*
Final commodity price	0.3037	−1.708	−1.2224
Scrap price	−2.659*	−2.3855	*−1.5234
Transportation cost (scrap)	−2.972 **	0.04224*	−2.9593**
Transportation cost (final)	−3.7052***	−2.8702*	−1.124

Significance level: *: 10%, **: 5%, ***: 1%

be the minimum mean squared error. Then it is said that there is a Granger causality from $\{y_t\}$ to $\{x_t\}$ if the following relationship is satisfied:

$$\sigma^2(x_t \mid x_{t-1}, x_{t-2}, \cdots; y_{t-1}, y_{t-2}, \cdots) < \sigma^2(x_t \mid x_{t-1}, x_{t-2}, \cdots) \tag{9}$$

Once vector autocorrelation regression (VAR) model is estimated, it is relatively easy to calculate the Granger causality because the null hypothesis of the Granger causality is the same as testing the F statistic for the original VAR model.

Because our interest is the transportation cost, we include the following five variables; (i) exchange rate, (ii) oil price index, (iii) commodity price, (iv) quantity traded, and (v) transportation cost.[4] Thus we build the VAR model below:

$$
\begin{bmatrix} x_{1,t} \\ \vdots \\ x_{5,t} \end{bmatrix} = \begin{bmatrix} a_{10} \\ \vdots \\ a_{50} \end{bmatrix} + \begin{bmatrix} a_{11} & \cdots & a_{15} \\ \vdots & \ddots & \vdots \\ a_{51} & \cdots & a_{55} \end{bmatrix} \begin{bmatrix} x_{1,t-1} \\ \vdots \\ x_{5,t-1} \end{bmatrix} + \begin{bmatrix} e_{1,t} \\ \vdots \\ e_{5,t} \end{bmatrix},
\tag{9}
$$

where $x_{i,t}$ denotes the ith time-series variable in the data at time t while a_{kh} is the set of parameters to be estimated. Finally, $e_{1,t}$ is the error term which, we assume, satisfies *iid* property.

We include exchange rate because it affects a lot when it comes to import/ export, which is usually transacted by the US dollar. Since our focus is transportation cost, we assume that oil price index plays an important role. We add commodity price because the virgin material price – say, at LME – is a good measurement to check the degree of demand. As for the demand for transportation, quantity traded for each material is added.

Table 11.2 implies two insights. Firstly, four out of five variables are essential to explain its time-series fluctuation for ferrous regardless of final commodity or scrap commodity, but not for the other two materials, even though each of the three materials has a similar significant level in the VAR models. One reason that the case of ferrous is successful is because of its larger volume of trade. As Figure 11.8 shows, ferrous scrap trade quantity from Japan to China is much larger than copper and aluminum combined.[5] A larger number of participants in the market often leads to more efficient market transaction and follows the theory. The only variable that is not significant is quantity traded. The reason quantity traded has not played an important role might be its definition. Here we use the quantity for the Japan–China trade volume for the specific commodity, which might be too small to measure the total demand pressure for a shipping firm.

Table 11.2 Results of Granger causality test

	Final commodity			Scrap commodity		
	Ferrous	*Copper*	*Aluminum*	*Ferrous*	*Copper*	*Aluminum*
Exchange rate	3.1444**	3.796***	3.6115***	3.4442**	1.6871	1.4106
Oil index	2.0648*	0.9995	2.053**	1.7745	0.5182	0.5931
Commodity price	2.641**	1.1958	1.0948	3.3597**	2.6973**	1.1768
Quantity traded	0.6621	0.8325	0.2826	1.5167	0.8087	0.665
Transportation cost	3.2913**	0.6055	0.7697	3.3078**	2.0394*	0.6825

Significance level: *: 10%, **: 5%, ***: 1%

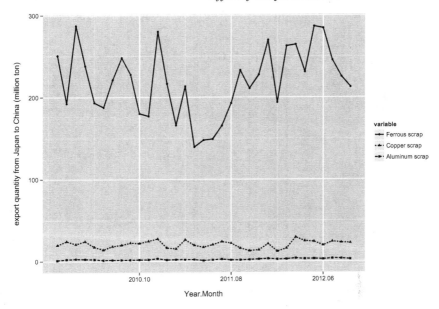

Figure 11.8 Quantity exported from Japan to China

Secondly, the exchange rate shows a strong importance in explaining the whole model. This is rather intuitive because both oil price and commodity prices are influenced by the exchange rate, and trade volume will be further influenced by all three. An interesting point to be mentioned is that the fluctuation effect of the exchange rate is limited for the scrap material. It is usually said that scrap metals are generated as by-products. As a result, scrap generation is rather inelastic to the related change of the prices. Table 11.2 could be considered evidence to indicate that scrap trade is generally slow to respond to the changes in its surrounding business environment.

For the further analysis of the dynamic relationship among the variables, the forecast error variance decomposition (FEVD) is conducted. FEVD allows the user to identify which variable is important to forecast by dividing MSE of forecast into the part of the contribution by each variable. The result of FEVD is derived by computing relative variance contribution (RVC) for each variable, which is defined by[6]

$$RVC_{ij}(k) = \frac{contribution\ of\ y_j\ to\ MSE\left(\hat{y}_{i,t+k|t}\right)}{MSE\left(\hat{y}_{i,t+k|t}\right)}. \tag{7}$$

Note that MSE($\hat{y}_{i,t+k|t}$) is a mean squared error of the VAR model. Using RVC(k), we can compare whether a variable has a strong short-term effect while another one has a rather longer contribution. Figures 11.9 to 11.11 are the

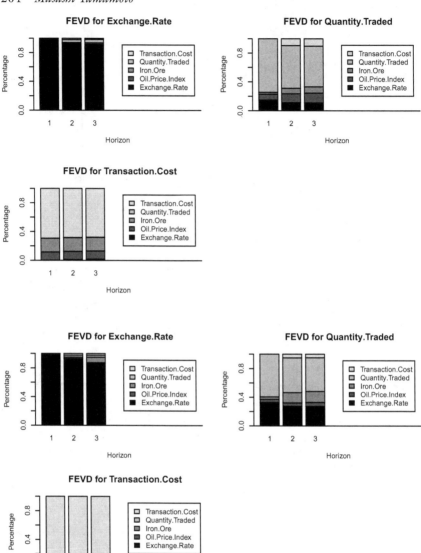

Figure 11.9 Comparison of FEVD (ferrous; upper: scrap, lower: final commodity)

result of the FEVD analysis. Following the VAR model's significance, 3 periods ahead of forecast error variance are plotted. In each figure, the results are limited only for exchange rate, quantity traded, and transportation cost. The cases of oil price index and resource prices are omitted because of the limited space.

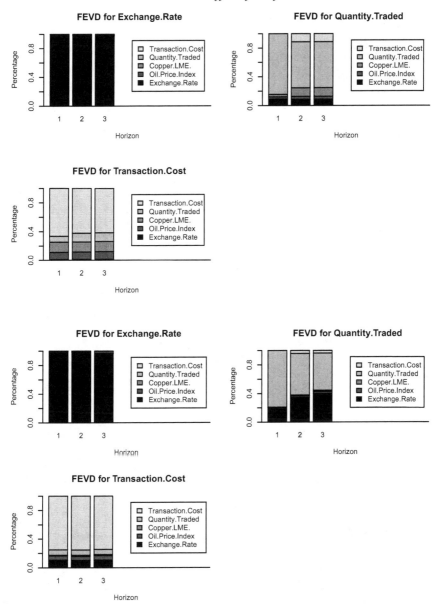

Figure 11.10 Comparison of FEVD (copper; upper: scrap, lower: final commodity)

We assume that exchange rate is the most exogenous variable in our analysis, and the results follow the assumption. In each material, the forecast error variances are almost dominated by their own effect on the exchange rate, at least in the short run. It is worth mentioning that within all materials, the contributions made by

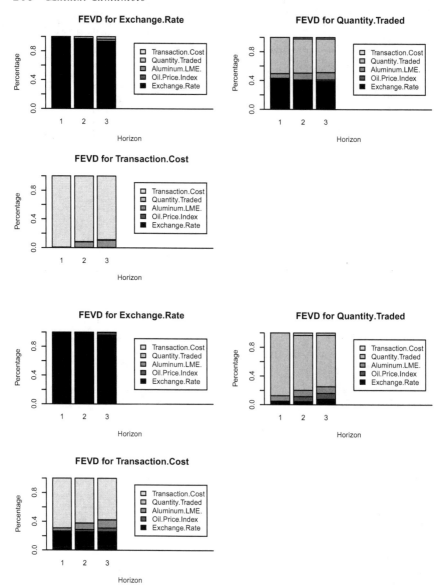

Figure 11.11 Comparison of FEVD (aluminum; upper: scrap, lower: final commodity)

other variables are (still small but) higher as the period goes by. This means the other four variables are relatively more important to forecast further into the future.

As for the quantity traded, its own variance is the major contribution in most of the cases. One thing that should be mentioned is that the role of the effect of quantity traded is decreasing in all three final commodities while the tendency is unclear for the cases of the scrap materials. Finally, for the transportation cost, it seems that the contribution is stable during these periods. This means the forecast of the transportation is so difficult that adding another period of information does not improve the forecast. Another notable thing is that, in the case of ferrous and copper, the transportation costs for scrap materials receive larger influences from other variables (and less from their own effects). As we mention in Section 2, suppose that a recycling firm in the formal sector competes against an informal one. Because the formal one needs more money to comply with environmental regulations properly, the firm would find it difficult to respond to a change in transportation cost due to the change in exogenous economic trend. This leads to less competitiveness for the formal sector firm; it would collect fewer and fewer recyclables. However, the case of the aluminum does not follow the same story. One of the reasons would be smaller volume of trade for aluminum. To clarify this difference of the transportation cost between scrap and final commodity, we need many more cases than the three materials we analyze in this paper. This will be the next step of our research.

5 Conclusion

This chapter analyzes the waste trade data between Japan and China. Through this research, it is revealed that a transportation cost is important, especially when there is a competition between a firm in the formal sector and one in the informal sector, which is often seen in the Chinese recycling industry. Furthermore, it is shown that the transportation cost of the scrap is more difficult to forecast compared to the transportation cost of the final commodity in the cases of ferrous and copper but not in aluminum's case. The fluctuations of the world market price affect the transaction of the scrap in a different way. Policy makers should be aware of this type of difference when making decisions about waste management policy

Notes

1 See http://eprc.kyoto-u.ac.jp/saigai/report/2011/03/001341.html.
2 For the complete list, please check Table A1 in Kellenberg (2013).
3 The data is available at http://www.imf.org/external/np/res/commod/index.aspx.
4 Note that the variables are listed by exogeneity (we assume exchange rate is the most exogenous in the five variables).
5 Note that the monetary value of the copper and aluminum could be higher than the ferrous because they have much higher unit prices.
6 The definition here is based on Okimoto (2012).

References

Agostini, C. (2006) "Estimating market power in the US copper industry," *Review of Industrial Organization*, Vol. 28, pp. 17–39.

Baggs, J. (2009) "International trade in hazardous waste," *Review of International Economics*, Vol. 17, pp. 1–16.

Basel Action Network (2002) *Exporting Harm: The High-Tech Trashing of Asia*. Retrieved from http://archive.ban.org/E-waste/technotrashfinalcomp.pdf (accessed on 30 January 2016).

Gomez, F., J. Guzman, and J. Tilton (2007) "Copper recycling and scrap availability," *Resource Policy*, Vol. 32, pp. 183–190.

Kellenberg, D. (2013) "Trading wastes," *Journal of Environmental Economics and Management*, Vol. 64, pp. 68–87.

Li, S., H. Zhu, and K. Yu (2012) "Oil prices and stock market in China: A sector analysis using panel cointegration with multiple breaks," *Energy Economics*, Vol. 34, pp. 1951–1958.

Okimoto, T. (2012) *Time-Series Analysis for Economics and Finance*, Asakura Shoten Publishing, Tokyo, in Japanese.

Slade, M. (1980) "An Econometric model of the US secondary copper industry: Recycling versus disposal," *Journal of Environmental Economics and Management*, Vol. 7, pp. 123–141.

Yamamoto, F. (2013) "Chapter 5: Overview of Waste Trade in East Asia," in N. Kakita, K. Nakamura, and F. Yasumoto, eds. *Creation of East Asian KYOSEI Studies*, March 2013, in Japanese.

Index

Note: figures and tables are denoted with italicized page numbers; end note information is denoted with an n and note number following the page number.